EJS 12.0

Korn Shell Programming

BY EXAMPLE

201 West 103rd Street
Indianapolis, Indiana 46290

Dennis O'Brien

Korn Shell Programming by Example

International Standard Book Number: 0-7897-2465-0

Library of Congress Catalog Card Number: 00-111668

Printed in the United States of America

First Printing: March 2001

02 01   4   3   2   1

Trademarks

Warning and Disclaimer

Associate Publisher
Dean Miller

Acquisitions Editor
Gretchen Ganser

Development Editor
Sean Dixon

Managing Editor
Thomas F. Hayes

Project Editor
Tricia Sterling Liebig

Copy Editors
Cynthia Fields
Megan Wade

Indexer
Chris Barrick

Proofreader
Harvey Stanbrough

Technical Editor
Paul Love

Team Coordinator
Cindy Teeters

Interior Designer
Karen Ruggles

Cover Designer
Maureen McCarty

Contents at a Glance

Table of Contents

About the Authors

Dennis O'Brien started his technical career as a COBOL programmer during the early 1970s. He has participated in each daring step made by the industry since then and stands in awe of all that has transpired.

This is his first book-writing effort, although he has delivered many symposium sessions and papers, and portions of his published code lives in private software. Through his company, Bruden Corp. (www.bruden.com), he has created materials for many technical classes with focus on C language programming, Shell programming, UNIX User, UNIX Admin, UNIX Internals, and various OpenVMS courses.

Dennis is a co-owner of the Bruden Corporation. He started working in the computer industry in 1972, began working with and delivering training on OpenVMS in 1983 with Digital Equipment Corp., and has been providing UNIX training and development since 1989 with Vastek Co. and Bruden Corp. He was a co-founder of the Vastek Company. He won five *Instructor Excellence* awards while working for Digital Equipment Corporation. He provides training and development in UNIX from the user to the internals level. He also provides training in OpenVMS and C programming languages.

He has trained many Compaq Computer Corporation's customer support center engineers. He is known by many of Compaq's employees and customers as one of the best technical instructors in the industry. He has a unique ability to address the needs of the most novice and the most technical audiences in a manner that makes learning technical details easy and fun.

Dennis lives in Danvers, Massachusetts with his wife Cheryl Dyment and his stepsons Scott Manley and Christopher Manley.

Dennis can be reached at dennis.obrien@bruden.com.

David Pitts (dpitts@mk.net) has been a part of the writing of more than half a dozen books. He was the primary author for *Red Hat Linux Unleashed* (Second and Third Editions), *Red Hat Linux 6 Unleashed*, and *Linux Unleashed, Fourth Edition,* for Sams Publishing. David has been a supporting author on Que's *Using Unix, Using Linux*, and *Programming CGI in Perl, Visual Basic, and C.* In addition, David writes a regular column on Perl for internet.com.

David is the president and CEO of Pitts Technical Resources, Inc. (http://www.dpitts.com), a company that specializes in programming and development consulting around the world. In addition, PTRi develops off-the-shelf software, including the increasingly popular CorPortal, which—according to one source—is "doing for the business world what AOL has done for the home user."

David lives in Lexington, Kentucky (`http://www.visitlex.com`), with his wonderful, intelligent, and compassionate wife Dana, whom he loves and adores more than any human on earth. A graduate from Asbury College (`www.asbury.edu`), David has been programming commercially since high school—1983. His goal in life is to appear in every type of media available. He is still looking for a nationally televised television show (Oprah, you have a book list!!) and a movie role.

David is a founding member of TM3. His favorite quote comes from Saint Francis of Assisi: "Preach the Gospel, and, if necessary, use words."

Dedication

This book is dedicated to my beautiful wife, Cheryl Dyment. Her belief in me and her encouragement throughout this project have been an inspiration. After listening to my plaintive technobabble, she would always provide some real-world insight and praise when I desperately needed it. Thanks, beautiful lady!

Acknowledgments

I'd like to thank the folks at Que for helping me with my first book project. Their sensitivity to my needs has been outstanding. Thanks in particular to Gretchen Ganser, Sean Dixon, Megan Wade, Paul Love, and Tricia Liebig for scrubbing it all up for me.

Thanks to David Pitts for outlining and starting the project.

I'd also like to thank my partner and friend, Bruce Ellis, for his encouragement and for providing the inspiration for some of the example scripts. Thanks to all the folks at Bruden Corp. for their understanding while I toiled in the darkness. Thanks to Susan Ellis, Glenn Oehms, Laurel Zolfonoon, Keith McLaughlin, and Scott Fafrak.

Many thanks to Robert Katz, a spectacular Korn Shell script writer from Compaq. His scripts opened my eyes to the nooks and crannies of the Korn Shell.

I have been blessed with a wonderful family, all of whom have provided support and emotional nourishment throughout this project. Thanks to my loving parents, Mary and Cliff O'Brien (always my biggest fans), and to my brothers Cliff (Linda, Erin, and Mike), Clint (Sue, Greg, and Scott), and Mark O'Brien. I love you guys.

Thanks to Scott and Chris Manley and all their friends for providing an infinite variety of teenager metaphors.

Cheryl, you have inspired me. You do inspire me. You will forever inspire me. Thank you. I love you.

Introduction

What is this book that you are holding? It is a book that teaches you, the system administrator or user, how to program using the Korn shell. For my Linux friends out there who say, "What, not in bash??" let me say a couple of things. First of all, ksh is a wonderful shell (ksh is the name of the Korn shell program; bash is the name of the Born again shell, common in many Linux systems). It has many features that make it an excellent choice for creating scripts as a system administrator. Second, ksh is and has been a standard in the UNIX community for a number of years. My goal is to help you become a better system administrator by showing you how to automate many of your daily tasks. I plan on accomplishing that goal without making you cry from boredom.

I have been in the computer industry for many years (since 1972) and have helped many administrators and users create many useful tools. But throughout my career, I have consistently found the following things to be true. I have seen good quality IT (and other) professionals placed way too often in positions where they are asked to either develop some process or update some tool that they are unfamiliar with, and that is written in some language that they do not understand. I have also seen these same talented IT professionals buy a book, find an answer, and leave the book on the shelf never to be opened again after that one use. If the book is good, it comes off the shelf many times; if it is bad, it stays there.

What these professionals need, what they are looking for, and what you are probably looking for right now, is a good book that will help you automate processes, produce information, and take the boredom and monotony out of your day. And that is what you have in your hands right now!

Having said all that, the following should be obvious. This book is not a history of Unix/Linux. It will not tell you how things were done in the good old days. Great lengths were taken to ensure that this book does not resemble academia. This is a practical, hands-on book jammed with useful examples.

Assumptions About the Reader

I have two assumptions about you, the reader. First, you have access to a UNIX/Linux box, or ksh on Win98 or NT. Second, you have some familiarity with UNIX/Linux commands and the command line. Appendix A does include many pages of useful commands, and we use many of them throughout this book. The examples are based on Korn Shell 93. I have tried to point out places where I use syntax that will not work on earlier releases of the Korn shell. Korn Shell 93 is freely available on the Web for personal use. Perform a general search for Korn Shell and you will find locations from which to download the program.

What This Book Will Give You

This book will give you good, usable, tested scripts. It will give you easy-to-follow and easy-to-use examples that will help you to write your own scripts. Many times this will mean that I will give you more information than you were probably looking for, but I follow the adage that if I give you all the information, you will be able to apply it yourself.

What This Book Will *Not* Give You

This book will not give you

- A history of UNIX or of Linux. Some good books are out there that do that; get one of those if you don't want to learn how to program.

- A tutorial on UNIX/Linux. Some great books on UNIX and Linux are available. When delivering introductory UNIX material, I sometimes suggest *A Practical Guide to the UNIX System* by Mark Sobell, but many others are available.

- A history on shells, shell scripting, types of shells, and so forth. As a matter of fact, great effort has gone into this work to not bore you with this stuff. Besides, you likely wouldn't read it anyway!

- Probably most importantly, you will find absolutely no references to XXX.edu for where to get errata, answers to questions, or other information. I am not in school, and this is not a class project. These are real-life examples from real systems programmed by real systems administrators that you can use in your real life as a real, live systems administrator. (Really!)

Conventions

- Code lines, commands, statements, variables, and any text you type or see onscreen appear in a `computer typeface`. **`Bold computer typeface`** is used to represent the user's input.

- Placeholders in syntax descriptions appear in *`italic computer typeface`*. Replace the placeholder with the actual filename, parameter, or whatever element it represents.

- *Italics* highlight technical terms when they first appear in the text and are being defined.

- ➥This special icon will be used before a line of code that is really a continuation of the proceeding line. Sometimes a line of code is too long to fit as a single line on the page, given this book's limited width. If you see this special symbol before a line of code, remember that you should interpret that line as part of the line immediately before it.

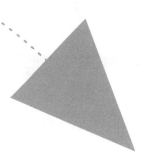

The Environment

The assumption of this book, and particularly this chapter, is that you are at least familiar with a shell. You have typed in some commands—such as changing your password—and are fairly comfortable with the environment. The chapter begins by explaining a few items common to all scripts, including comments and the cryptic #!/bin/ksh that mysteriously lurks on the first line of most shell scripts. After that, a few environment issues are explained.

This chapter teaches you the following:

- The meaning of #! /bin/ksh
- How to understand file and directory permissions
- How to use the chmod and umask commands
- How to provide comments in your script
- How to use the .profile file
- What the Korn shell environment options are
- How to use shell variables and environment variables
- How to use the history file and command-line recall

What Is a Shell?

A *shell* is a program that enables the user to enter commands. The commands entered by the user are checked and interpreted by the shell. The shell produces a prompt (typically the $) and waits for the user to type a command.

The command might be executed within the context of a new process (for example, ls), cause some functionality within the shell program itself to execute (for example, print), or cause an error to be reported (for example, non existent_command).

If you are totally new to the shell environment, you probably are envisioning a shell covering over the critical essence of something, much like a peanut shell covers and protects the peanut. Consider the shell as a neighborhood through which you can pass to get to downtown. Downtown, in this case, is the kernel of your operating system. Any program, including the shell, might need to communicate with the UNIX kernel for low-level activities such as file access.

The shell discussed in this book is the Korn Shell created by David Korn of Bell Labs. We will also include features of the ksh 93 version of his program.

When used interactively, a shell prompts the user for input. The input is a string in the form of a command. Each interactively entered command is interpreted by the shell. The interpretation checks the syntax of the command and performs other shell-level processing before the interactive command is actually executed.

For example, if you type in a command of ls -l obrien, the shell interprets the line as a series of tokens consisting of the following: the ls, the -l, and the obrien. The shell must locate the command file, check to see whether this user is actually permitted to execute the command, and perform other sanity checks before it actually runs the ls command. When the ls program runs, it checks the -l and the obrien and uses them appropriately, or issues an error if necessary.

The ls program runs in the context of a process. All programs run within their own process contexts. I like to think of the process as the ocean in which the program floats. The context provided by a process is used to support the running of a program. (You learn more about processes later in the book.)

What Is a Shell Script?

When Hollywood actors are given a script to read, they follow the sequence of dialogue as it appears in the document. Likewise, a shell script is a pre-defined sequence of dialogue to be presented to a shell. A shell *script* is a file full of commands to be executed.

#!/bin/ksh Explained

As discussed previously, a shell script is nothing more than a set of commands saved in a file. When the script is executed, the set of commands in the file are passed to an interpreter for processing. Several shells are available that a script writer can choose. How do you indicate that your script is a Korn Shell script, and is to be interpreted by ksh (and not csh, sh, bash, tcsh, or any other shell program)?

In shell scripting, the way to do this is to make the first line of the script file contain special characters that will precede a file specification locating the program responsible for interpreting the remaining lines in the file.

Normally a pound sign (#) begins a comment. *Comments* are lines in the script file that are not to be interpreted by the shell, but usually provide some documentation or description for script maintenance purposes. As soon as the shell sees a # within a line, it does not interpret any characters that appear after that point. Therefore, if the # appears as the first character in a line, the whole line is taken as a comment. If, on the other hand, the pound sign is followed immediately by an exclamation point (!), and is in the first line and first two characters in the file, the currently running shell interprets the file spec following the #! as being the program to run to interpret the rest of the script file.

In fact, a separate process is created within which the ksh program runs. The rest of the script file is presented to the ksh program as its stream of input. The input is interpreted and executed, provided no errors occur.

Therefore, a simple shell script could look like this:

EXAMPLE

```
#!/bin/ksh
echo "Hello World!"
```

This script would produce the following output:

```
Hello World!
```

Note that your system's Korn shell program might be in a directory other than /bin. If so, just change the first line of your script to match the location and name of your ksh program. In the case of this simple introductory script, you could have typed **echo Hello World!** at the interactive prompt and done the same task.

What happens if you have a file containing just the second line (in other words, the #!/bin/ksh is not there)?

If the shell you are currently executing can understand the command(s) in the script file, it runs them; if it cannot, it produces some kind of error message and exits from the script. A simple example such as displaying some text should work in just about any shell.

By having the #!/bin/ksh in the first line of the script, you ensure that the script will do exactly what you want it to do regardless of the environment or default interactive shell of the user, because you have explicitly told it to use the Korn shell to interpret the rest of the contents of the file. You should realize that the #! is a very special line, not just an ordinary comment line. The #! must be the first two characters in the first line of the file.

Now, you might have had some problems getting your simple program to run. If you edited a file and tried to run it, you might have gotten the error **Permission denied**. The reason for this has to do with, you guessed it, permissions. Permissions are discussed in detail in this chapter. In essence, *permissions* determine who can do what with a file. You must tell the computer that the file you have just created should be treated as an executable.

The following example shows a simple script that displays output onscreen. The permissions indicate that the file is not executable (no x in the permissions); therefore, the attempt to execute the script fails. The example then uses the chmod command to add execute access for the owner (u) and group (g) categories (ug+x—more later). After changing the permissions, the script runs successfully.

EXAMPLE

```
$ cat hello-k
#! /bin/ksh        # Uses Korn shell to execute the rest of the file (one line)
print hello
$
$ ls -l hello-k  # No execute permission
-rw-r--r--   1 obrien   users        27 Sep 28 17:36 hello-k
$
$ hello-k
ksh: hello-k: cannot execute
$
$ chmod ug+x hello-k   # Add execute permission
$
$ hello-k              # Script runs now
hello
```

What happens if you try to run your Korn shell script from an interactive C shell? Because the script starts with the #! /bin/ksh, it should be capable of executing from any environment.

The following example starts a C shell interactive environment by running the csh program. Notice that the prompt changes from $ to %. The Korn shell script still runs properly, and the exit command exits from the csh program and returns to the ksh interactive shell.

EXAMPLE

```
$
$ csh                 # Start C shell
%
% hello-k             # Runs in C shell also
hello
%
% exit
$
```

The next example uses the sed stream editor command (discussed in Chapter 9, "File and Directory Manipulation") to create a new file (hello-g) with the #! line removed from the script. This provides the opportunity to see whether the script can succeed in a non-ksh environment without the #! /bin/ksh. The result is that the altered script will not run within the C shell because it tries to interpret the contents of the script as if it were C shell script syntax, not Korn shell script syntax. Once again, the example uses the chmod ug+x command to give execute access to the user (owner) and group categories:

```
$ sed 's/^#.*//' hello-k > hello-g    # Create script without #! in the
                                      # first line
$
$ cat hello-g
print hello                           # Single line file
$
$
$ ls -l hello-g
-rw-r--r--   1 obrien    users        16 Sep 28 17:41 hello_g
$
$ chmod ug+x hello-g                  # Add execute permission
$
$ hello-g                             # runs fine in Korn shell
hello
$
$ csh
%
% hello-g
```

```
hello-g: print: not found              # Errors out in C shell
%
% exit
$
```

File Attributes

If a new file, such as the previous echo `hello` program, is created, the permissions assigned to the file are based on the user's umask. The default umask on most systems is 022. This default can be changed globally by the system administrator and individually in one of several files in a user's directory, or interactively. The most common place to change this setting is in the user's profile file (typically named .profile). The entry would look like this:

```
umask 002
```

Assuming you have created a temporary file (use touch `david` for now), have saved it in your home directory, and have called the file david, a long listing of the file would look like this:

```
$ ls -l david
-rw-rw-r--   1 Pitts     users        24 May 13 16:57 david
```

NOTE

The $ is the default Korn shell prompt; it is not typed when you run the listing command. What was typed was **ls -l david**.

Technically, nine pieces of information are given when you perform a long listing of a file (or directory):

- Type of file
- Permissions
- Number of hard links
- Owner
- Group
- Size
- Month last modified
- Day last modified
- Time last modified
- Name of the file

The permissions, owner, group, and name of the file are what is important to us presently.

The permissions for the file are rw-rw-r--. The first character on the line shows the type of file; - means regular file; d means directory; and the others are listed in Table 1.1.

- The owner is Pitts.
- The owning group is users.
- The name of the file is david.

The permissions for files are split into four sections:

- A special file type field (one character)
- Permissions for the owner of the file (three characters)
- Permissions for the group associated with the file (three characters)
- Permissions for everyone else (the world—three characters)

Each section has its own set of three file permissions, which provide the capability to read, write, and execute (or, of course, to deny the same). These permissions are called the file's *filemode*. Filemodes are set with the chmod command.

The object's permissions can be specified in two ways—the numeric coding system or the letter coding system. Using the letter coding system, the three sections are referred to as follows:

- u for user
- g for group
- o for other
- a for all three

The following are three basic types of permissions:

- r for read
- w for write
- x for execute

Combinations of r, w, and x with each of the three groups of users provide the complete set of permissions for the files. In the following example, the owner of the file has read, write, and execute permissions, and everyone else has read access only:

EXAMPLE

```
$ ls -l test
-rwxr--r--  1 obrien    users          24 May 13 16:57 test
```

The command ls -l test tells the computer to retrieve a long (-l) listing (ls) of the file (test). The second line is the result of the command.

Therefore, the permissions are made up of 10 character positions. A dash (-) indicates no permission granted for that category of user (user, group, others) for that capability (read, write, execute). The user category would probably be better served if it were named owner, but that would lead to confusion between o for others and o for owner. The first field is a little different. Refer to Table 1.1 to identify many entries that could be found in the first position.

Table 1.1: Object type identifier

Character	Description
-	Plain file
b	Block special file
c	Character special file
d	Directory
l	Symbolic link
p	Named pipe
s	Socket

Following the file type identifiers are the three sets of permissions: rwx (user), r-- (group), and r-- (other).

NOTE

A small explanation needs to be made as to what read, write, and execute actually mean. For files, a user who has *read* permission can see the contents of a file; a user with *write* permission can write to it; and a user who has *execute* permission can execute the file. If the file to be executed is a script, the user must have read and execute permissions to execute the file. If the file is a binary file (created through a compile and link sequence), just the execute permission is required to execute the file.

A compiled and linked binary file is created when a high-level language program (C, COBOL, FORTRAN, Pascal, Ada, C++, and so on) is presented to a program called a *compiler*, which translates the C code into machine instructions to be executed when the program is run. The compiler sends its output to the linker program, which resolves any global references and produces a binary executable file.

This type of executable runs four or five times faster than a shell script in which each line must be interpreted and potentially executes a separate process per line. In contrast, a compiled and linked program is more difficult to write, but executes more quickly. A script should be faster to write (and easier), but executes more slowly.

The interactive shell can distinguish between a request to execute a compiled and linked binary program versus a shell script by examining the first two bytes of the file. If it finds the #!, it knows it is about to execute a script. If it finds some other values in the first two bytes, the shell assumes that the file is a compiled and linked executable and prepares to execute the program. The first two characters of a file contain the magic numbers (see man magic) identifying the type of file.

Directories

The permissions on a directory are the same as those used by files: read, write, and execute. The actual permissions, however, mean different things. For a directory, read access provides the capability to list the names of the files in the directory, but does not allow the other attributes to be seen (owner, group, size, and so on):

The following example demonstrates that a directory without the execute permission bit set disallows the display of file attributes. However, it allows the display of filenames within the directory. The ls -ld ob command requests that permission information be displayed for the ob directory file, not the files within the directory. Here's the example:

EXAMPLE

```
$
$ mkdir ob      # Make a test directory named ob
$
$ ls -ld ob
drwxr-xr-x   2 obrien    users        8192 Sep 27 19:00 ob  # Note r and x
                                                            # permissions
$
$ cd ob
$
$ cat > tmp1  # Create a file in ob directory
junk in file
$
$ ls -l       # No problem getting new file's attributes
total 1
-rw-r--r--   1 obrien    users          13 Sep 27 19:01 tmp1
$
$ cd ..
$
$ ls -ld ob   # Show directory permissions
drwxr-xr-x   2 obrien    users        8192 Sep 27 19:01 ob
$
$ chmod ugo-x ob  # Remove execute permissions from all categories
$
$ ls -ld ob   # No execute permission for the directory
```

```
drw-r--r--   2 obrien   users        8192 Sep 27 19:01 ob
$
$ ls -l ob      # Displays no attribute info without
                # execute permission on the directory
ls: ob/tmp1: No permission
total 0
$
$ ls ob         # No problem viewing filenames
tmp1
```

Write access provides the capability to alter the directory contents. This means the user could create and delete files in the directory.

The following example demonstrates that an attempt to create a file within a directory that does not have write permission will fail. After adding execute permission, the file creation request is tried again, successfully. The cat command is used to create a small file. To terminate the creation activity begun by the cat > command, you must press Ctrl+D at the beginning of a blank line:

EXAMPLE

```
$ pwd
/usr/users/obrien/ob
$
$ ls -ld                 # Note no write permission
dr-xr--r--   2 obrien   users        8192 Sep 27 19:01 .
$
$ cat > tmp3             # File create fails
ksh: tmp3: cannot create
$
$ chmod u+w ../ob        # Add write permission
$
$ cat > tmp3             # Success
ddddd
$
$ ls -ld
drwxr--r--   2 obrien   users        8192 Sep 27 19:16 .
$
```

Finally, execute access enables the user to make the directory the current directory:

```
$ ls -ld ob              # No execute permission of the directory file
drw-r--r--   2 obrien   users        8192 Sep 27 19:01 ob
$
$ cd ob                  # Can't cd to the directory
ksh: ob: permission denied
$
$ chmod u+x ob           # Add execute permission
$
$ cd ob                  # Success
```

Execute access on a directory file also provides list capabilities, but browsing is supported by read permission.

The following example shows successful browsing of a directory due to read access. After removing read access, but retaining execute access, browsing is not allowed. However, access is successful provided that the user already knows the name of the file to be accessed:

```
$ ls -ld                # Directory allows browsing
drwx------    2 obrien   users        8192 Sep 27 19:16 .
$
$ ls                    # Browsing away
tmp1   tmp3
$
$ chmod u-rw ../ob      # Remove read access (write also just because!)
$
$ ls                    # Can't browse
.: Permission denied
$
$ ls tmp3               # Can get info if I know filenames
tmp3
$
$ ls -l tmp3            # Attributes too
-rw-r--r--    1 obrien   users           6 Sep 27 19:16 tmp3
$
```

Table 1.2 summarizes the differences between the permissions for a file and those for a directory.

Table 1.2: File permissions versus directory permissions

Permission	File	Directory
r	View the contents	Search the contents, browse
w	Alter file contents	Alter directory contents (delete files, add files)
x	Run executable file	Make it the current directory, list but no browse

Combinations of these permissions also allow certain tasks. It was previously mentioned, for example, that it takes both read and execute permissions to execute a script. This is because the shell must first read the file to see what to do with it. (Remember that the #!/bin/ksh tells the shell to execute a Korn shell and pass the rest of the file's contents to the Korn shell as input.) Other combinations allow certain functionality. Table 1.3 describes the combinations of permissions and what they mean, both for a file and for a directory.

Table 1.3: Comparison of file and directory permission combinations

Permission	File	Directory
`- - -`	Cannot do anything.	Cannot access it or any of its subdirectories.
`r - -`	Can see the contents.	Can see the contents.
`rw -`	Can see and alter the contents.	Can see and alter the contents.
`rwx`	Can see and change the contents, as well as execute the file.	Can list the contents, add or remove files, and make the directory the current directory (cd to it).
`r - x`	If a script, can execute it. Otherwise, it provides read and execute perms.	Provides capability to change to directory and list contents, but not to delete or add files to the directory.
`- - x`	Can execute if a binary.	Users can execute a binary they already know about.

As stated, the permissions can also be manipulated with a numeric coding system. The basic concept is the same as the letter coding system. As a matter of fact, the permissions look exactly alike—the difference is in the way the permissions are identified when using the chmod command. The numeric system uses binary counting to determine a value for each permission and sets them. Also, the find command can accept the numeric form of the permissions as an argument, using the -perm option, providing the capability to locate files containing certain permission values.

With binary, you count from right to left for each set of values. Therefore, if you look at a file, you can easily come up with its numeric coding system value. The following file has full permissions for the owner and read permissions for the group and the rest of the world:

```
$ ls -l test
-rwxr--r--  1 shell     shell         24 May 13 16:57 test
```

This would be coded as 744. Table 1.4 illustrates how this number was developed.

Table 1.4: Permission access values

Permission	Value
Read	4
Write	2
Execute	1

Permissions use an additive process; therefore, a person with read, write, and execute permissions to a file would have a 7 (4 + 2 + 1). Read and execute would have a value of 5. Remember that three sets of values exist (for user, group, and others categories), so each section would have its own value.

Table 1.5 shows both the numeric system and the character system for the permissions.

Table 1.5: Numeric permissions

Permission	Numeric	Character
Read-only	4	r - -
Write-only	2	- w -
Execute-only	1	- - x
Read and write	6	rw -
Read and execute	5	r - x
Read, write, and execute	7	rwx

You can change permissions by using the chmod command, which is explained in the next section.

chmod

With the numeric system, the chmod command must be given the value for all three fields. Remember, the numeric system uses numbers to define permissions. The nine permissions (rwxrwxrwx) are represented as three series of three-bit fields. An on bit (set to 1) means the particular permission is present for this category of user (user, group, others) for this particular file. An off bit means the opposite. Quite often, you will see permissions of 777 used in a chmod command. Each 7 represent 3 on bits, or rwx. Therefore, to change a file to read, write, and execute for everyone, issue the following command:

```
$ chmod 777 <filename>
```

The character system uses characters such as u for user, g for group, o for others, and a for all three at once—as well the rwx to reflect permissions. To add a permission, use a plus (+); to remove a permission, use a minus (–). To perform the same task as the numeric example shown previously, with the character system, issue the following command:

```
$ chmod a+rwx <filename>
```

Of course, more than one type of permission can be specified at one time. The following command adds write access for the owner of the file and adds read and execute access to the group and everybody else:

```
$ chmod u+w,og+rx <filename>
```

The advantage that the character system provides is that you do not have to know the previous permissions. You can selectively add or remove permissions without worrying about the rest. With the numeric system, each section of users must always be specified. The downside of the character system is apparent when complex changes are being made. Looking at the preceding example, (chmod u+w,og+rx <filename>), an easier way might have been to use the numeric system and replace all those letters with three numbers: 755.

Coming Full Circle—Back to umask

As you recall, the default umask on many systems is 022. Now that you understand the numeric system, it is easy to explain what this number means. When a non-directory file is created, the umask value is subtracted from 666 (directories subtract from 777) to come up with the default permission value to be assigned to the newly created file. Therefore, a umask of 022 makes the permissions of the file 644. This gives the owner read and write access, and gives the group and the rest of the world read permission.

When a new directory is created, the umask is subtracted from 777 instead of 666 to set the default permissions. Therefore, a umask of 022 would give a newly created directory permissions of 755. This means the owner has read, write, and execute permissions, while the owning group and the rest of the world have read and execute permissions.

Now that you are starting to feel as if you understand permissions and their relationship to the umask value, you are ready to handle the truth. The subtraction technique described in the previous paragraphs will suffice in most situations. But what if the umask value is set to something like 027? What would the resulting file permissions be? How do you subtract a 027 from 666? Do we borrow a one from the middle 6 as in normal subtraction and put permissions of 639 (666–027) on any new non-directory files created?

The truth is that the bitwise one's complement (described in the next paragraph) of the umask value is bitwise-anded (described in the next paragraph) with octal 777 for directories or octal 666 for regular files to produce the default permissions placed on newly created files. (I'll wait while you get up off the floor.)

Are you ready? A umask of 027 is 000010111 in binary. The one's complement of 027 is 111101000 (just flip the bits—0s become 1s, and 1s become 0s). Octal 666 is 110110110 in binary. A bitwise-and operation analyzes each bit combination and produces a result of 1 if the bit on top AND the bit on bottom are both on (1). The bitwise-and operation produces a 0 otherwise. So, 111101000 bitwise-anded with 110110110 (666) yields 110100000, or 640, or rw-r-----.

111 101 000	(1's complement of 027)
110 110 110	(666)
-----------	(bitwise and)
110 100 000	(640 which is rw-r-----)

Feel free to erase the previous merriment from your memory banks. Most of the time, the good old subtraction method will work just fine for you. But now you know the truth about umask. You also know why the command is called "umask." It is the user file creation bitmask filter.

The following example demonstrates the permissions on a newly created file given a umask value of 022. It then changes the umask to 027 and generates a different set of permissions for a subsequently created file:

EXAMPLE

```
$ umask              # Current umask value
022
$
$ touch newfile      # Create empty new file
$
$ ls -l newfile      # Check permissions
-rw-r--r--   1 obrien   users          0 Sep 27 20:22 newfile
$
$
$ umask 027          # Alter umask
$
$ touch newfile2     # Create another new file
$
$ ls -l newfile2     # Note permissions
-rw-r-----   1 obrien   users          0 Sep 27 20:23 newfile2
$
```

#—Comments Explained

As you would expect, someone who has been a part of the writing of nine different books would be pushing documentation. And it is true, I am. More importantly, documenting what I have done while it is fresh in my mind has saved me countless hours of work. I usually take a few minutes and provide some simple headers and some quick explanations of what I am doing in a script. *Comments* are the way to add these simple headers and quick explanations within your script. In shell scripting, a comment runs from where the pound sign (#) begins to the end of the line. Therefore, something like this is feasible:

```
$ ls -l # give a listing of all files in the current directory!
```

But the shell will interpret this as follows:

```
$ ls -l
```

This is because the shell ignores everything from the pound sign to the end of the line unless it is the first line of the program and the character following the pound sign is an exclamation point. This means that a comment can either be a part of a line with a command, such as this:

```
$ ls -l  # this command gives a listing of all files in the current directory
```

Or it can be on a line by itself, such as this:

```
$ # The next command gives a listing of all files in the current directory
$ ls -l
```

The .profile Script

In its simplest form, a *script* is nothing more than one or more commands lumped together in a file. The file has had its permissions adjusted so that the intended user(s) has both read and execute permissions. The most obvious reason for such a file is user friendliness. Using a script can save typing. Instead of typing the same thing over and over again, you can save the commands in a file and execute the commands by typing in the name of the script.

In reality, scripts are much more than that. Scripts typically contain a large number of commands, logic flow statements, and other information that simplifies a task. One other nice thing about a script is that it enables you to automate some process. For example, in my home directory a program called .profile runs automatically every time I log on:

The following example shows a typical user's .profile file. It sets up the user's PATH variable (used to locate command files), creates a non-default prompt, sets the umask value, and defines several environment variables.

Have no fear, we cover all these topics in this and upcoming chapters.
Here's the example code:

EXAMPLE

```
$ cat .profile
# /etc/profile
# Systemwide environment and startup programs
PATH="$PATH:/usr/X11R6/bin"
# PS1="\$ "
typeset -uxL5 HOSTCHAR=$(uname -n)
PS1="$HOSTCHAR"':${PWD#HOME/}:!$ '
ulimit -c 1000000
if [ 'id -gn' = 'id -un' -a 'id -u' -gt 14 ]; then
        umask 002
else
        umask 022
fi
USER='id -un'
LOGNAME=$USER
MAIL="/var/spool/mail/$USER"
HOSTNAME='/bin/hostname'
HISTSIZE=100
HISTFILESIZE=1000
LINES=53
INPUTRC=/etc/inputrc
set -o vi
export PATH PS1 USER LOGNAME MAIL HOSTNAME HISTSIZE HISTFILESIZE INPUTRC LINES
for i in /etc/profile.d/*.sh ; do
        if [ -x $i ]; then
                . $i
        fi
done
unset I
```

This script sets up the environment the way I want it. Because it runs
every time I log on, I do not have to bother making changes to my environment every time I log on. It is automated for me.

Shell scripts are used for the following:

- Saving time in typing

- Automating processes

- Enabling complex processes to occur without user intervention

- Providing program-like functionality without having to learn a programming language

To maximize their productivity, and be comfortable in their computing environment, system administrators and other computer professionals should learn how to write shell scripts.

Aliases

Another shell technique that can save you a few keystrokes is using an alias. An *alias* is a way of doing something in shorthand. An alias is defined using a name/value pair. For example, the following alias takes the command ls -la and assigns it to the alias ll:

```
alias ll='ls -la'
```

After this alias has been created (either in a script, such as .profile, or manually at a shell prompt), the user can type **ll** and get a long listing:

```
$ ll
total 56
drwx------    6 shell    shell       4096 May 16 10:32 .
drwxr-xr-x   22 root     root        4096 Mar 27 14:26 ..
-rw-r--r--    1 shell    shell       1422 Mar 27 14:26 .Xdefaults
-rw-r--r--    1 shell    shell         24 Mar 27 14:26 .bash_logout
-rw-r--r--    1 shell    shell        230 Mar 27 14:26 .bash_profile
-rw-r--r--    1 shell    shell        173 Mar 27 14:26 .bashrc
drwxr-xr-x    3 shell    shell       4096 Mar 27 14:26 .kde
-rw-r--r--    1 shell    shell        435 Mar 27 14:26 .kderc
-rw-r--r--    1 shell    shell        634 May 16 10:32 .profile
-rw-r--r--    1 shell    shell       3394 Mar 27 14:26 .screenrc
drwxr-xr-x    5 shell    shell       4096 Mar 27 14:26 Desktop
drwxr-xr-x    2 shell    shell       4096 Mar 27 14:26 public_html
drwxrwxr-x    2 shell    shell       4096 May  1 19:51 scripts
-rwxr--r--    1 shell    shell         24 May 13 16:57 test
```

The unalias command is used to remove an alias:

```
$ unalias ll
$ ll
ksh: ll: not found
```

The value of an alias can be seen by typing the alias command:

```
$ alias
autoload='typeset -fu'
functions='typeset -f'
hash='alias -t'
history='fc -l'
integer='typeset -i'
local=typeset
login='exec login'
newgrp='exec newgrp'
```

```
nohup='nohup '
r='fc -e -'
stop='kill -STOP'
suspend='kill -STOP $$'
type='whence -v'
```

As you can see, several predefined aliases are listed here. If I were to add my alias back in, it too would be added to the list:

```
$alias ll='ls -la'
$ alias
alias ll='ls -la'
MOOSE:/home/shell:10$ alias
autoload='typeset -fu'
functions='typeset -f'
hash='alias -t'
history='fc -l'
integer='typeset -i'
ll='ls -la'    # There it is
local=typeset
login='exec login'
newgrp='exec newgrp'
nohup='nohup '
r='fc -e -'
stop='kill -STOP'
suspend='kill -STOP $$'
type='whence -v'
```

Notice that the `alias` command returns all the aliases in alphabetical order. Therefore, my `ll` is in the middle of the list, not at the end.

Ksh Environment Options

The Korn shell is itself an executable program. This is why you put the `#!/bin/ksh` at the beginning of the file. Several environment options are set by default, and others can be set manually either when Ksh is invoked or afterward with the `set` command. Options can do many things, including affecting how Ksh processes commands. By typing **set -o**, you can see how your current options are set:

EXAMPLE

```
$ set -o
Current option settings
allexport     off  keyword     off  nolog      off  trackall   off
braceexpand   on   login       on   notify     off  verbose    off
bgnice        off  markdirs    off  nounset    off  vi         on
emacs         off  monitor     on   physical   off  viraw      off
```

errexit	off	noclobber	off	posix	off	vi-show8	off
gmacs	off	noexec	off	privileged	off	vi-tabcomplete	off
ignoreeof	off	noglob	off	restricted	off	vi-esccomplete	off
interactive	on	nohup	on	stdin	on	xtrace	off

This happens to be the output from my Linux box (named "Moose"). The man pages will tell the inquisitive user what each option means. An option can be changed from off to on by supplying the option after the set -o command. For example, the command line

```
set -o vi
```

sets vi to be the default built-in editor for Ksh. To turn off an option, use a plus sign instead of a minus sign, as shown in the next example:

```
set +o vi
```

If it seems like the plus and minus should be reversed, remember that this came about as an option to a command. Options for commands are indicated by the minus sign (–), such as ls -l or shutdown -r. The plus sign (+) indicates to turn something off.

Variables

Variables are used to store values. In the following equation, two variables—x and y—are given:

```
x + y = 4
```

In this particular case, you can infer that the values associated with the variables are numeric. But variables can just as easily be character-based. Variables are used extensively in programming, so more will be discussed later. A variable is a name/value pair. The variable has a name, called a *varname*—x and y, previously shown—and a value, such as 2 or /home/shell as seen in the following example:

EXAMPLE

```
$ echo $HOME
/home/shell
```

The dollar sign ($) is placed in front of the varname to indicate that you are accessing the value of the variable. It forces the shell to check its table of variables to see whether it contains a variable matching the name appearing after the $. If the varname is followed immediately by other characters or the underscore, the varname must be enclosed in curly braces ({ }). This can be useful if you are trying to concatenate two variables. The curly braces can be used even when not necessary.

The following example shows an instance in which the curly braces are mandatory. Without them, the shell looks for a variable named USERisadude, which doesn't exist. Surrounding USER with the curly braces indicates you want the shell to look for the variable named USER—not USERisadude—and concatenate the contents of the variable $USER with the string isadude. Here's the example code:

```
$ echo $USER              # Works without curly braces
obrien
$
$ echo ${USER}            # Works with curly braces
obrien
$
$ echo $USERisadude       # Looks for 'USERisadude'
                          # Not found

$
$ echo ${USER}isadude     # Looks for USER, concatenates 'isadude'
obrienisadude
$
```

Three types of variables exist: shell variables, built-in variables, and environment variables. Each of these is discussed in the following sections.

Shell Variables

Shell variables are name/value pairs. Some shell variables are set automatically when the shell is instantiated. Many of these variables change on their own as the user performs certain tasks. For example, two such shell variables are PWD and OLDPWD. PWD stands for present working directory. Its value is the current directory to which the user has set his default. If the user has changed directories then the second variable, OLDPWD—old present working directory—stores the default working directory that the user had set previous to the current working directory. This makes switching back to the previous directory much quicker, as is demonstrated in the following text.

First, view the contents of the two variables (you might need to change directories before OLDPWD will instantiate itself):

```
$ cd /usr/local/vmware
$ echo $PWD
/usr/local/vmware    # Current directory
$ echo $OLDPWD
/home/shell          # Previous directory
```

From the current directory (/usr/local/vmware), switching back to the previous directory (/home/shell) without typing in or even remembering the name of the directory is easy. The change directory command (cd) followed by a dash and no arguments tells the shell to change directories to the old present working directory, as is evident in the following example:

```
$ cd /usr/local/vmware
$ echo $PWD
/usr/local/vmware
$ echo $OLDPWD
/home/shell
$ cd -
/home/shell
```

Some shell variables are local variables, and others are environment variables. Environment variables are discussed in a later section. Briefly, however, the difference between an *environment variable* and a *local variable* is that an environment variable's value is accessible to any child process of the current shell, but the same is not true for a local variable. Typically, a variable used in a script is a local variable and has no contextual value outside the script of which it is a part. The set command shows all currently set variables within an environment:

```
$ set
HISTFILESIZE=1000
HISTSIZE=100
HOME=/home/shell
HOSTCHAR=MOOSE
HOSTNAME=moose.qx.net
IFS='
'
INPUTRC=/etc/inputrc
KDEDIR=/usr
KSH_VERSION='@(#)PD KSH v5.2.14 99/07/13.2'
LANG=en_US
LC_ALL=en_US
LINES=55
LINGUAS=en_US
LOGNAME=shell
MAIL=/var/spool/mail/shell
MAILCHECK=600
OLDPWD=/usr/local/vmware
OPTIND=1
PATH=/usr/local/bin:/bin:/usr/bin:/usr/X11R6/bin:/usr/X11R6/bin
PPID=715
PS1='MOOSE:${PWD#HOME/}:!$ '
PS2='> '
PS3='#? '
PS4='+ '
PWD=/home/shell
QTDIR=/usr/lib/qt-2.0.1
RANDOM=20850
SECONDS=1271
```

```
SHELL=/bin/ksh
TERM=ansi
TMOUT=0
USER=shell
_=set
kdepath=/usr/bin
```

One more variable to spotlight is PS1. The value of this variable is displayed as the user's prompt. The one I use displays the name of my server, the present working directory, and which command I am on in the history file along with the dollar sign:

```
MOOSE:/home/shell:20$ cd /tmp
MOOSE:/tmp:21$
```

For clarity, in most of the examples, I have replaced my customized prompt with the standard Korn shell dollar sign prompt. Later in the chapter when the history file is discussed, you will see the true value of my customized prompt. If you have terminal windows emanating from several servers displaying on your workstation, it is helpful to be able to quickly discern from which machine the prompt comes. This is accomplished by the MOOSE part of the prompt.

Similarly, it can be efficient to be reminded of what the current working directory is. This is accomplished by the /tmp part of the last prompt.

The last part of my customized prompt displays a number from the history file. This indicates which number command I am about to type in. These numbers can be used to recall previously issued commands. All of this is discussed at the end of this chapter.

Shell variables are set with the equal sign. No spaces are allowed in the setting of the varname value pair. If spaces are needed in the value then the value must be placed between quotes to let the system know that it is only one value and that you are not trying to do multiple things at once. The following example shows setting a varname of ME equal to David and then unsetting the value with the unset command:

EXAMPLE

```
$ ME=David      # Setting a variable
$ echo $ME      # Displaying a variable
David
$ unset ME      # Unsetting a variable
$ echo $ME

                # Blank
```

There is a blank line after the command because the Ksh returned nothing:

The following example demonstrates the shell's misinterpretation of a request to set a nonquoted variable containing a space:

```
$ echo $ME

$ ME=David Pitts         # Shell assigns David
ksh: Pitts: not found    # But thinks Pitts is a command
$ echo $ME               # So it aborts the entire line

$ ME="David Pitts"       # Works with quotes
$ echo $ME
David Pitts
```

You should notice the error stating that `Pitts` could not be found. Because an error occurred, even the seemingly valid `ME=David` did not occur.

Built-In Variables

A number of *built-in* variables change as the environment changes. Specifically, the values change as commands are executed. The values of these variables hold information relevant to the current shell, the current process, or the most recently completed process. These are similar to shell variables, but the values are generated when the value is accessed. The following example shows this. Notice that no error is generated:

EXAMPLE

```
$ echo $0      # $0 contains command name
-ksh
$ set 0=Moose  # Reset upon access
$ echo $0
-ksh
```

Because the value is generated each time it is accessed, the previous command really did set the value of shell variable `0` equal to `Moose`. But when you asked for it to be displayed, it was reset to the name of the current program, which is ksh (the shell itself). This is the reason no error was generated. Many of these variables can be used in scripts. Table 1.6 shows these variables and gives a brief explanation as to what each means.

Table 1.6: Built-in variables

Variable	Explanation
$0	Name of the command or script being executed.
$n	Argument passed as a positional parameter (for example, n is a number between 1 and 9) indicating which value is passed to the script from the command line. Arguments can exceed 9 if enclosed in curly braces—for example, ${14} indicates the 14th positional parameter.
$#	Number of positional parameters passed as arguments to the script from the command line.
$*	A list of all command-line arguments.

Table 1.6: continued

Variable	Explanation
$@	An individually double-quoted list of all command-line arguments.
$!	PID (process ID) number of the last background command.
$$	PID (process ID) number of the current process.
$?	A numerical value indicating the exit status of the last executed command.

Environment Variables

As already mentioned, the values associated with an *environment variable* are visible by child processes of the shell. For a variable to be part of the environment, it must be exported to the environment. This is done with the export command. Earlier, we examined a .profile script. In that file several variables were set, including the PATH, the prompt setting (PS1), and the hostname of the computer. After all the values were set, the varnames were exported to the environment:

EXAMPLE

```
PS1="$HOSTCHAR"':${PWD#HOME/}:!$ '        # Set the prompt variable PS1
PATH="$PATH:/usr/X11R6/bin"               # set the path variable PATH
HOSTNAME='/bin/hostname'                   # Set the hostname variable
                                          # HOSTNAME
export PATH PS1 USER LOGNAME MAIL HOSTNAME HISTSIZE HISTFILESIZE INPUTRC LINES
# Export them all
```

As you can observe from the export list, several varnames can be exported on a single line delimited with spaces. The lines could have just as easily been written like this:

```
PS1="$HOSTCHAR"':${PWD#HOME/}:!$ '
export PS1                                # Export individual variable
PATH="$PATH:/usr/X11R6/bin"
export PATH
HOSTNAME='/bin/hostname'
export HOSTNAME
export USER LOGNAME MAIL HISTSIZE HISTFILESIZE INPUTRC LINES
```

Many times commands can be included on a single line or split onto several lines.

Typically, environment variables use uppercase names, and shell variables use lowercase names. Note that this is a convention and not a rule.

Either type of variable can be created using the same syntax: name=value. The shell assumes you are creating a shell variable, not an environment variable. You must describe your intention to make your variable an environment variable by using the export command export name. This can be accomplished in a single line with the following syntax:

```
$ export name=value
```

The following example creates an environment variable (DENENV), and then uses the ksh command to create a subshell. It shows that the environment variable is known to the subshell. It then exits from the subshell, creates a local shell variable (den), and then creates another subshell to show that the local variable is not known in the subshell:

```
$ export DENENV=Valkyrie          # Create environment variable
$
$ echo $DENENV                    # Display contents
Valkyrie
$
$ ksh                             # Create sub shell
$
$ echo $DENENV                    # Accessible in sub shell
Valkyrie
$
$ exit                            # Exit from sub shell
$
$ den="local Valkyrie"            # Create local variable
$
$ echo $den                       # Display local variable
local Valkyrie
$
$ ksh                             # Create sub shell
$
$ echo $den                       # Not accessible from sub shell

$
$ exit                            # Back to original shell
$
$ echo $den                       # Still available in local shell
local Valkyrie
$
```

Environment File

Many systems have an *environment file* that the system administrator uses to set some basic environments for all users. Typically, this file is located in the /etc directory and can be called env, ENV, environment, or environments. If your system has such a file, another file (such as .profile) contains a line that invokes this script. In addition, some systems have a universal profile that is called as well. A typical Linux system, for example, has one or more files in the /etc/profile.d/ directory that execute at the end of a user's customized profile. The following is an example of such a call:

EXAMPLE

```
for i in /etc/profile.d/*.sh ; do
        if [ -x $i ]; then
                . $i
        fi
done
unset i
```

This snippet of code sets up a variable (i) containing the names of all the files in /etc/profile.d/ whose filenames end in .sh. It then checks each one. If the file is executable, it runs that file in the context of the current shell using the dot command (. $i). After it has finished, it unsets the value of i. Don't worry, the for loop is explained in Chapter 6, "Flow Control."

It seems as if ksh has several startup files. We have just discussed the .profile file, which is a script that runs each time you log on. In addition, system-wide profile files and environment files exist. But what about a script that runs each time a new shell is created?

Each time a new shell is created, ksh searches to see whether the environment variable named ENV is defined. If it is, the script that it points to is executed.

This is useful because it executes each time a shell is created, not just when you log on (although it is executed then also):

```
$ cat .profile
#! /bin/ksh
print "In the profile file"
set -o emacs
PS1='$ '
PATH=$PATH:.
alias ll='ls -la'                       # Set up an alias named ll
$
$ alias ll                              # Display alias ll
ll='ls -la'
$
$ ll                                    # The alias works
total 643
-rw-rw-r--   1 obrien    obrien          0 Nov  4 16:05 !
drwx------  11 obrien    obrien       1024 Nov  9 10:22 .
(…)
$
$ ksh                                   # Create a sub shell
$
```

```
$ alias ll                         # Alias is gone
ll: alias not found
$
$ ll                               # Won't work in sub shell
ksh: ll: not found
$
$ exit                             # Back to parent shell
$
```

The point is that aliases are treated differently from variables. No capability to export aliases exists. (Although an earlier ksh version supported the -x option, that option no longer has any effect.) The only way to get your aliases to be in effect in a subshell is to recreate them. Fortunately, a way to automate the process of recreating your aliases does exist.

As mentioned previously, the ENV environment variable can be used to point to a script that will run as each new ksh is begun. Usually, this variable points to a script in your home directory named .kshrc. But the script can be named anything as long as it is pointed to by the ENV variable. The .kshrc file is a perfect place to put any aliases you want to have available within your subshells.

While experimenting with this functionality, you might want to include a line that displays a message indicating you are currently executing the .kshrc file. You might be surprised at how often the .kshrc script executes!

The following example shows the ENV variable pointing to a script that will run as each new ksh is started. It creates an alias when it executes:

```
$ echo $$                          # Parent pid is 606
606
$
$ alias ll                         # Alias ll exists
ll='ls -la'
$
$ echo $ENV                        # ENV variable not yet set

$
$ ksh                              # Create sub shell
$
$ alias ll                         # Alias ll does not exist
ll: alias not found
$
$ echo $$                          # Child pid is 8435
8435
$
$ exit                             # Exit from sub shell
$
```

```
$ echo $$                              # Back to parent pid 606
606
$
$ export ENV=/home/obrien/.kshrc       # Set up ENV variable
$
$ echo $ENV
/home/obrien/.kshrc
$
$ ksh                                  # Create another sub shell
Executing the .kshrc file
$
$ alias ll                             # Alias exists now
ll='ls -la'
$
$ echo $$                              # Child pid is 8439
8439
$
$ exit                                 # Back to parent 606
$
$ echo $$
606
$
```

History File and Repetition

Earlier it was discussed that my customized prompt gives a number associated with the command that was run. As commands are run, they are saved in the *history file*. Think of it as building a script as you go along. A couple of benefits of having this file are evident. First is the ability to repeat a command without having to retype it, and second is that the commands can then be saved in a different file for later scripting. For ease of viewing, here is the prompt string again:

```
PS1="$HOSTCHAR"':${PWD#HOME/}:!$ '
```

Notice that it looks slightly different from the output the set command provides:

```
PS1='MOOSE:${PWD#HOME/}:!$ '
```

This is because the value for the varname HOSTCHAR is interpreted in the set command.

The prompt looks like this:

```
MOOSE:/home/shell:35$
```

By typing the history command, the user can see the last several commands that were executed, preceded by a number:

```
MOOSE:/home/shell:36$ history
20      clear
21      man set
22      export LINES=50
23      clear
24      ls
25      cat test.pl
26      vi test.pl
27      man man
28      clear
29      ls
30      script
31      ls -la
32      cat .profile
33      set -o
34      set
35      h
```

It is the number in the leftmost column that is important. By typing an r for repeat, any command in the history file can be repeated:

EXAMPLE

```
MOOSE:/home/shell:38$ r 32          # Repeat command number 32
cat .profile
# /etc/profile
# Systemwide environment and startup programs
PATH="$PATH:/usr/X11R6/bin"
# PS1="\$ "
typeset -uxL5 HOSTCHAR=$(uname -n)
PS1="$HOSTCHAR"':${PWD#HOME/}:!$ '
(...)
```

The size of the history file is set with the environment variable HISTFILESIZE. In addition, a number of the commands are kept in memory with the environment variable HISTSIZE. Each of these is set (and exported) in my .profile file.

A second way of repeating commands is available. The shell comes with a choice of built-in editors. My editor of choice—and the most popular for UNIX/Linux—is vi (pronounced "vee eye," not "vie," although, in jest, you can refer to it as "six"). If you have vi enabled, and you should, you can use the editing keystrokes of vi to move up and down, left and right through your history file. To do this, ensure that vi is your editor. (You can do this with Emacs, but I do not cover Emacs in this book. I do, on the other hand, provide a guide to vi in Appendix B, "vi Tutorial.") To set vi as your editor permanently, place the command inside your .profile or some other appropriate environment file. The command is as follows:

```
set -o vi
```

The following example shows my environment options. Notice that vi is turned off. Then, the command is run to turn on vi as my default editor. The options are then rechecked to ensure that the value was set to on:

```
$ set -o
Current option settings
allexport      off  keyword     off  nolog       off  trackall        off
braceexpand    on   login       on   notify      off  verbose         off
bgnice         off  markdirs    off  nounset     off  vi              off
emacs          off  monitor     on   physical    off  viraw           off
errexit        off  noclobber   off  posix       off  vi-show8        off
gmacs          off  noexec      off  privileged  off  vi-tabcomplete  on
ignoreeof      off  noglob      off  restricted  off  vi-esccomplete  on
interactive    on   nohup       on   stdin       on   xtrace          off
$ set -o vi                        # Turn on vi command-line editing
$ set -o                           # Display shell option settings
Current option settings
allexport      off  keyword     off  nolog       off  trackall        off
braceexpand    on   login       on   notify      off  verbose         off
bgnice         off  markdirs    off  nounset     off  vi              on
emacs          off  monitor     on   physical    off  viraw           off
errexit        off  noclobber   off  posix       off  vi-show8        off
gmacs          off  noexec      off  privileged  off  vi-tabcomplete  on
ignoreeof      off  noglob      off  restricted  off  vi-esccomplete  on
interactive    on   nohup       on   stdin       on   xtrace          off
```

With the option set to on, you can press the Esc key, which is the equivalent to switching from insert mode to command mode. You can then use the J key to move down, the K key to move up, the H key to move left, and the L key to move right—just as if they were arrows. This enables you to move up and down through the history list. After you have the desired command at the prompt, you can edit it with the standard editing keystrokes used in vi. If you need to insert something, the command i places you back in insert mode.

Despite the fact that we focus on vi as the editor of choice, you should also be aware of the emacs editor. In particular, the emacs editor might be a more intuitive choice for your command-line editor, even if you use the vi editor for your file edits. You can enable emacs as your command-line editor using the same syntax as shown with vi:

```
$ set -o emacs
```

The emacs editor enables the use of the up and down arrow keys to move forward and backward through the history list, and the left and right arrow keys to move the cursor through the selected line. The actual edits are achieved through the Backspace key (to delete characters), and inserting characters occurs as you type.

The emacs editor might not be present on all systems. The vi editor, however, most likely is available on all systems.

What's Next

When writing this chapter, it seemed like a lot of jumping around, hitting highlights, and juggling was going on. This is because some of the day-to-day shell activities are typically performed by rote and not given much thought as to what is actually happening. So, I thought we should sort out the meanings and uses of environment variables, shell variables, startup files, and other shell items.

Having a basic understanding of the environment will help you regardless of how you use UNIX/Linux. It will make you a more efficient programmer, a better-qualified DBA, a better system administrator, and just an all-around better human being!

You have probably figured out by now that most of the shells are similar, particularly ksh, bash, and sh. Although they are not exactly alike, they are close enough that if you are using any of these three, this book will be a wonderful guide for your adventure to come.

After you are comfortable with the environment, the step to programming in ksh is a relatively small, simple, baby step! Having read this chapter you are prepared for the next step. You are able to take a script, change its permissions as appropriate—based on the users, groups, and other people who need access—and are able to run the script. An old adage states, "History repeats itself." Whoever said this must have been a UNIX guru!

In Chapter 2, "Process Control," we examine how to control the script, enabling it to run either in the foreground or the background and how to have it run automatically. Stay tuned!

Process Control

The previous chapter introduced you to the Korn shell environment. This chapter helps you take that information a step further. You take a closer look at the concept of a process. The environment discussed in Chapter 1, "The Environment," is part of the process context within which a script or command runs. You find out how to schedule the execution of scripts (or commands) at predefined times and examine the difference between background processing and foreground processing. You also discover ways to interact with a process during its execution through signals. In essence, this chapter looks at processes and shows some ways of interacting with them.

This chapter teaches you the following:

- What has to happen for your script to run
- How to start and stop a process
- How to move jobs between foreground and background
- How to schedule jobs to run at specified times
- How to obtain process status
- How to kill, suspend, or terminate a process

How to Run a Script

Simply speaking, executing a script is as easy as typing its name at the shell prompt. Of course, if that were all there was to it, a whole section wouldn't be dedicated to it, now would it? A number of pieces must fall into place for a script to be executed. Here are a few of the prerequisites for script execution:

- The permissions must be correct.

- You must be able to locate the script through the PATH variable or through an absolute file specification.

- System resources must be available to support the execution of the script.

- The correct shell must be invoked to interpret the script's contents.

- The script's syntax must be correct.

- All files referenced during the run must be available.

- The user interaction must be reasonable.

As discussed in the previous chapter, the permissions must be such that the user has both read and execute permissions on the file. Execute access is needed for the actual execution, and read access is needed because the file is not a binary and the shell (which is running under the user's ID) must be able to read the contents of the file.

In addition, the shell must be capable of locating the script file. The directory where the file is located must either be part of the user's PATH variable or the full path and filename must be used at the shell prompt. In the following sample code, the path setting is such as might be established in a .profile file:

```
PATH="$PATH:$HOME:$HOME/bin:"      # Adds two locations to current PATH
export PATH
```

EXAMPLE

Although it does not look like much, it is really doing something. In this particular command, the PATH variable is having two additional directories appended to it. Notice that the current value of PATH (as indicated by $PATH) is included in the assignment. This enables the additional directories to be appended. Had the $PATH not been there, any directories already a part of the $PATH would have been lost. Echoing out the PATH provides the following results:

EXAMPLE

```
$ echo $PATH
/usr/local/bin:/bin:/usr/bin:/usr/X11R6/bin:/home/david:/home/david/bin
```

Two things should be noticed at this point. The first is that each directory is delimited by a colon (:). The second is that $HOME is expanded out to be the location of the user's actual directory of /home/david. This means that the user named david can execute any script in any of the directories listed in the user named david's PATH statement. Permissions still are used to determine whether the script can be executed. Finding the location of a script is just half the battle.

CAUTION

It is legal to place a dot (.) in the path. Many users do this so they can execute files in their current directory. Under no circumstances should a privileged user have the dot directory in her path. This is a HUGE security hole because the root user might cd to a directory where, for example, a script named ls might have been placed. The ls script might show filenames as the real ls command would, but maybe it also removes the password field from the root account (or some similar dastardly act). This is more likely to be a problem if the . appears early in the PATH. This is a famous security hole exploited by hackers over the years!

Because this PATH was for a non-privileged user, /sbin, /usr/sbin, and /usr/local/sbin were not a part of the string. These directories are traditionally reserved for commands and scripts usable only by privileged users and are typically for system (the s in sbin) programs. Many of these scripts and binaries look like they can be run by the ordinary user, but the "dangerous" ones have safeguards built in. The shutdown command is an example of a command containing safeguards:

EXAMPLE

```
$ /sbin/runlevel
N 3
$ /sbin/shutdown    # Attempt to shut down the system
shutdown: must be root.
$
```

First, the user runs the runlevel command. This is a fairly innocuous program that returns the previous and current runlevel (see the man pages on runlevel for more information). Then, the user decides to try a different command—shutdown. If the user is successful then the system comes down. Fortunately, a built-in safeguard checks to see whether the user is root (privileged), and—because the user david does not have a UID of zero (the root account's UID)—the program aborts with an error. Later in the book you will see how to set up such error checking.

Jobs and Processes

When a script is run, the shell goes through several steps to begin the execution. Basically, the current shell opens the executable file, sees that it is a script (not a compiled and linked program executable), and creates a new process, running the shell indicated in the first line of the script file. If the script file does not have the #! /bin/ksh in the first line, the current shell creates a process running the same shell program as the shell from which the script was executed.

Most of what happens is internal and of no concern unless you are studying the kernel, in which case you want a book on UNIX internals and C programming, not on shell programming. From the scripter's perspective, what happens is that a process is added to the system's process table. The process contains several pieces of information that can be viewed using the ps command. The ps command has a wealth of options capable of producing many process statistics. A partial process table is shown for reference. The -ef options request a display showing full information about every process:

```
$ ps -ef |more
UID       PID  PPID  STIME TTY       TIME CMD
david    6724  6702  23:54 pts/2  00:00:00 ps -ef
david    6725  6702  23:54 pts/2  00:00:00 -ksh
```

EXAMPLE

Seven columns (that we are interested in) are associated with a process as indicated by the first line of headers. There are, or can be (depending on your OS) other columns that provide additional information, but we are not concerned with those at this point. The meaning of the ps -ef columns is presented here:

UID	This is the user ID of the person who called the executable.
PID	This is the process ID assigned to the process. This ID is unique to each process. More about this ID is discussed later in this chapter.
PPID	This is the parent process ID. This is the process ID of the process that actually created the process you are examining.
STIME	This is the time the process started.
TTY	The terminal type is listed next. The pseudo-terminal (pts/#) contains the terminal number. This number indicates which pseudoterminal the user was using when he executed the command.

TIME	This indicates the execution time of the process. Note: This is not how long the process has been running, but how much processor time it has used.
CMD	The command being executed is the final field.

Starting a Process

Starting a process is as easy as executing a command. A simple command that can be captured in the process list (as an example) is the man command. The man command requests a display of the manual page for some command. Therefore, the following example uses the man command to display the manual pages for the kill command (in Linux):

```
$ man kill

KILL(1)              Linux Programmer's Manual              KILL(1)

NAME
       kill - terminate a process

SYNOPSIS
       kill [ -s signal | -p ]  [ -a ] pid ...
       kill -l [ signal ]

DESCRIPTION
kill sends the specified signal to the specified process.
       If no signal is specified, the TERM signal is sent. The
       TERM signal will kill processes which do not catch this
       signal. For other processes, it may be necessary to use
       the KILL (9) signal, since this signal cannot be caught.

       Most modern shells have a built-in kill function.

OPTIONS
       pid ...
               Specify the list of processes that kill should sig-
               nal. Each pid can be one of four things. A pro-
               cess name in which case processes called that will
                be signaled. n where n is larger than 0. The pro-
               cess with pid n will be signaled. -1 in which case
               all processes from MAX_INT to 2 will be signaled,
               as allowed by the issuing user. -n where n is
               larger than 1, in which case processes in process
               group n are signaled. IFF a negative argument is
```

EXAMPLE

given, the signal must be specified first; otherwise,
it will be taken as the signal to send.

-s   Specify the signal to send. The signal may be
given as a signal name or number.

-p   Specify that kill should only print the process id
(pid) of the named process, and should not send it
a signal.

-l   Print a list of signal names. These are found in
/usr/include/linux/signal.h

SEE ALSO
     bash(1), tcsh(1), kill(2), sigvec(2)

AUTHOR
Taken from BSD 4.4. The ability to translate process
     names to process ids was added by Salvatore Valente <sva-
lente@mit.edu>.

Linux Utilities   14 October 1994

The man command has to retrieve the appropriate manual pages holding the
information describing a particular command. Usually, the man pages are
compressed in some way. The result is that the process running the man
command must create a subprocess running an uncompress program of
some kind (gunzip in this case) to prepare the data for display. The last
thing the man command has to do is actually display the manual page information.

Most implementations present the output of the unzip to the UNIX more
command. My Linux system uses the less command to do the display work.
(The less command is a newer, more streamlined version of more.) If the
output display is longer than one screen's worth, the less command waits
until the user requests the next page.

The behavior of the less command enables you to get the following example
of some data describing the processes involved with executing a man command:

EXAMPLE

UID	PID	PPID	STIME	TTY	TIME	CMD
shell	27375	27329	10:23	pts/4	00:00:00	man kill
shell	27376	27375	10:23	pts/4	00:00:00	sh -c /bin/gunzip -c /var/catman
shell	27378	27376	10:23	pts/4	00:00:00	/usr/bin/less -is

In reality, three processes were spawned. The first is the command that was run, man kill. This command is the first one in the previous list. The second process that was run was a child process of the first command, sh -c /bin/gunzip -c /var/catman. Notice that the parent process ID of this second process is the process ID of the first process. Finally, the third process was spawned from the second—again, with the parent process ID of the third command being the process ID of the second command. Also notice that the command appeared to take no time. It actually did, but it was such a small amount of process time that it rounds down, becoming zero.

When this command is run from a terminal, the result of the command is displayed on the terminal. This means that the terminal is busy until the command finishes. For an example such as looking at a man page, this is very reasonable and expected. When the command finishes executing, the system will, of course, remove the processes from the process list.

Stopping a Process

Suppose a running process is tying up your terminal. (And suppose you aren't working on a Windows-based workstation on which you could just bring up another terminal window.) What are the options for getting the running process to stop tying up your terminal?

If the goal is to make the process cease and desist, you could kill the process (assuming you are the owner or root). More realistically, you want to get the process to run in the background. *Running in the background* means that the process is running without tying a terminal. If the background job needs input from a terminal, it sends a message to the terminal and waits until it is brought back to the foreground and given its input.

Getting a process that is currently running in the foreground to be running in the background requires two steps. The first step is to stop the process. Note that you are stopping it, not killing it. You can stop a foreground process by pressing Ctrl+Z. This control sequence puts the current process in the background and stops it. In effect, you have suspended the execution of the process. It still exists, but is not eligible to use the processor until it is "unsuspended."

A process that has been *suspended* is still a "live" process in that it still exists within memory, has its own environment, and is listed on the process list. A process that has been *killed*—the method used will determine the actual process involved—is not a "live" process. It does not exist in memory, it no longer has its own environment, and it is not included in the process list. More on killing a process is discussed later in this chapter.

Suspending a process means putting it on hold. It is allowed no more processing time and is in a wait state.

In the following example, a man page is displayed and then the Ctrl+Z key combination is pressed:

EXAMPLE

```
$ man man    # Man page for the man command
man(1)                                                          man(1)


NAME
man - format and display the online manual pages
       manpath - determine user's search path for man pages


SYNOPSIS
       man [-acdfFhkKtwW] [-m system] [-p string] [-C con-
       fig_file] [-M path] [-P pager] [-S section_list] [section]
       name ...


DESCRIPTION
       man formats and displays the online manual pages. This
       version knows about the MANPATH and (MAN)PAGER environment
       variables, so you can have your own set(s) of personal man
       pages and choose whatever program you like to display the
       formatted pages. If a section is specified, man only looks
       in that section of the manual. You may also specify the
       order to search the sections for entries and which prepro-
       cessors to run on the source files via command-line
       options or environment variables. If name contains a /
       then it is first tried as a filename, so that you can do
:          # Ctrl+Z was pressed here
[1]+  Stopped                 man man
$
```

Notice that a couple of things happened. First, the system informed the user that the process had stopped:

```
[1]+  Stopped                 man man
```

Second, the user was returned to the prompt. (On some systems, you must press the Enter key after the Ctrl+Z combination to get the prompt to appear.) Looking at the process list confirms that the process is still running:

```
$ ps -ef |grep man
david     8894  8870  23:18 pts/4   00:00:00 man man
david     8895  8894  23:18 pts/4   00:00:00 sh -c /bin/gunzip -c /var/catman
david     8896  8895  23:18 pts/4   00:00:00 /bin/gunzip -c /var/catman/cat1/
david     8926  8870  23:20 pts/4   00:00:00 grep man
```

By the way, the |grep man part of the command does two things. The first part is the pipe symbol (|). This tells the system to take the output of the command ps -ef and pass it to whatever follows the pipe instead of sending the output to standard output (the screen). The second part, grep, is a way of searching for specific text. Whatever follows the grep command is what is being sought. So, in the previous example, the grep command says to return any line that contains the text "man".

Hopefully, you saw something else that intrigued you when the system suspended the process. Here is another look at the output when the system informed the user that the process had stopped:

```
[1]+  Stopped                 man man
```

Four pieces of information are here. In reverse order are the command (man man), what the system is doing to the command (Stopped), and then two other pieces of information—[1]+.

The [1] is the job number. A *job* is a command or sequence of commands (like a pipeline) presented to the shell on one line. The + after the job number indicates that this is the most recent job that was placed in the background.

The command jobs will list out all jobs currently in the background or stopped for the current user. In the following example, two more commands are started and then put in the background with the Ctrl+Z sequence:

EXAMPLE

```
$ jobs
 [3] + Stopped              more .Xdefaults
 [2] - Done                 ls -la /usr |
       Stopped              more
 [1]   Stopped              man man
```

Note that now three jobs are displayed, and that the job with the + next to it has changed. As mentioned earlier, the + indicates the job most recently placed in the background. The job with the - next to it is the job second most recently placed in the background. Maybe you're thinking that the job numbers would suffice to define the order, so who needs the + and -? Consider that a job can be moved from background to foreground many times during its execution. This means that the + can move from job to job based on recent activities.

The shell keeps track of the most current and previously most current jobs. The most current job is indicated by the + sign. (Some operating systems use the percent [%] sign.) The previously most current job is indicated by the - sign.

The job can fall into one of three status categories: *running*, *stopped*, and *done*. The Done and stopped status categories could have a code after them indicating how the process was stopped or indicating the exit status of the done (finished) process.

Each of the processes listed previously is in a stopped state. You will recall that this means they are not receiving any processing time and are not doing anything. These processes can be started again either in the background or in the foreground. Each of these terms is explained in the following sections.

Background

The bg command resumes a suspended process in the background. This means the process will continue to run in the background until it either finishes or requires access to the terminal. If it requires access to the terminal, it stops on its own, and displays a message to the terminal.

The bg command, if executed without any parameters, assumes you mean to take the most current job (+) and make it run in the background. The following example shows this:

EXAMPLE

```
$ bg                                    # Operates on job number 3
[3] more .Xdefaults
$ jobs
jobs
[3] + Stopped (tty output) more .Xdefaults  # Waiting for input
[2] - Done                 ls -la /usr |
        Stopped            more
[1]     Stopped            man man
```

When the jobs command is run, you can see that the job placed in the background has stopped. The reason for this is indicated by (tty output) and means that the job needs to access the terminal before it can proceed.

Jobs that are known to require the terminal—such as the ones we have been using—are poor candidates for background execution, but it provides some insights into the world of job control.

> **NOTE**
>
> If you attempt to exit from a shell that has jobs either running in the background or in a stopped state, the shell reminds you of these processes and will not let you exit without informing you of your stopped jobs:
>
> ```
> $ exit
> You have stopped jobs
> ```
>
> A second exit command must be given to allow the user to exit the shell. The shell then kills (discussed following) the jobs and then kills the shell.

More jobs than just the most current one can be resumed in the background. As implied earlier, the bg command can have parameters. These parameters fall into one of two categories. Either a plus (+) or minus (-) symbol can be used to indicate the most current or previously most current process, or %job_number can be used, where job_number is the bracketed number as shown in bold here:

```
        $ jobs
  [3] + Stopped                 more .Xdefaults
  [2] - Done                    ls -la /usr |
        Stopped                 more
  [1]   Stopped                 man man
```

Therefore, an example of getting a different background command to start executing in the background would be as shown here:

```
        $ bg %1
  [1] man man
```

You might have guessed that the process man man was restarted. However, it immediately stopped because that particular process requires access to the terminal to continue, as shown in the following output:

```
        $ jobs
jobs
[1] + Stopped (tty output) man man
[3] - Stopped                 more .Xdefaults
[2]   Done                    ls -la /usr |
        Stopped                 more
```

Now that you have a process that needs to run with repetitive interaction from the terminal, the question becomes, "How can this be done?" The fg command can be used to take care of this.

Foreground

When a command is executed from the command line, it is automatically run in the foreground. This means that it has access to (and control of) the terminal, and the user must wait for the command to finish executing before the shell can be used for other purposes. The fg command can be used similarly to the bg command to bring a stopped command or a command currently running in the background into the foreground. This is the situation we were left with in the background discussion.

In the previous section, a process had stopped because it needed access to the terminal. The jobs listing is repeated here for easy reference:

```
$ jobs
jobs
[1] + Stopped (tty output) man man
[3] - Stopped              more .Xdefaults
[2]   Done                 ls -la /usr |
      Stopped              more
```

Originally, when job number one (man man) was run, it was suspended after showing the first page of the man page for the command man. Remember that suspending a process puts it in the background and stops its execution. Also note the man command uses the more command (or a more-like command) to display text on the terminal in a controlled fashion (pressing the spacebar shows the next page, Enter shows the next line, the slash allows searching, B brings you back a page, F brings you forward a page, G takes you to the end of the file, 1G takes you back to the beginning of the file, and ? gets a help display). When you bring the process back into the foreground, it picks up where it left off displaying the next page of text.

The following example brings job number one to the foreground:

```
$ fg %1
```

When the spacebar is pressed, the more command associated with the man command displays another page of text from the man pages describing the man command. After the command has finished, it is removed from the process list and from the job list. The new jobs listing shows this:

```
$ jobs
[3] + Stopped              more .Xdefaults
[2] - Done                 ls -la /usr |
```

Notice that the previously most current job is now the most current job and a new previously most current job is assigned.

Just like the bg command, the fg command can be used to start up any of the stopped jobs in the jobs list. Additionally, it brings the job to the foreground, which provides convenient terminal interaction. The fg command uses the same parameters as the bg command. Either the plus (+) or minus (-) symbol is used, or %job_number is used to indicate which job to continue execution in the foreground, where job_number is the bracketed number from the jobs command output.

NOTE

A third way to move processes to either the background or the foreground has not been discussed. A prefix can be used with the percent sign (*%prefix*), where the prefix is enough of the command to ensure uniqueness within the job list. For example, instead of bringing the command man man to the foreground with the job number, it would have been just as correct to use *%prefix*, as shown in the following example:

```
$ fg %ma

[1] man man
```

Sometimes, the user wants to have a command run in the background when the command is issued. As mentioned before, the default is to have the process run in the foreground. In order to run a command in the background, you must place an ampersand (&) at the end of the command, as shown in the following example:

EXAMPLE

```
$ sleep 10000 &
[1] 13947
$
```

The shell responds by placing the sleep command in the background. Note that this technique puts a job in the background, but does not stop it. The shell returns the PID of the process as well as the job number of the process:

```
$ jobs
[2] + Stopped              more .Xdefaults
[1] - Running              sleep 10000   # Running, not stopped
```

If another command is also sent to the background then that new process's PID and job number are shown:

```
$ sleep 99999 &
[3] 13959
$
```

A quick peek at the jobs listing ensures that everything is running smoothly:

```
$ jobs
[2] + Stopped              more .Xdefaults
[3] - Running              sleep 99999
[1]   Running              sleep 10000
```

The ampersand is very useful in that it allows processes that do not require access to the display to run, and at the same time allows the user to continue using the terminal.

Signals

I recently watched the movie *The Bachelor*. In the movie, one of the supporting cast playing the character of Margo is driving a limousine. The light changes, and the car in front of them sits there. Margo yells at the driver, "What, not your shade of green?!?" Apparently, in New York there are various shades of signals. The same (sort of) holds true for UNIX/Linux. There are different kinds of signals, but, unlike green traffic lights, the differences do matter.

A signal can occur any time during the execution of a command or script. A *signal* is an interrupt sent to the command or script that indicates something has happened that requires attention.

Every UNIX/Linux variant has a slightly different set of signals, but the capability they present is common. The signals that are most commonly used are shown in Table 2.1.

Table 2.1: Signals

Name	Value	Description
SIGHUP	1	Hang up detected on controlling terminal or death of controlling process
SIGINT	2	Interrupt from the keyboard (Ctrl+C)
SIGQUIT	3	Quit signal from the keyboard (Ctrl+\)
SIGKIL	9	Kill signal
SIGTERM	15	Termination signal

Depending on your system, several ways exist to see all your system's particular signals. For the most part, the `kill -l` command lists the signals available for your system. Note that the command is `kill dash ell`, not `kill dash one`. The letter l stands for list in this case. The following are the signals for Linux:

EXAMPLE

```
$ kill -l
 1    HUP Hangup                        33    33 Signal 33
 2    INT Interrupt                     34    34 Signal 34
 3   QUIT Quit                          35    35 Signal 35
 4    ILL Illegal instruction          36    36 Signal 36
 5   TRAP Trace trap                    37    37 Signal 37
 6   ABRT Abort                         38    38 Signal 38
 7    BUS Bus error                     39    39 Signal 39
 8    FPE Floating point exception      40    40 Signal 40
 9   KILL Killed                        41    41 Signal 41
10   USR1 User defined signal 1         42    42 Signal 42
11   SEGV Memory fault                  43    43 Signal 43
12   USR2 User defined signal 2         44    44 Signal 44
```

13	PIPE	Broken pipe	45	45	Signal 45
14	ALRM	Alarm clock	46	46	Signal 46
15	TERM	Terminated	47	47	Signal 47
16	STKFLT	Stack fault	48	48	Signal 48
17	CHLD	Child exited	49	49	Signal 49
18	CONT	Continued	50	50	Signal 50
19	STOP	Stopped (signal)	51	51	Signal 51
20	TSTP	Stopped	52	52	Signal 52
21	TTIN	Stopped (tty input)	53	53	Signal 53
22	TTOU	Stopped (tty output)	54	54	Signal 54
23	URG	Urgent I/O condition	55	55	Signal 55
24	XCPU	CPU time limit exceeded	56	56	Signal 56
25	XFSZ	File size limit exceeded	57	57	Signal 57
26	VTALRM	Virtual timer expired	58	58	Signal 58
27	PROF	Profiling timer expired	59	59	Signal 59
28	WINCH	Window size change	60	60	Signal 60
29	IO	I/O possible	61	61	Signal 61
30	PWR	Power-fail/Restart	62	62	Signal 62
31	UNUSED	Unused	63	63	Signal 63
32		32 Signal 32			

According to the table, only the first 30 signals are defined. Many vendors also provide a man page for viewing this information. In Linux, the command is man 7 signal; in HP-UX, the command is man 5 signal. The suggestion would be that you read the man page associated with your version of UNIX/Linux to see the particulars. For example, some of these signals have default actions—such as stopping a program's execution—whereas others have the default of being ignored.

NOTE

The number between man and the command indicates the section number. Therefore, in HP-UX it is explained in section 5 of the man pages, and in Linux it is explained in section 7. Read the man pages on man to find out more on this.

Generally, UNIX man page sections are as follows:

- **1**—User commands

- **2**—System calls

- **3**—Library routines

- **4**—File formats

- **5**—Miscellaneous

- **6**—Games (usually empty)

- **7**—Special files, drivers, networking,

- **8**—Administrator commands

You can usually get a quick summary of a man page section by typing **man 7 intro**:

```
$ man 8 intro
Reformatting page. Please wait... completed

intro(8)

NAME

  intro - Introduction to system maintenance and operation commands

DESCRIPTION

  This section contains information related to system operation and
maintenance.  In particular, commands (such as newfs) used to create new
file (...)
```

You can generate a one-line description of each man page in a particular section by typing **man -k "(8"** or **apropos "(8"**:

```
$ man -k "(8"

ac (8)                      - Outputs connect-session records
acct, chargefee, ckpacct, dodisk, lastlogin, monacct, nulladm, prctmp,
prdaily,
prtacct, remove, shutacct, startup, turnacct (8)   - Provide accounting
commands for shell scripts
acctcms (8)                 - Produces command usage summaries from
accounting
records
acctcom (8)                 - Displays selected process accounting record
summaries
acctcon1, acctcon2 (8)  - Display connect-time accounting summaries
acctdisk, acctdusg (8)  - Perform disk-usage accounting
acctmerg (8)                - Merges total-accounting files into an
intermediary
file or a daily accounting file
acctprc1, acctprc2, accton (8)   - Perform process-accounting procedures
addgroup (8)                - Adds a new group interactively
adduser (8)                 - Adds a new user interactively
addvol (8)                  - Adds a volume to an existing file domain
(...)
```

Finally, these signals can be seen in the signal.h file, which is typically located in /usr/include/sys/signal.h, but can also be in /usr/include/asm/ signal.h. The following command finds the file for you:

```
$ find /usr/include -name signal.h -print
```

An understanding of C is helpful in understanding this file.

Control Key Signals

Control key signals are a fancy way of referring to a key sequence in which the Ctrl key is held down and another key is pressed. One such signal has already been discussed, the Ctrl+Z signal. As you will recall, this signal stops the foreground process and puts it in the background. Some programs use control key signals to perform tasks.

One program that is not discussed in this book is emacs. There is a huge discussion, with people very devout on both sides, as to which is a better editor—vi or emacs. Given that there is an appendix at the back of this book on vi, you probably have a good idea of which editor the author prefers. The vi editor is the more commonly available editor and is therefore recommended here.

When you see something that begins with the letters Ctrl followed by a plus sign and then another letter, it means you hold down the Ctrl key and then press the other character. For example, when you see Ctrl+C, it means you hold down the Ctrl key, press the C key once, and then let up on the Ctrl key.

The following is not an exhaustive list of the control key signals available on your system. They are, however, many of the default key signals available on almost all systems:

- **Ctrl+**—The Ctrl+\ key signal is the quit signal. It is basically a stronger signal than the Ctrl+C (interrupt) signal. Stronger means that it stops some programs that ignore the interrupt signal and produces a core file also. Core files can be used by programmers for debugging purposes.

- **Ctrl+C**—Ctrl+C is the default interrupt signal. The user wanting to interrupt a process would use this key sequence. In the following example, a simple but long running ls command is set up. The output of this command is being redirected into a special file (/dev/null) that accepts all data sent to it and ignores it. Shortly after its execution, Ctrl+C is pressed:

```
$ ls -lR / > /dev/null
 (ctrl+c)
$ jobs
$
```

EXAMPLE

Following the Ctrl+C being pressed, the list of jobs is shown to emphasize that the ls command was not suspended, but was actually interrupted and the process was removed from execution and from the process list with the Ctrl+C signal.

- **Ctrl+D**—This key sequence is the default end-of-file interrupt. See the at command near the end of this chapter for an example of its use.

- **Ctrl+H**—The default key sequence to erase a character is to use the Ctrl+H key sequence. On many systems, the default is to bind the Backspace key to perform a Ctrl+H signal. Sometimes, however, the Backspace key does not work, and either the Ctrl+H key sequence or the Ctrl+Backspace key sequence must be used.

- **Ctrl+Q**—This is the signal that tells the shell to restart output to your terminal that had been previously stopped with the Ctrl+S signal. It is important to note that whatever is typed at the keyboard still goes to the computer; it just does not echo to the display. See the example after the Ctrl+S signal.

- **Ctrl+S**—The Ctrl+S signal stops output from echoing to your terminal. The Ctrl+Q key sequence is used to restart echoing to your terminal. From the user's perspective, the terminal is frozen. But, as mentioned in the Ctrl+Q discussion, after the output has been restarted, all the buffered output is sent to the screen.

  In the following example, Ctrl+S is pressed; a command is then run (ls -la). After this, Ctrl+Q is pressed:

  ```
  $ (Ctrl+S)
  ```

EXAMPLE

  Ctrl+S has been pressed and the command entered. Now, Ctrl+Q is pressed to turn on output (you will either have to take my word on this, or try the experiment yourself):

  ```
  $ ls -la
  total 96
  drwx------   6 david    shell       4096 Jun  8 22:29 .
  drwxr-xr-x  23 root     root        4096 May 25 18:09 ..
  -rw-r--r--   1 david    shell       1422 Mar 27 14:26 .Xdefaults
  -rw-r--r--   1 david    shell        695 Jun  8 22:29 .profile
  -rw-r--r--   1 david    shell       3394 Mar 27 14:26 .screenrc
  drwxr-xr-x   5 david    shell       4096 Mar 27 14:26 Desktop
  -rw-rw-r--   1 david    shell        836 May 22 17:14 man.set
  -rw-rw-r--   1 david    shell      22840 May 23 00:01 ps.man
  -rw-rw-r--   1 david    shell        126 May 22 17:44 test
  ```

- **Ctrl+Z**—This is the control key sequence discussed earlier in the chapter, and it is used to suspend a foreground operation. See the earlier discussions of foreground and background for examples of using this key sequence.

ps

So far, we have only looked at the jobs that a user has had suspended or that are running in the background. In reality, many processes are usually running that are owned by that user but do not show up on the jobs list. In addition, any number of other jobs are running on the system, from other users' programs to daemons taking care of the system itself. Obviously, the jobs command will not show these processes. These processes can be seen, however, by using the process status command, ps.

The ps command by itself shows the processes running for the current user. In the following example, the jobs command is run, followed by the ps command. In this example, neither of the commands use any parameters or arguments:

EXAMPLE

```
$ jobs
 [2] + Stopped                more .Xdefaults
 [1] - Stopped                ls -la /etc | more
$ ps
  PID TTY          TIME CMD
 7776 pts/1    00:00:00 ksh
12462 pts/1    00:00:00 ls
12463 pts/1    00:00:00 more
12475 pts/1    00:00:00 more
12565 pts/1    00:00:00 ps
```

Notice that the jobs command shows two stopped processes. These processes have been given the process job numbers of 1 and 2.

The ps command shows that five processes are running. In this default display of the output, four columns are shown, PID (process identifier, TTY (terminal), TIME (CPU time used), CMD (command).

NOTE

Some UNIX variants support two implementations of the ps command. Be aware that your default PATH might execute the Berkeley flavor of the ps command, or it might execute the System V flavor of the command. A difference in the columns of information displayed and the command options supported for each type of ps command will exist. Check your man pages for details.

Your UNIX might discern whether your ps command is BSD (Berkeley Software Distribution) or System V by the way you present the options. For example, ps lax (no dash before the options) would request a BSD interpretation, and ps -ef would request a System V interpretation.

Fortunately, most UNIX commands do not suffer from this type of schizophrenia.

You might need more or different information than the actual process status command shows. A number of columns can be retrieved using this powerful command. I refer you to your man pages for more specifics, but I list a few more here because of their importance later:

EXAMPLE

```
$ ps -f
UID         PID  PPID  C STIME TTY        TIME CMD
shell      7776  7775  0 Jun10 pts/1   00:00:00 -ksh
shell     12462  7776  0 16:04 pts/1   00:00:00 ls -la /etc
shell     12463  7776  0 16:04 pts/1   00:00:00 more
shell     12475  7776  0 16:05 pts/1   00:00:00 more .Xdefaults
shell     12710  7776  0 17:04 pts/1   00:00:00 ps -f
```

The two that are important additions when using the full option (-f), are PPID and STIME. The C column is obsolete and won't be discussed. The following explains PPID and STIME:

PPID

This is the parent process ID from which the current process has been instantiated. In this example, processes 12462, 12463, 12465, and 12710 are all child processes of process ID 7775. Process ID 7775 is the parent process of those processes, and in turn, is the child process of 7775, which is not shown.

STIME

STIME shows the time the process was started, if it was started during the same day the process list was shown. If the process has been running longer than the current day, the day the process was started is shown. In this example, the first process (-ksh) was started sometime on June 10th, but the other processes were started today at the time indicated. For example, the ps -f process was started at 17:04 (5:04 p.m.).

The everything option (-e) can be used to see all the processes currently running on the system. It is commonly used with the full option (-f) to give a more complete picture of the processes running on the system. That command would look like this: ps -ef. On a minimal system, at least 60 or 70 processes would be running. A BSD ps command to see all the processes on the system might be ps -laxw (the options are long listing, all processes, even the extra ones not associated with a terminal, and wrap the lines if they are too long for the display).

kill

Such a daunting word, kill. If you are not used to UNIX/Linux, you probably find this word a little aggressive. Just imagine you are applying it toward Barney, the purple dinosaur, and a smile will unfold across your face and the apprehension will vanish.

As a shell programmer, you will have many opportunities to use the `kill` command. The `kill` command sends a signal to a running process and tells it to do something. The signals are distinguished by their signal numbers. A program or script can be prepared to handle, ignore, or take a default action when interrupted by a signal.

The `kill` command uses the following syntax:

```
/usr/bin/kill -s signal pid
/usr/bin/kill [-signal#] pid
/usr/bin/kill -l exit_status
```

The part inside the square brackets is optional. The difference between the first two listed is the signal part. A signal can be identified either by its number or by its symbolic name. If the symbolic name is used, the `-s` signal variant is used. If the signal number is used, the `-#` variant is used, in which the pound sign (#) is replaced by the appropriate signal number.

These are the same signals discussed earlier in the chapter, and you can refer to that earlier discussion for more information. The signal table is repeated in Table 2.2 for ease of viewing.

Table 2.2: Signals (again)

Name	Value	Description
SIGHUP	1	Hang up detected on controlling terminal or death of controlling process
SIGINT	2	Interrupt from the keyboard
SIGQUIT	3	Quit Signal from the keyboard
SIGKIL	9	Kill Signal
SIGTERM	15	Termination Signal

Table 2.2 shows that you can send a number of signals to a process. The default signal used if no explicit signal is given is 15, SIGTERM. Therefore, if a process were running that you owned, which you wanted to terminate, the `kill` command is for you. Of those listed, the two most commonly used are 15 and 9.

The first signal, 15, as stated earlier, is the default signal. This tells the program to stop running. If the process is in the middle of a write or read, the `kill` command allows it to finish its work first. This is the polite way of killing the process. This is also the preferred method to use because it allows the program to clean up after itself.

The second signal, 9, is the mean and nasty killer. It is a signal that can't be handled. It does not allow any signal handlers or termination handlers built into the script or program to execute. On many occasions the `-9` option is the only way to go. Signal number nine is one of the few signals a script writer or programmer does not have the ability to handle. Only one result is possible when number nine is received—process termination.

With any `kill` command, you can identify the target process using either the PID or job number. You must, however, precede the job number with a percent symbol to distinguish it from a PID number. The first example shows taking a command that is running and stopping it by killing it using its process ID. First, you look to see which jobs and processes are running:

EXAMPLE

```
$ jobs
[2] + Stopped              more .Xdefaults
[1] - Stopped              ls -la /etc | more
$ ps
  PID TTY        TIME CMD
 7776 pts/1   00:00:00 ksh
12462 pts/1   00:00:00 ls
12463 pts/1   00:00:00 more
12475 pts/1   00:00:00 more
13532 pts/1   00:00:00 ps
```

After you know which process you are going to kill, carefully enter the `kill` command, making sure you got the process ID (PID) correct:

```
$ kill 12462
$ ps
  PID TTY        TIME CMD
 7776 pts/1   00:00:00 ksh
12462 pts/1   00:00:00 ls
12463 pts/1   00:00:00 more
12475 pts/1   00:00:00 more
13533 pts/1   00:00:00 ps
```

Next, glance at the process status listing again, and you see that the process is still running. You want it dead, and you want it dead now, so reissue the `kill` command—but this time, add the `-9`:

```
$ kill -9 12462
$ ps
  PID TTY        TIME CMD
 7776 pts/1   00:00:00 ksh
12463 pts/1   00:00:00 more
12475 pts/1   00:00:00 more
13534 pts/1   00:00:00 ps
[1] + Killed               ls -la /etc |
        Stopped            more
```

The process status shows it is dead, and job control indicates it is dead as well. A follow-up of the jobs command further proves this:

```
$ jobs
[1] + Killed                ls -la /etc |
      Stopped               more
[2] - Stopped               more .Xdefaults
```

When I was in college, I watched a movie called *The Princess Bride*. In that movie, Westley is dead. His body is taken to Miracle Max to see whether he can be brought back to life. Miracle Max declares that Westley isn't dead, but is mostly dead.

Like Westley, the job is also mostly dead. The job listing cannot remove it from the list until the process associated with it is also killed. And, when the process control listing is examined, it is not obvious which process is the correct more to kill:

```
     $ ps
  PID TTY          TIME CMD
 7776 pts/1     00:00:00 ksh
12463 pts/1     00:00:00 more
12475 pts/1     00:00:00 more
13537 pts/1     00:00:00 ps
```

Fortunately, the -l option with the jobs command can be used to find out the process IDs of the remaining jobs:

```
     $ jobs -l
[1] + 12462 Killed          ls -la /etc |
      12463 Stopped         more
[2] - 12475 Stopped         more .Xdefaults
```

The process ID 12463 is now identified as the one associated with the previously killed command. If the user were killing it with the PID number as was done before, the user would enter the following command:

```
$ kill -9 12463
```

Because the user can also kill it with the job ID, this route is shown for completeness:

```
     $ kill %1
     $ jobs
[1] + Killed                ls -la /etc |
      Terminated            more
[2] - Stopped               more .Xdefaults
$ jobs
[2] + Stopped               more .Xdefaults
```

The jobs command was run twice quickly after the kill command. By doing so, the user was able to take a glimpse at what was happening. It seems that the more command was first terminated. Then, after that process was released, the killed process could be released.

The third way of using the kill command is shown here:

```
/usr/bin/kill -l exit_status
```

The kill -l was used by itself earlier in the chapter to get the exit status list available on the system. If a status number is provided, kill -l returns the text name assigned to that particular value. In the following example, the text name "HUP" is displayed as assigned to the value 1 (one):

```
$ kill -l 1   # Kill dash ell one
HUP
```

You might recall from the discussion on background processing that when processes are running in the background, and the shell is shut down, the shell informs you that processes are running and that you must exit a second time to kill the processes and exit the shell. This is the default response of the shell when it receives the HUP signal (HUP stands for hangup). If a process is a child of the shell and that shell goes away, so do its children:

```
$ ps -ef |grep pts
root      7775  7774  0 Jun10 pts/1    00:00:00 [login]
david     7776  7775  0 Jun10 pts/1    00:00:00 -ksh
david    12475  7776  0 16:05 pts/1    00:00:00 [more]
david    13642  7776  0 21:26 pts/1    00:00:00 ps -ef
david    13643  7776  0 21:26 pts/1    00:00:00 -ksh
```

In the previous listing, the logon process is the parent process of ksh. Also, ksh is the parent of the other commands.

Now, about this time you are probably thinking, "Does this mean that if I start a process, I cannot log out until that process finishes? What if I just want the process to run all night, or at least until it finishes?"

Well, I am glad you asked. This shows you are paying attention. Fortunately, there is a way of having a process run where it ignores the hang up. This is accomplished through the nohup command and is explained next.

nohup Explained

The command nohup is used to ensure that a process will run even if it loses contact with the terminal in which it is attached.

The syntax is simple:

```
/usr/bin/nohup command
```

Showing how the `nohup` command works requires the use of two terminals. In the first terminal, a simple `sleep` command is executed with `nohup`:

```
$ nohup sleep 10000
nohup: appending output to `nohup.out'
```

EXAMPLE

You might recall that the problem with a process existing in the background is that it gets into trouble when it needs to access the display. To get around this, `nohup` appends all output to a file in the current directory called `nohup.out`. This is the meaning of the line following the `nohup` command in the previous example.

The `sleep` command is a way of having a pause. The number following the `sleep` command is how long the process should sleep in seconds. Therefore, you are telling the shell to run the `sleep` command for 10,000 seconds (just over 27 hours), which provides plenty of time to kill the shell and watch what is happening from another shell.

First, you must ensure that the process is running:

```
$ ps -ef |grep sleep
david    13793 13774  0 22:02 pts/2   00:00:00 sleep 10000
```

After killing the parent shell of the command, existence of the `sleep` command is again checked. To find out what has happened with the command, the `ps -ef` command is run with the output passed through the `grep` command searching for "137". This is a simple way of seeing all the process lines that have that number in them. This number was chosen because it is the first three numbers of the PID for the process (13793) and also the first three numbers of the PPID for the process (13774):

```
$ ps -ef |grep 137
david    13774     1  0 22:01 ?       00:00:00 -ksh
david    13793 13774  0 22:02 ?       00:00:00 sleep 10000
david    13811  7776  0 22:05 pts/1   00:00:00 grep 137
```

Killing the process requires nothing special; however, a `HUP` or signal 1 will not work. Therefore, a simple `kill` (which sends signal 15) will work to kill the process:

```
$ kill 13793
$ ps -ef |grep 137
david    13903  7776  0 22:32 pts/1   00:00:00 grep 137
```

Because the command had no output, the file nohup.out is empty, as shown in the following example:

```
$ ls -la nohup.out
-rw-------   1 david     shell           0 Jun 11 22:02 nohup.out
```

Just a reminder, the nohup.out file is placed in the current directory where the command is executed. If the user does not have permission to write to that directory, nohup notices this and informs the user that it is writing the output to the user's home directory. This is shown here:

```
$ cd /opt
$ nohup sleep 10000
/usr/bin/nohup: nohup.out: Permission denied
nohup: appending output to `/home/shell/nohup.out'
```

Because the process runs in the foreground, the user does not have access to the shell. This process is a fine candidate for the ampersand to place it in the background.

Scheduling Jobs

Two utilities are available to manage job scheduling. Which utility the user chooses should depend on what he is trying to accomplish. The first utility is cron. The cron utility is used to schedule events that will occur repeatedly at a fixed time. The second utility is at. The at utility is used to schedule events that will occur only once. I explain each of these utilities in the next sections.

cron

Commands, including scripts, can be set to run on a schedule. This schedule allows fine-tuning for any combination of minutes, hours, day of the month, month of the year, day of the week. The cron file contains crontab entries. A crontab entry is one scheduled event. The following is the syntax of a crontab entry for a Linux system:

```
1 2 3 4 5 user command
```

For a UNIX system it is

```
1 2 3 4 5 command
```

Each number corresponds to the time entries previously mentioned (minutes, hours, day of month, month, day of week). The following table describes each of those times and gives the valid entries for each.

Value	Time	Valid Entries
1	Minute	(0–59)
2	Hour	(0–23)
3	Day of the month	(1–31)
4	Month of the year	(1–12)
5	Day of the week	(0–6, with 0 = Sunday)

Several valid patterns are legal for each time entry. The following table shows these values and gives a description of what they mean.

Value	Description
*	Any valid entry for that time entry
Comma-separated list	Indicates which times are valid for that time increment
Two numbers separated by a dash (-)	Indicates a range of times inclusive of the two numbers

To better understand the `crontab` entries, think of the minutes and hours falling into one section, the days of the month and the months of the year falling into a second section, and the days of the week falling into a third section. Within each section, the numbers are inclusive of each other, and each section is additive. Therefore, a minute of 15 and an hour of 15 means to run the command at 15 minutes past the 15th hour (3:15 p.m.). A day of the month of 15,30 and a month of the year of * would mean to run the command on the 15th and 30th of the month, and on any month of the year. A day of the week of 1 would mean run this on Mondays. Because an example is worth a thousand misunderstood words, look at the following example:

```
0,15,30,45  15  1,16  *  1 /run/your/script/here
```

EXAMPLE

In this example, the script `/run/your/script/here` would run on the 1st and the 16th of every month. It would also run every Monday, and it would run at 3:00 p.m., 3:15 p.m., 3:30 p.m., and 3:45 p.m.

Because flexibility promotes ambiguity, the following table shows some examples of `crontab` entries and a brief explanation of what they mean.

Time	Command	Explanation
01 * * * *	run-parts /etc/ cron.hourly	Run this command if it is 1 minute past the hour, and it is any hour, and it is any day of the month, and it is any month of the year, and it is any day of the week.
02 4 * * *	run-parts /etc/ cron.daily	Run this command if it is 2 minutes past the hour, and it is 4 hours past midnight, and it is any day of the month, and it is any month of the year, and it is any day of the week.

Time	Command	Explanation
22 4 * * 0	run-parts /etc/ cron.weekly	Run this command if it is 22 minutes past the hour, and it is 4 hours past midnight, and it is any day of the month, and it is any month of the year, and it is the 0 day (Sunday) of the week.
42 4 1 * *	run-parts /etc/ cron.monthly	Run this command if it is the 42nd minute of the hour, and it is the 4th hour past midnight, and it is the 1st day of the month, and it is any month of the year, and it is any day of the week.
*/10 * * * *	/sbin/rmmod -as	Run this command if the minutes past the hour can be evenly divided by 10, and it is any hour of the day, and it is any day of the month, and it is any month of the year, and it is any day of the week.
0,10,20,30,40, 50 * * * *	/sbin/rmmod -as	This is the same as the previous example, but the minutes are explicitly given instead of using the division.
15 3 * * 1-5	find $HOME -name nohup.out 2>/dev/ null | xargs rm -f	Run this command if it is 15 minutes past the hour, and it is 3 hours past midnight, and it is any day of the month, and it is any month of the year, and it is Monday, Tuesday, Wednesday, Thursday, or Friday.
0,12-15,27-30 * 21 12 *	/do/something/to/ remind/me/of/my/ wife's/birthday	Run this command if it is 0 minutes, 12 to 15 minutes, and 27 to 30 minutes past the hour, and it is any hour, and it is the 21st day of the month, and it is the 12th month of the year, and it is any day of the week.

It is improper to edit the cron file directly. The proper way of adding a cron entry to the crontab file is by using the -e option to the crontab command. The -e option makes a copy of that user's cron file (or creates a new one if one does not exist), and brings it up in the default editor. When the user exits out of the file, it replaces the original file with the edited one and notifies the cron daemon (called cron or crond) that a new cron file is in place.

The cron daemon then re-reads the file. If the crontab file is edited directly, the cron daemon does not get informed of this, and it then continues to read the crontab file it has cached in memory. This means the changes would be ignored.

at

Use of cron is excellent for tasks that need to be repetitive. But for tasks that need to occur once, the way to go is to use the at utility.

The at utility reads commands from the keyboard and groups them together to be executed at a later, specified time. An at job runs as a separate invocation of the shell (with a separate process group); has no controlling terminal; and inherits the environment variables, umask, the current working directory, and the system resource limits that are in place when the at job is scheduled. Two ways of setting up an at job exist. Their syntaxes are shown here:

```
at [-c|-k|-s] [-m] [-f file] [-q queuename] -t time
at [-c|-k|-s] [-m] [-f file] [-q queuename] timespec...
```

The -c|-k|-s causes the process to run through a C shell, Korn shell, or Bourne shell. These options are not available under most Linux systems. The -m sends mail notification to the user that the job has completed. Conversely, the -f file reads from the indicated file the list of what is to be executed instead of reading from standard input.

The -q queuename indicates on which queue to schedule the job. The options are lowercase letters, a–z (some UNIX variants also support uppercase letters A–Z), with a couple of exceptions. The queuename of a is the default queue for at jobs. The queuename of b, on the other hand, is used for batch processing (this is started with the batch command and executed when the system is not busy with other processing). The queuename of c is used for cron jobs and is not allowed to be used with the at job on most UNIX/Linux systems. Any letter higher than c is valid, but as the queuename approaches z, some UNIX systems increase the *niceness* under which the queuename runs.

NOTE

A process can be *nice* by indicating a willingness to utilize the CPU less often than it would if it were not being nice. This is accomplished with the nice command. The higher the specified nice factor, the nicer you are being. The root user can be nasty with the nice command by specifying a negative number. This makes a process utilize the CPU more heavily than normal. The following is an example:

```
$ nice -n 19 sleep 200 &   # runs sleep (or some other command) niced
[1]     68773
$
$ ps -o nice,pid,comm,pri  # shows nice factor, pid, command, priority
 NI    PID COMMAND         PRI
  0  68767 ksh             44
 19  68773 sleep               63 # The higher the number, the less
➥important you are
```

The only difference between the two is how you specify the time. Some differences (particularly with options) from what I describe here depends on your particular operating system, so be sure to read the man pages for at for your version of UNIX/Linux. For the most part, though, the following examples should work across the board:

EXAMPLE

```
$ at -m now + 1 min    # Execute the sort command 1 min from now
at> sort < test > test.sorted
at> <EOT>              # Ctrl+D
warning: commands will be executed using /bin/sh
job 1 at 2000-06-12 01:57
```

In this example, the file named test is sorted and the output of the command sent to a file called test.sorted. The <EOT> was not typed, but the control key signal Ctrl+D was used, indicating the end of the commands to be run. Notice that the -m option was used so the user would receive email notification that the process ran. That email on a Linux system looks like this:

```
$ mail
Mail version 8.1 6/6/93.  Type ? for help.
"/var/spool/mail/shell": 1 message
>   1 shell@moose.qx.net    Mon Jun 12 01:57  11/341    "Output from your job "
& 1
Message 1:
From shell  Mon Jun 12 01:57:00 2000
Date: Mon, 12 Jun 2000 01:57:00 -0400
From: shell@moose.qx.net
Subject: Output from your job        1

&
```

Had there been any output from the job, that information would have been mailed to the user. This would include any standard output, such as echoes or print statements, as well as any standard errors. The following example is designed to produce an error. Notice that when the at job is invoked, no validation takes place. All validation is done at the time of the execution of the command (technically, validation is done to ensure the at job was set up properly, but the commands the at job contains are not validated):

```
$ at -m now + 1 min
at> sort < not_a_real_file > not_a_real_file.output
at> <EOT>
warning: commands will be executed using /bin/sh
job 2 at 2000-06-12 02:03
```

The output from the at job is listed next:

```
$ mail
Mail version 8.1 6/6/93.  Type ? for help.
"/var/spool/mail/shell": 1 message
> 1 shell@moose.qx.net    Mon Jun 12 02:03  13/389   "Output from your job "
&
Message 1:
From shell  Mon Jun 12 02:03:48 2000
Date: Mon, 12 Jun 2000 02:03:48 -0400
From: shell@moose.qx.net
Subject: Output from your job      2

sh: not_a_real_file: No such file or directory   # Error message

&
```

It is important, as this example shows, to make sure the commands are entered correctly. Also, you should make sure that either all files are reachable in the path of the user executing the at utility or the full pathname is indicated; otherwise, you too will receive a not a real file error.

Relative times are not the only times that are allowed. Depending on your system, you can list a day and time. For example, you could tell it to run at 5 p.m. on Friday with the following command:

```
$ at 5 pm FRIday
at> sort < test > test.input
at> <EOT>
warning: commands will be executed using /bin/sh
job 4 at 2000-06-16 17:00
```

at jobs can be listed with the -l option, as shown with the following syntax:

```
at -l [-q queuename] [at_job_id...]
```

If no queuename is used, the default is the a queue. For example, the following code performs a sorting routine 20 minutes from the time the user executed the command. Again, the system sends the user an email indicating that the process finished:

```
$ at -m now + 20 min
at> sort < test > test.sorted.2
at> <EOT>
warning: commands will be executed using /bin/sh
job 3 at 2000-06-12 02:29
```

Next, the at utility is run with the -l option to show all currently queued jobs:

```
$ at -l
2000-06-12 02:29 a
```

Finally, at jobs can have their jobs removed with the -r option (on most UNIX systems):

```
at -r at_job_id...
```

For the Linux people out there, the atrm command is used to remove a job:

```
atrm job
```

In either case, as long as you are the owner of the at job or superuser of the system, you can delete the job before it has time to execute.

What's Next

At this point, you should know how to run a command. The command can be a system-supplied command, such as ls, or it can be a shell script that either you or someone else has supplied.

In addition, you now know how to find information about processes you have running, as well as other processes running on the system. You have learned how to suspend processes, move processes to the background, and even kill processes.

This chapter also showed you how to schedule a process to run at a later time either repetitively with the cron utility or on a one-time basis using the at utility.

Now that the environment is a more comfortable place, you can start building your own scripts. Chapter 3, "Variables," introduces the use of temporary variables used during the execution of a script.

Variables

When I was in first grade, my teacher gave us this problem:

$$\_ + 3 = 5$$

As a budding mathematician, my job was to figure out what number went in the blank space. When I was in ninth grade, my algebra teacher gave us the following problem:

$$X + 3 = 5$$

As a budding mathematician, my job was to figure out what number the X represented.

Now that I am older and wiser, I have moved away from such nonsense. Today, I know that it was wrong to use X because it has no meaning. Today, I know that the problem should have been written something like this:

$$Number\_Of\_Oranges + 3 = 5$$

As a budding programmer, I have learned that the use of descriptive variables is better than either a blank space or an X.

In all three examples—blank space, X, and Number_Of_Oranges—what is really happening is that a variable is put in place of a value. We know, because we have been doing this since first grade, that each of these variables has the value of 2.

This chapter talks about variables. It explores the various types of variables allowed in shell programming and shows how to set and unset the variables. Along the way, common errors are pointed out.

This chapter teaches you the following:

- How to use variables in a script
- How to use the typeset command
- How to avoid common errors with variables

- How to use arrays in a script

- How to customize variable attributes

Case Sensitivity

The basics of variables were discussed in Chapter 1, "The Environment."
In review, a *variable* is simply a way of expressing a value with a name.
Hence, variables are called *name-value pairs*. When designing your own
variable, you should keep a number of things in mind. The first is case sensitivity.

Case sensitivity means that the case—uppercase and lowercase—of each
letter in the varname is significant. Therefore, two variables can look alike,
but if one or more of the letters is of a different case in one of the variables
then they are two different variables.

For example, each of these is a different variable:

```
Apple    APple    APPle    APPLe    APPLE
aPple    aPPle    aPPLe    aPPLE    applE
apPle    apPLe    apPLE    appLE    ApPle
appLe    appLE    ApLe     ApPLE    AppLE
```

Some standards in programming concerning uppercase and lowercase are
probably wise to follow. You might remember from Chapter 1 that environment variables are conventionally (but not necessarily) all uppercased. As
an example, here are two environment variables shown in Chapter 1. A
shell variable that is exported becomes an environment variable, whether it
is uppercase or not:

EXAMPLE

```
PS1='$ '
PATH=/usr/local/bin:/bin:/usr/bin:/usr/X11R6/bin:/usr/X11R6/bin
```

Other variables, such as the ones you use to program, should be all—or at
least mostly—lowercase. A simple rule when naming a variable is that its
name should be as descriptive as its value is important. Therefore, a temporary variable used to hold a value or as a counter could have a name as
simple as counter or even x. Another simple rule to remember is that the
program you code can be the program you have to change six months from
now—so do yourself a favor and name the variables wisely! Variable names
should document their purposes.

Valid Characters

Part of naming variables wisely is knowing which characters are *valid*
characters to be used in the varname. Valid characters for varnames are

the letters of the alphabet (both upper- and lowercase), numbers, and the underscore character. One caveat is that the varname cannot start with a number. For example, consider the following varnames:

```
Peaches
2Peaches
PeachesAndCream
Peaches4
_2Peaches
```

The second is not a legal varname, but the rest are. Notice that the last example begins with an underscore, which is valid. The second one is not valid because it begins with a number.

Scalar

Two types of variables exist in the Korn shell. The first is a string; the second is a number. Of the numbers, two types are available: integers and floating-point. Most Korn shell implementations support integer numbers only. Korn shell 93, however, supports floating-point numbers. *Integers* are whole numbers, such as 14 and -999. *Floating-points* are numbers that can contain a fraction, such as 3.14159 or -99.54.

A *scalar* is your basic name-value pair that has been discussed in this book. A scalar has a varname and a value. That value can be accessed and assigned by the programmer, as is shown in the next two sections.

Accessing

To this point, the discussion has indicated that a variable has a value. The question therefore becomes, How do you access the value of the variable? Fortunately, the answer is simple. The dollar sign ($) preceding the variable name is used to access the value of the variable.

As an example, look at the following work that was done at the command line:

EXAMPLE

```
$ echo PS1
PS1
$ echo $PS1
$    # Displays the contents of PS1 which is the $
```

The command echo is used to show values. In the first line of the previous code, PS1 is echoed. Sure enough, the shell returns PS1. When the dollar sign is placed before the varname, $PS1, the shell returns the value associated with the variable PS1 (PS1 means prompt string number one).

Assigning

Assigning a value to a varname can be accomplished by placing an equal sign between the varname and the value. A space can't exist either before or after the equal sign. Although you might not have thought about it, you have already seen the assigning of variables in action when you looked at the .profile file in Chapter 1. Here are some examples from that file:

```
HISTSIZE=1000
HISTFILESIZE=1000
```

If a space is used in the value, the value must be placed within quotes, as seen in the following examples:

```
KSH_VERSION='@(#)PD KSH v5.2.14 99/07/13.2'
PS1='$ '
```

More on quoting is discussed in Chapter 5, "Quoting." In the following example, three variables are defined as integers:

```
integer x=0
integer y=1000
integer Num=0
```

typeset

The typeset command is used to define variables. Many variables have aliases that are actually typeset commands. For example, integer, from the previous section, is an alias for typeset -i. The syntax for typeset is

```
typeset [+-AHlnprtux] [+-ELFRZi[n]] [name[=value]]
```

This command is used to set and unset attributes for variables, or to list the varnames and attributes of all variables.

Table 3.1 lists many commonly used attributes and their meanings. Note that not all of these are compatible with all versions of UNIX/Linux. Some of these are specific to Korn Shell 93. Check the man pages for your distribution of UNIX/Linux for a complete listing.

Table 3.1: **Typeset** *attributes*

Attribute	Meaning
-	Used to set attributes after setting value(s)
+	Used to unset attributes after setting values
-A	Associative array
-E	Exponential number; *n* specifies the significant digits
-F	Floating-point number; *n* specifies the number of decimal places (ksh 93)
-i	Integer; *n* specifies the arithmetic base
-l	Lowercase

Table 3.1: continued

Attribute	Meaning
-L	Left justifies; *n* specifies field width
-LZ	Left justifies and strips leading zeros; *n* specifies field width
-n	Name reference
-p	Displays variable names, attributes, and values of all variables
-R	Right justifies; *n* specifies field width
-r	Read-only
-RZ	Right justifies; *n* specifies field width and fills with leading zeros
-u	Uppercase
-x	Export
-Z	Zero-filled; *n* specifies field width; same as -RZ

Here are some examples using typeset. The first displays the names and attributes of all variables:

EXAMPLE

```
$ typeset -p   # Print typeset variables
readonly HISTFILESIZE=1000
readonly HISTSIZE=1000
readonly HOME=/home/shell
readonly HOSTCHAR=MOOSE
readonly HOSTNAME=moose.net
readonly IFS='
'
readonly INPUTRC=/etc/inputrc
readonly KDEDIR=/usr
readonly KSH_VERSION='@(#)PD KSH v5.2.14 99/07/13.2'
readonly LANG=en_US
readonly LC_ALL=en_US
readonly LINES=53
readonly LINGUAS=en_US
readonly LOGNAME=shell
readonly MAIL=/var/spool/mail/shell
readonly MAILCHECK=600
readonly OPTIND=1
readonly PATH=/usr/local/bin:/bin:/usr/bin:/usr/X11R6/bin:/home/shell:/home/
shell/bin:/usr/X11R6/bin
readonly PPID=28568
readonly PS1='$ '
readonly PS2='> '
readonly PS3='#? '
readonly PS4='+ '
readonly PWD=/home/shell
readonly QTDIR=/usr/lib/qt-2.0.1
readonly RANDOM=5837
readonly SECONDS=13191
```

```
readonly SHELL=/bin/ksh
readonly TERM=vt100
readonly TMOUT=0
readonly USER=shell
readonly _=-p
readonly kdepath=/usr/bin
```

The next two examples show initializing and assigning values to two new variables:

```
$ typeset Program=$0
$ typeset host='hostname'
```

The following example (note, this does not work in Linux or any ksh earlier than 93 because they do not recognize the -F attribute) makes salary a floating-point variable that prints two spaces after the decimal point:

```
$ typeset -F2 salary
```

Throughout this book, if an alias for a typeset is available, it usually is used because it is easier to remember (and tends to be a little more cross-platform friendly).

Four Common Errors

You should watch out for four common errors when assigning and accessing variables. These errors do not necessarily produce syntax errors, which makes them an even worse enemy.

The first common error is accessing the variable incorrectly. The following example shows this error:

EXAMPLE

```
$ WIFE=Dana
$ echo $WIFE
Dana
$ $WIFE=Computer
ksh: Dana=Computer: not found
```

More than likely, the previous example is an attempt to set the varname WIFE equal to Computer. However, with the dollar sign there, the shell returns the value of WIFE and is left with Dana=Computer, which is not correct. If the value of WIFE were not previously set, a slightly different error would occur, as shown in the next example:

```
$ $WIFE=Dana
ksh: =Dana: not found
```

The second common error is in not having the dollar sign. The following example shows this error, which is the same error shown previously in the chapter:

EXAMPLE

```
$ echo PS1
PS1
```

In this example, the user is trying to access the value associated with the varname PS1. By not having the dollar sign, it returns the string PS1 instead of the value of PS1. This type of error is much more difficult to catch because no error occurs from the computer's perspective; it just did what the programmer told it to do.

The third common error is assigning a variable that has been previously defined. This is an error despite the fact that it works. This one, similar to the previous one, falls into the category of the computer doing what you said, and not what you meant. The following code shows an example of this:

EXAMPLE

```
$ cat  assigning
#!/bin/ksh

x=4
y=10

while [ $x -le $y ]
do
        echo $x
        ((x=x+1))
        if [ $x -eq $y ]
        then ((x=4))
        fi

done
```

This code, although syntactically accurate, is an endless loop because reassigning x means that whenever x becomes equal to y, its value is reset to 4:

```
$ assigning
4
5
6
7
8
9
4
5
6
7
8
```

```
9
4
5
6
7
(This continues ad infinitum or until Ctrl+C is pressed!)
```

Finally, the fourth common error that a programmer can make is assigning a variable if that variable is not previously defined. A small modification to the previous script accomplishes this. The modification has been bolded to make it easier to find:

EXAMPLE

```
#!/bin/ksh

x=4
y=10

while [ $x -le $y ]
do
        echo $x
        ((x=x+1))
        if [ $x -eq $y ]
        then ((x=z))
        fi

done
```

The change is that when x equals y, x is set to z. Unfortunately, z has not been previously defined. The question therefore is what happens when the program is executed? The following code shows the result:

EXAMPLE

```
$ assigning
4
5
6
7
8
9
0
1
2
3
4
5
6
7
```

```
8
9
0
```
(This continues ad infintum or until Ctrl+C is pressed!)

The shell automatically sets the undefined z to have a value of zero. Notice that the script will still run forever and that no error is ever produced.

Array

A simple definition for an *array* is that it is a single variable (varname) that can store one or more values. The Korn shell has two types of arrays: indexed and associative.

In an *indexed* array, each element of the array is indexed with an arithmetic expression. The index is valid as long as the value of the arithmetic expression is at least zero. The upper value of the arithmetic expression is dependent on the implementation, but in all versions of Linux and UNIX, it is at least 4,095.

NOTE

On a sample Red Hat Linux 6.1 system, a simple program to increment an indexed array had a memory fault after 13088. This means that 13,088 values were stored in one array before a memory error caused the system to crash the program.

In an *associative* array, the subscript is an arbitrary string, such as "Yankees," "Red Sox," or "Tigers."

Declaring

Associative arrays must be declared with typeset -A:

```
$ typeset -Ai Alteams    # values will be integers
$ Alteams["Yankees"]=92
$ Alteams["Red Sox"]=88
```

EXAMPLE An indexed array does not have to be previously declared. If the programmer knows or wants to specify the maximum size of an indexed array, he can use the typeset -u *variable*[*n*] command, where *n* is the upper bound of the array and *variable* is the name of the array, as seen in the following example:

```
typeset -u children[2]
```

There are two ways of assigning values to array elements, and there are two ways of accessing arrays. These are explained next.

Assigning—Two Ways

The first way of assigning a value to an array is similar to what would be done with scalars. Just as a scalar is a variable name with a single value associated with it, an individual array element is treated as a scalar. Using an array name without an element number in square brackets is the equivalent of referencing the zero element of the array. The syntax is varname=value, as shown in the following example:

```
$ Children="Meshia"
```

This example looks identical to a scalar. It could also have been written like this:

EXAMPLE

```
$ Children[0]="Meshia"
```

The arithmetic expression inside the square brackets indicates which array element is being referenced. In most computer languages, including shell programming, indexes begin with the zero value. Therefore, Children[2] actually is a reference to the third indexed value of Children.

The second way of assigning a value to an array is to assign multiple elements at the same time. The syntax is set -A varname value1 value2 ... value*n*, as shown in the following example:

```
$ set -A Children Meshia Andy Ashley Tommy
```

NOTE

In other shells, such as bash, it is written slightly differently and looks like this:

```
Children=(Meshia Andy Ashley Tommy)
```

The following are a couple of items to note:

- The arithmetic expression used for the index must be a positive integer. This means that it cannot be negative, nor can it have a decimal point.

- The term *arithmetic expression* means that the value does not have to be a number, but can be a variable or even an equation, as long as the result of the expression is a positive integer.

The following two examples show using a variable for the indexvalue when assigning a value to an array:

```
$ Cmd[x]="hostname"
$ Cmd[x]="uname -a"
```

These two examples are part of the CHECKIT program used in Chapter 13, "Pulling It All Together."

Accessing—Two Ways

Now that some values are assigned to the arrays, the next question becomes how to access the values. Both indexed and associative arrays are accessed the same way. Just as there are two ways of assigning values to arrays, there are also two ways of accessing those values.

The first way of accessing the value of an array is with the following syntax:

```
${varname[index or string]}
```

The following example uses the `Children` array assigned earlier and returns one of its values:

```
$ echo ${Children[2]}
Ashley
```

EXAMPLE

The second way of accessing the value of an array is to access more than one value at a time. Two characters can be placed in the index portion of the command that allows this. These are shown here:

```
$ echo ${Children[*]}
Meshia Andy Ashley Tommy
```

```
$ echo ${Children[@]}
Meshia Andy Ashley Tommy
```

You are thinking, and rightfully so, that these two commands produce the same output. The difference would have existed if one or more of the values had contained spaces. To further explain this, we will set up a new array for `Children`:

```
$ Children="Meshia Davidson"
$ Children[1]="Ashley Davidson"
```

Now, if the array is accessed, a slightly different output is produced:

```
$ echo ${Children[*]}
Meshia Davidson Ashley Davidson
$ echo ${Children[@]}
Meshia Davidson
Ashley Davidson
```

In most versions of UNIX, the echoing of the children with the * produces four items. In contrast, in most versions of UNIX, the echoing of the children with the @ produces two items, as shown in the previous example. Linux's version of the Korn shell, however, produces four items either way.

Read-Only

The shell provides a way of making a variable read-only. After a variable is declared as read-only, its value cannot be changed. This is shown in the following example:

EXAMPLE

```
$ Children=Meshia
$ readonly Children    # Sets the readonly attribute
                       # on the Children variable
$ echo $Children
Meshia
$ Children=David
ksh: Children: is read only
```

You cannot have any more children because when an attempt to change its value occurred, the shell produced an error and would not allow the value associated with Children to change.

This brings up an interesting problem. If a value is set, such as when you assigned multiple children to the varname Children, how can it be changed? Better yet, when a variable has been set to readonly, how do you get rid of it?

This is addressed next through the use of the unset command.

Unsetting

When going through the examples earlier in the chapter, the variable Children was used several times. What was not shown was the command that was run in between to free up that variable so it could be used again. Here is a more complete listing of commands to let you see what was really going on:

EXAMPLE

```
$ echo ${Children[*]}
Meshia Andy Ashley Tommy
$ unset Children
$ echo ${Children[*]}

$
```

As you can see from the previous code, the unset command is followed by the variable to be freed. If the variable's value is not freed from memory, it cannot be set to something else. But, what about when you made Children a read-only variable? How do you get rid of it?

The quick answer is that you cannot. If you could, it would go against the basic idea of identifying the variable as crucial and unchangeable.

The long answer is that the variable will remain as long as the shell or program environment of which it is a part exists. Therefore, a variable that is set as a part of the environment, such as KSH_VERSION in the following example or the variable Children that you set earlier to be readonly, remains part of the environment until that environment goes away:

```
$ readonly    # Displays all readonly variables
Children
KSH_VERSION
```

If a new environment is instantiated, that new environment will not have the variable Children. It will have the variable KSH_VERSION instead because it is set with each new login. This is shown in the next example:

```
$ su - dennis
Password:
$ readonly
KSH_VERSION
```

When the environment in the previous code is exited, and the previous environment is back in control, the read-only variable Children again returns:

```
$ exit
$ readonly
Children
KSH_VERSION
```

After the environment that contains the variable Children is terminated, the variable is released from memory.

What's Next

As a summary, what can I say? We started out in first grade with

$$\_ + 3 = 5$$

and advanced to defining what went in place of the blank space with a variable. Along the way, we looked at how to assign and access the two types of variables allowed in shell programming—scalars and arrays.

Remember, if a variable is read-only, do not attempt to change it; just put your keyboard down and back away slowly!

In Chapter 4, "Regular Expressions," you look at one of the most powerful ways of manipulating values. You explore regular expressions and delve into pattern matching.

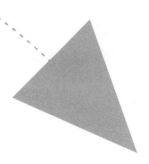

Regular Expressions

Many UNIX programs, languages, editors, and shells use *regular expressions*. They are a way of describing a set of strings through pattern-matching. When you use the expression, "That's cool," you are not presenting literal information on the temperature of the object. You probably are trying to indicate that the object is good, or interesting, or well done, or acceptable, or neat, or...cool.

Similarly, expressions are used by the shell and by utilities to represent an aggregate of string information in a succinct manner.

This chapter teaches you the following:

- The value of regular expressions in scripts
- How to represent groups of characters through character classes
- How to use special pattern-matching characters

Regular Expressions Versus Wildcards

The Korn shell uses a form of regular expressions similar to those used by grep, awk, sed, and other programs. Be aware that the regular expressions used by utilities such as sed and grep are not to be confused with filename expansion used by the shell.

Unfortunately, most syntax used for filename expansion expressions (sometimes called *wildcards*) is the same as the syntax used for string pattern-matching regular expressions. You must take a breath and ask yourself what you are trying to do. Does it involve filenames, or does it involve string patterns? The next sequence shows some filename expansion (wildcards) expressions being used:

EXAMPLE

```
$ ls
obr  obrr  obrrr  regextest   # four files in the directory
$
$
$ ls obr           # no wildcards used
obr
$
$ ls obr?          # single character match wildcard (?)
obrr
$
$ ls obr*          # multiple character match wildcard (*)
obr  obrr  obrrr
$
$ ls obr.*         # pattern '.*' has no special meaning
ls: obr.*: No such file or directory
$
```

The next sequence shows regular string expressions being used. Note that you can start off by thinking of any string as a regular expression, but their power is shown when the special characters are used for pattern matching:

```
$ cat regextest        # file  contents
obr
obrr
obrrr
obrrabcrrr
$ grep 'obr' regextest    # uses regular expression
                          # containing no 'special' characters
obr
obrr
obrrr
obrrabcrrr
$
```

```
$ grep 'obr$' regextest    # looks for 'obr' anchored to the end of a line
obr
$
$ grep 'obr?$' regextest   # question mark has no special meaning
                           # in this context
$
$ grep 'obr*$' regextest   # asterisk means zero or more repeats
                           # of previous R.E.
obr
obrr
obrrr
$
$ grep 'obr.*$' regextest  # Dot means match any single character,
                           # so '.*' means any sequence
                           # of zero or more characters
obr
obrr
obrrr
obrrabcrrr
$
$ grep obr.*$ regextest    # Are the apostrophes superfluous?
obr
obrr
obrrr
obrrabcrrr
$
```

As you will see in the next sequence, using apostrophes is a good habit to
develop when using regular expressions as string pattern input to a utility.
Recall that the shell was happy to expand an asterisk to mean multiple
character match for filenames in the first set of examples in this chapter.
Given the context of a command, unless you tell it differently, the shell
assumes it has the responsibility to filename expand any wildcards you present on the command line. This next sequence uses the xtrace debugging
option, which is discussed further in Chapter 11, "Diagnostics," but which
is used here to expose the shell's actions:

EXAMPLE

```
$ grep obr* regextest # No apostrophes surrounding the R.E.
regextest:obr
regextest:obrr
regextest:obrrr
regextest:obrrabcrrr
$
$ set -o xtrace         # Turn on extended tracing to see what
                        # the shell does
$
$ grep obr* regextest
```

```
+ grep obr obrr obrrr regextest  # Looks for string 'obr' in files
                                 # named 'obrr, obrrr, regextest'
regextest:obr
regextest:obrr
regextest:obrrr                  # Output includes the name of the file
                                 # in which it found string matches
regextest:obrrrabcrrr
$
$ grep 'obr*' regextest
+ grep obr* regextest            # Use apostrophes to avoid any surprises
obr
obrr
obrrr
obrrrabcrrr
$
```

This chapter examines how ksh uses regular expressions. The topics include character classes, pattern matching, back references, and metacharacters. Although this is a fairly short chapter, the information contained herein is powerful and extremely useful.

Mastering regular expressions will save you hours because complicated processing can be performed with simple lines of code that, if they had to be programmed by hand, would be tedious and error prone.

Character Classes

When I was in school, I took a number of classes, but none of them were on character. Ten years after graduation, I learned that my class was having a class reunion. Apparently, someone—in their wisdom—had associated me with 226 other people and had called us the "Class of 1985." Although I am an individual and am unique (just like everybody else), I have been categorized as part of this larger group of people and am forever associated with them whether I like it or not. I recall that when I was in high school there were always four classes. There were then these other people who could also be categorized into parents, teachers, administrators, and staff.

Similarly, characters are thrown together into classes. These classes are broken down according to function. Therefore, a class exists for all the letters and another for numbers. Several classes cover the types of characters, as well. Table 4.1 shows the character classes recognized by ksh and gives a brief description as to why they are grouped together. Be aware that most of these classes were created in Korn Shell 93 and will not work in earlier releases of ksh.

Table 4.1: Character classes

Class	Description
alnum	All digits, all uppercase characters, and all lowercase characters
alpha	All uppercase characters and all lowercase characters
blank	Tabs and spaces
cntrl	Any control character:
digit	0–9
graph	Any digit, uppercase, lowercase, or character
lower	Any lowercase letter
print	Any digit, uppercase, lowercase, character, or the space character
punct	Any punctuation character

Character	Explanation of Special Use
!	Negation operator
"	Grouping quoting
#	Comment Character
#	Substring operator, left truncate
#	Default primary prompt for superuser
$	Default prompt
$	Parameter expansion
$	Special parameter
%	Substring operator, right truncate
%	Job identifier
&	Asynchronous background execution
'	Single quote
-	No options
(	Subshell grouping
)	Subshell grouping
*	Wildcard match on pattern
.	(dot) Working directory
/	Name of root directory
:	Null built-in command
;	Command delimiter
?	Single character match in patterns
@	All Arguments
[	Escape quoting; begin single character match options
\	Escape next character
]	End single character match options
^	Anchor to beginning of line
_	(underscore)
+	Plus sign; performs addition
<	Redirects command input
=	Used in variable assignments
>	Redirects command output

Table 4.1: continued

Class	Description
>	Built-in command to create empty file
>	Default secondary prompt
/	Pathname delimiter
{	Command grouping
|	Pipe command output
}	Command grouping
~	Tilde substitution
space	Tab and spacebar (same as blank)
upper	All uppercase letters
xdigit	All numbers and the letters A–F, both uppercase and lowercase

Now that the classes of characters have been defined, what does this all mean? It means a great deal when pattern-matching is discussed later in the chapter. Suffice it for now to say that it enables the programmer to match any character within a set without having to identify every character within that set. For example, if you want to refer to all characters that are between A and Z and all characters between a and z (remember case is important), it could be written as one of the following:

```
[a-zA-Z]
```

```
[[:alpha:]]
```

Examples of using these can be found later in the chapter in the sections "Pattern Matching" and "Metacharacters."

Pattern Matching

For those familiar with regular expressions in other programs—including Perl, awk, grep, and sed—remember the context, but forget the format. The format of regular expressions is different. A fairly easy way of converting the format into the shell format so that it can be used within a shell script exists. The %P format of printf converts the formats for most versions of UNIX, but it is not an option with older versions of printf. The printf command is discussed in Chapter 10, "Output Control."

The following is an example of printf with the %P modifier. It shows the shell equivalent of the regular expression obr.*$. This regular expression matches any string containing obr and then 0 or more characters up to the end of the line:

```
$ printf "%P\n" 'obr.*$'
*obr*
$
```

EXAMPLE

The ksh uses four pattern characters for pattern processing. These characters are `"*"`, `"?"`, `"["`, and `"]"`. The pattern characters can appear anywhere in a word and any number of times within a word. If a pattern character is quoted, as they are previously shown, the special meaning associated with the pattern character is removed and the shell treats the character just like a regular character instead of a pattern.

Square brackets (`[ ]`) delimit a set of characters from which to choose for a single character match. This was alluded to earlier with the illustration of a character class. Within the brackets, several characters take on special meaning and are handled differently from the way they would normally be handled. The first is the minus sign (`-`), which indicates a range of characters. For example, `a-z` tells the shell to match any one character that is any of the lowercase letters. In the previous section, the following was used to indicate all alphabet characters:

`[a-zA-Z]`

The brackets indicate that a successful match is any one of that set of characters. The following example shows a more complicated example of matching any of a set of characters:

`[Cc]hapter[1-6]`

Notice that more than one bracket is used. This particular example would match any of the following words:

Chapter1   chapter1   Chapter2   chapter2   Chapter3   chapter3

Chapter4   chapter4   Chapter5   chapter5   Chapter6   chapter6

This simple example should help illustrate how much typing, time, and programming energy is saved with a bare minimum of pattern matching.

Simple pattern matching can include the character classes as well. Character classes are distinguished from the characters used to make their names by the brackets and colons placed around them. Consider the following two regular expressions:

`[[:digit:]]`
`[:digit:]`

Although they look similar, the second has only one set of brackets. When you apply each of these to a pattern-matching routine—such as a grep—you get vastly different results. To illustrate this, a sample file has been set up. That file is listed here for reference:

```
$ cat david
#!/bin/ksh

#   Written by David Pitts
#   written on July 2, 2000
```

EXAMPLE

```
#   Pitts Technical Resources, Inc.
#   3175 Custer Drive, Suite 203
#   Lexington, Kentucky  40515
#   Phone:  859-552-3262
#
```

```
first_variable="This is a test of the Emergency System.  This is only a test."
second_variable="If this had been an actual emergency, you would have been"
third_variable="instructed on what to do.  Now, go back to your game of "
forh_variable="Quake. "
```

The first regular expression is used here. The example uses the grep command to search the lines in the file and display all lines that contain at least one digit:

EXAMPLE

```
$ grep [[:digit:]] david   # Searches for digit class
#   written on July 2, 2000
#   3175 Custer Drive, Suite 203
#   Lexington, Kentucky  40515
#   Phone:  859-552-3262
```

As expected, the lines containing digits were returned. Now the second regular expression is used. It searches for any lines that contain any of the set of characters inside the brackets:

EXAMPLE

```
$ grep [:digit:] david      # Single character match request
#!/bin/ksh
#   Written by David Pitts
#   written on July 2, 2000
#   Pitts Technical Resources, Inc.
#   3175 Custer Drive, Suite 203
#   Lexington, Kentucky  40515
#   Phone:  859-552-3262
first_variable="This is a test of the Emergency System.  This is only a test."
second_variable="If this had been an actual emergency, you would have been"
third_variable="instructed on what to do.  Now, go back to your game of "
```

Notice that any line containing any of the characters d, i, g, t, or : was returned. You might have noticed that the fourth variable was spelled differently to allow this example to be shown.

The following is another regular expression example. This time, the search is for any use of the word "emergency":

```
$ grep [Ee]mergency david   # Upper or lowercase E, then mergency
first_variable="This is a test of the Emergency System.  This is only a test."
second_variable="If this had been an actual emergency, you would have been"
```

EXAMPLE Notice that with both the uppercase and lowercase "e" between the brackets, it returns all lines containing either "Emergency" or "emergency".

Sometimes you might want to find instances in which an expression begins or ends with a particular set of characters.

Front

To find a set of characters that match the front of a line, the caret (^) is used. The following example finds all the lines that begin with the comment character (#) in the file `david` using this method:

```
$ grep ^# david    # shows lines that start with the #
#!/bin/ksh
#    Written by David Pitts
#    written on July 2, 2000
#    Pitts Technical Resources, Inc.
#    3175 Custer Drive, Suite 203
#    Lexington, Kentucky  40515
#    Phone:  859-552-3262
#
```

EXAMPLE

Another example would be to find all the lines that begin with an `f` or an `F`:

```
$ grep ^[fF] david
first_variable="This is a test of the Emergency System.  This is only a test."
forh_variable="Quake. "
$
```

EXAMPLE

This example returns two matching instances.

Back

Just as a special character can be used to match the front of a line, another character can be used to match the end of a line. That character is the dollar sign ($). In the following example, all lines are found that end in a number:

```
$ grep [[:digit:]]$ david    # Dollar sign anchors the expression
                             # to the end of the line
#    written on July 2, 2000
#    3175 Custer Drive, Suite 203
#    Lexington, Kentucky  40515
#    Phone:  859-552-3262
```

EXAMPLE

Obviously, this could have also been done this way:

```
$ grep [0-9]$ david
#    written on July 2, 2000
#    3175 Custer Drive, Suite 203
#    Lexington, Kentucky  40515
#    Phone:  859-552-3262
```

EXAMPLE

One further example is needed to show how to handle special characters. Later in the book, you learn that the double quote (") is a special character. To use the double quote in the search pattern, it must be indicated that it is not to be used for its specialness, but as a regular character. This is done with a backslash (\):

```
$ grep  ' \"'$ david
third_variable="instructed on what to do.  Now, go back to your game of "
forh_variable="Quake. "
```

The previous example actually takes the next step. It uses single quotes to indicate that the space before the double quote is included as a character. Two lines end with a space and a double quote, and that is exactly what is returned.

Metacharacters

"I have never meta character I didn't like." No, that is not what is meant here. A *metacharacter* is a character that has a special meaning. Five characters have special meanings. They are shown in Table 4.2 with an explanation of each of their meanings.

Table 4.2: Metacharacters for sub-patterns

Symbol	Meaning
!	Matches all strings except those matched by the pattern-list
*	Matches zero or more occurrences of the pattern-list
?	Matches zero or one occurrence of the pattern-list
@	Matches exactly one occurrence of the pattern-list
+	Matches one or more occurrences of the pattern-list

A *pattern-list* is one or more patterns separated by an ampersand (&) or a vertical bar (|). An & between two patterns indicates that both patterns must be matched. A | between two patterns indicates that either one pattern or the other must be matched. The pattern-list is placed inside a set of parentheses. The parenthesized pattern-list optionally might be preceded by one of the special characters from Table 4.2. Pattern-lists can be used within [[...]], for filename expansion (wildcards), matching in the case statement, and substring expansion.

The following example shows a pattern match of any instance that does not contain the string David or the string Pitts:

```
!(David|Pitts)
```

EXAMPLE

The following example shows a pattern match for any occurrence in which the pattern-list is found only one time:

```
@(Custer & Suite)
```

The following example requests a match on zero or more occurrences of the pattern-list. It will match Den, Dennis, Dennie, or Denny:

EXAMPLE
```
Den*(nis|nie|ny)
```

The following example requests a match on one or more occurrences of the pattern-list. It will match Dennis, Dennie, or Denny:

```
Den+(nis|nie|ny)
```

The following example requests a match on zero or one occurrence of the pattern-list. It will match Den123, Dennis123, Dennie123, or Denny123:

EXAMPLE
```
Den?(nis|nie|ny)123
```

Back References

Some versions of ksh allow for back references. *Back references* allow a sub-pattern to be referred to by number. The number refers to the instance of the open parentheses (counting from the left) starting with 1. Within a pattern, back references are referred to by a backslash followed by the number just mentioned. Therefore, the following example will match any string that begins and ends with the same letter, such as "mom", "dad", or "dumb-founded":

```
@(?)*\1
```

EXAMPLE
Here is the breakdown of the expression. The @ means to match exactly one pattern; the (?) says to match exactly one character. The * says to match zero or more characters, and the \1 says to go back and reference what was after the first parenthesis. Therefore, it matches the same character matched with the (?). The following example is similar to the previous one, but by adding the additional *\1, it says to match any string which begins and ends with the same letter and contains that letter somewhere within the expression. Therefore, it would match "dumb-founded", but would not match "mom" or even "mommy":

```
@(?)*\1*\1
```

EXAMPLE
The next example uses the back reference pattern-matching capability to request that the sed command rearrange the data in a file. I'll explain the pattern after you check out the example:

```
$ cat names        # current contents
obrien, dennis m
ellis, bruce a
```

```
dyment, cheryl c
$
$ sed '1,$s/\([^,]*\), \(.*\)/\2 \1/' names
dennis m obrien    # revised output
bruce a ellis
cheryl c dyment
$
```

This one can give you a headache pretty quickly. Take your time and make sure you understand each of my explanations before you move on to the next part of the pattern. First of all, it is a stream edit request (sed) to be applied to the contents of the file named names. The entire edit request is placed in a set of apostrophes to make sure the shell keeps its hands off of it (no filename expansion or other shell interpretations). The edit should be presented to sed as it exists on the command line.

The edit can be broken into two pieces. The first part indicates which lines should be edited. The 1,$ indicates from line one to the end of the file. The second part indicates that there should be a substitution(s) of the pattern between the first pair of slashes, with the pattern between the second pair of slashes. The trouble comes when trying to pick out the slashes!

If the request were s/a/b/, it would be pretty easy to pick out the slashes. With the more complex edit, your eyes are deceived into seeing teepees and other bizarre constructs. The first slash is after the s; the second slash is before the \2; and the third slash is at the end. Draw over those three slashes with your pen to make them obvious. Therefore, the substitution says to take the stuff between the first pair of slashes and replace it with the stuff in the last pair of slashes. (The slash in the middle is in both pairs.)

The last pair of slashes encompasses a \2 \1 sequence. These represent back references to the second pattern of matched data (\2), and the first pattern of matched data (\1). Now you want to know what was the first pattern of matched data, don't you? The first pattern is represented by \([^,]*\). Focus on the \(and the \). They surround what matched data should go in back reference location number one. The square brackets indicate a single character match; the ^ inside the square brackets says match any characters other than what is in the square brackets; and the asterisk after the brackets means multiple instances of the previous match. So, it gathers all characters on the line up to a comma into back reference location number one.

The next things that appear are a literal comma and a space, which means it must match those two characters exactly, but you are not requesting that they be captured in a back reference location.

After that, you see another \(, which begins the second back reference location match. The contents of the back reference match parentheses is the .* combination, which indicates multiple character match (*) of any characters (.). So, the second back reference location gets the characters after the comma and space (the rest of the line).

So now that sed knows what it is supposed to match, the next question is what is it supposed to replace the pattern with? The final pair of slashes contain the \2 \1 sequence. As you have probably figured out by now, they indicate the contents of back reference location two, a space, and the contents of back reference location one.

What could be easier than that?

Although the back reference capability is probably not one you will use every day, it is a very powerful tool to have in your arsenal. When the need occurs, grab this book off the shelf, refresh your memory, and have a go at it.

What's Next

The way regular expressions are used varies between the Korn shell and many other applications and programming languages. Not only that, the implementation of regular expressions is the most widely varied topic within the Korn shell environment. This means that some of the topics discussed in this chapter might not work with your particular implementation of the Korn shell.

Most of the basic regular expressions used in this chapter should work across the board, with the back references section being the obvious exception to this rule.

As a summary, regular expressions are a way of describing a set of strings through pattern matching. Learning the basics of regular expressions will save you hours of coding and logic problem-solving.

Up to this point, quoting has been used without much explanation as to when and when not to use it. Chapter 5, "Quoting," delves into quoting and gives examples of how to use various quotes to get the desired results and to ensure that the program does exactly what you intend.

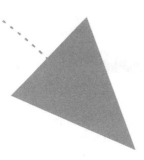

Quoting

Freud has been credited with the saying, "Sometimes a cigar is just a cigar." The same concept holds true in shell scripting, "Sometimes an * is just an *." In the time that I have spent writing and helping others write shell scripts, the single biggest confusion has come from quotes. When do you need to single quote? When do you need to double quote? How do you make a special character, such as an *, just be an *?

This chapter looks at examples of using the escape character and single and double quotes. From there, it moves to cover line continuation. After that, command substitution and parameter expansion are explored. The chapter finishes with arithmetic expansion and arithmetic evaluation.

This chapter teaches you the following:

- The various quoting techniques in the Korn shell

- How to perform command substitution

- How the shell performs parameter and arithmetic expansion

Escape Character

The shell has a number of special characters available. Many times these are called *metacharacters*. These characters are special because the shell interprets them to mean something other than the actual character value. For example, the * is a metacharacter. When the shell sees an *, it replaces it with a 'glob' of stuff. The term *glob* is used in UNIX to represent a bunch of characters—I believe the letters stand for great lot of bytes.

Asterisk with No Escapes

For example, a simple `find` command using an * (and using no escape character) would look like the following example:

EXAMPLE

```
$ find . -name C*
./CHECKIT
```

In the previous example, the shell interprets the `C*` to mean "anything that starts with a capital C and has zero or more characters following it." Therefore, the entire command means "Find from the current directory any file that has as its first character a capital C and has zero or more characters in its name. For every file that you find, list its location relative to the current directory."

What if there were a file literally named `C*t`? Certainly, the `find` command could have found it because it met the criteria. But, without some way of telling the system that we literally mean `C*t`, trying to do anything with that file would be close to impossible.

This is where the escape character comes in. The escape character tells the system that the character being referred to is literally that character, and not some metacharacter. To better show this, a file literally called `C*t` has been added to the current directory. The following is a listing of the directory:

```
$ ls
C*t   CHECKIT   array_index   assigning   integers
```

Now that this file exists, a `find` command is again run. You will notice that, with the exception of the additional file, nothing has changed. Here is the `find` command again:

```
$ find . -name C*
find: paths must precede expression
Usage: find [path...] [expression]
```

Now, an error exists. What happened? The shell did not know how to interpret the `C*` this time because it could not decide whether you meant find all the files that are named `C*` or find all the files that begin with a capital C and contain zero or more characters after that.

Asterisk with Escape

This problem is solved as soon as the escape character is used. The escape character is a backslash (\). Here is the same find command with a backslash (escape character) placed before the *:

```
$ find . -name C\*
./CHECKIT
./C*t
```

EXAMPLE

This is an interesting case that needs some explanation of what is happening. There is always a hierarchy to any command. The *hierarchy* means the shell interprets the line and searches out any special characters. After expanding (or interpreting) the special characters, the shell presents the newly re-formed command line to the program.

The shell looks at the syntax of the line (with the backslash) and recognizes the escape character. It knows, therefore, to pass C* to the find command instead of trying to perform filename expansion. With the backslash (escape character) before the *, the filter within the find command says to ignore the special meaning that the shell assigns to the * character. Therefore, the find command is presented with the * as one of its command-line arguments. Because it is an *, however, the find command recognizes it as a metacharacter within its own program. It then lists out all files that begin with a capital C and contain zero or more characters after that.

Asterisk with No Escapes from a Different Directory

Now, to muddy the waters a little more, what if the command was run from a directory different from the current one? To ask this in a different way: If the user were to back up one directory, in which no files begin with C*, what would happen if the find command were run? If that is the case, as shown in the following example, then no confusion exists and either method works:

```
$ find . -name C*
./scripts/CHECKIT
./scripts/C*t
$
$ find . -name C\*
./scripts/CHECKIT
./scripts/C*t
```

EXAMPLE

The reason for this goes back to the syntax check the shell does. No files begin with C* exist in the current working directory, so the shell knows that the * is a metacharacter. It then passes on that metacharacter to the find command, which performs its recursive search and eventually finds the files in question.

Asterisk with Two Escapes

Before leaving this subject, the next level of complexity would be to find the file C*t without finding CHECKIT. The trick would be to escape the * as before, but then to escape the * again. The first escape would get us past the shell's syntax checker, and the second one would escape the * for the find command. The net result would be the non-special * for the find command. This double escaping is shown here:

```
$ find . -name C\\*t
./C*t
```

Aggregate Quoting Options

At this point, most readers think that there must be an easier way. Fortunately, there is. It is at this point that aggregate quoting becomes useful. I call it *aggregate quoting* because it enables a mechanism to indicate to the shell that a series of characters are not to have their special meaning.

The next sections describe two power levels of aggregate quoting.

Single Quotes

Simply speaking, single quotes around one or more characters are the equivalent of placing escape characters before each of the characters. In the previous example, the file C*t could be found by any of the following methods:

EXAMPLE

```
$ find . -name 'C*t'
./C*t
$ find . -name C'*'t
./C*t
$ find . -name C'*t'
./C*t
```

As long as the * is included in the single quotes, the correct interpretation is found. Notice that the single quotes in no way hurt the regular characters. In fact, quoting non-special characters is completely harmless. This is also true for the escape character and for the double quotes, which I explain in the next section.

A time does exist when a single quote has problems. Any time that an apostrophe (which is, in reality, a single quote) is used in the string, it must be escaped so that the shell does not assume it is a special character. The following shows an example of incorrectly using an apostrophe:

```
$ echo David's Book is Fantastic!!
> ^C
```

Notice that the shell gives the secondary shell prompt (>), assuming that a multiline command had been entered. The secondary shell prompt is exited with Ctrl+C, but this also kills the echo. Notice what happens when a single quote is placed at the secondary shell prompt instead of Ctrl+C:

```
$ echo David's Book is Fantastic!!
> '
Davids Book is Fantastic!!
```

This is obviously a better response because the echo command is allowed to execute, but we lost the apostrophe toward the end of the word "David's". Even placing single quotes around the whole string does not help:

```
$ echo 'David's Book is Fantastic!!'
> '
Davids Book is Fantastic!!
```

The escape character is needed to remove the specialness associated with the single quote, as shown here:

```
$ echo David\'s Book is Fantastic!!
David's Book is Fantastic!!
```

The other problem that occurs many times with single quotes is that they take away too much of the specialness. For example, what happens if you want to have a variable within the command? In the following example, the current logged-in user is being charged a fee for using the session. If the single quotes were around the variables, the following would result:

```
$ echo '$USER you owe us $0.01 per minute for using $HOSTNAME.'
$USER you owe us $0.01 per minute for using $HOSTNAME.
```

It is obvious that substitutions should have been made for both $USER and for $HOSTNAME but not for $0.01. One way around this is to move the single quotes so that they are not around the variables:

```
$ echo $USER' you owe us $0.01 per minute for using '$HOSTNAME'.'
david you owe us $0.01 per minute for using moose.qx.net.
```

Another option is to escape the dollar sign in front of the 0.01 and leave the rest of the sentence alone:

```
$ echo $USER you owe us \$0.01 per minute for using $HOSTNAME.
david you owe us $0.01 per minute for using moose.qx.net.
```

Because of how strictly the single quote blocks everything, a middle-of-the-road approach is available. This approach enables most things to act as if they are escaped—like the single quotes do—but keeps other things as if they are not escaped. This middle-of-the-road approach is achieved through the use of double quotes.

Double Quotes

Double quotes take an approach between escaping everything and escaping nothing. Double quotes take away the special meaning for everything except for the following:

"	End of double-quoted string
$	Variables
\	Escaping characters
`	Command substitution

This, however, does not help with our monetary problem in the previous example, because the dollar sign still needs to be escaped, as is shown in the following example:

```
$ echo "$USER you owe us \$0.01 per minute for using $HOSTNAME."
david you owe us $0.01 per minute for using moose.qx.net.
```

Double quoting saves some time and confusion when the commands begin to get more complex:

EXAMPLE

```
$ echo "$USER, Today's date is ***`date +%m/%d`***"
shell, Today's date is***07/09***
```

Line Continuation

Line continuation is the capability to have a command span more than one line. Two ways of causing a line continuation are available. The first was done accidentally earlier in the chapter; this method is not recommended. It is done by not closing a quote:

EXAMPLE

```
$ echo 'hell
> o world
> this
> is line
> continuation the
> non-
> recommended
> way!'
hell
o world
this
is line
continuation the
non-
recommended
way!
```

This happens because the newline character loses its specialness within the single quotes. This means that instead of signifying that the user is ready to submit a command for processing, the user wants to have the new line as part of the string. Here's the other method:

```
$ echo Hell\
> o world \
> this \
> is line \
> continuation the \
> recommended way!
Hello world this is line continuation the recommended way!
```

I do not recommend that you separate a line arbitrarily as this shows, but when necessary, the technique is a good way of breaking up a line to make it easier to read. Here is an example:

```
$ typeset Separator="#=======================================\
====================================="
$ echo $Separator
#===========================================================================
```

Command Substitution—Two Ways

The example in the "Double Quotes" section containing the syntax `date` is an example of command substitution. *Command substitution* occurs when a command is included as part of the line of code (such as `date`), and when the line is interpreted, the part of the line containing the embedded command is replaced with the output of the embedded command. Two ways of using command substitution are available. The first way is the way shown earlier in the chapter. This method simply places back tics around the command. The back tics are easily confused with the apostrophes. The apostrophe is near the Enter key on most keyboards, whereas the back tic is found above the Tab key in the upper-left of the keyboard (usually). The visual confusion introduced by these two characters looking so much alike has brought a change to the syntax of ksh.

The example from before is shown here for easy viewing:

EXAMPLE

```
$ echo "$USER, Today's date is ***`date +%m/%d`***"
shell, Today's date is***07/09***
```

The second method works on most implementations of the Korn shell. It should be the preferred method if your version supports it. Instead of using

back tics, the command is placed between $(and). The following is the
previous command but with the newer syntax for command substitution:

```
echo "$USER, Today's date is ***$(date +%m/%d)***"
shell, Today's date is***07/09***
```

The second way of performing command substitution is much clearer and
easier to follow than with the back tics.

Parameter Expansion

Parameter expansion substitutes the contents of the parameter in the command line. If the parameter is a variable name, the shell expands the value
of the variable and replaces the variable name with the value of the variable. If the parameter is a number, the parameter is a positional parameter
and represents a value on the command line. In the following example, two
variables are defined. A third variable is then defined that uses the first
two variables as parameters:

EXAMPLE

```
typeset Program=$0
typeset host=$(hostname)
typeset OutFile="/root/CHECKIT/checkout/${Program}.${host}.Current_Output"
echo $OutFile
```

To better illustrate this example, the example has been placed in a file
called Example51.ksh. The following is the execution of that file:

```
$ ./Example51.ksh
/root/CHECKIT/checkout/./Example51.ksh.moose.qx.net.Current_Output
```

If this were the extent of the parameter expansion, there would be no reason not to use the variable name instead, such as the following:

```
typeset OutFile="/root/CHECKIT/checkout/$Program.$host.Current_Output"
```

One strength of parameter expansion is evident when the value of the variable is null or undefined. Default values can be set, allowing the default
value to be used if the value of the variable is either null or undefined.

The file from the previous example has been modified and saved as
Example52.ksh. Here is a listing of the new file:

```
#!/bin/ksh
typeset OutFile=\
"/root/CHECKIT/checkout/${Program:-CHECKIT}.${host:-Moose.com}.Current
➥Output"echo "Outfile is $OutFile"

Program="Test.ksh"
echo "New program is $Program"
echo "Outfile is $OutFile"
```

```
OutFile="/root/CHECKIT/checkout/$Program.$host.Current_Output"
echo "Outfile is $OutFile"

Program=$0
echo "New program is $Program"
echo "Outfile is $OutFile"
OutFile="/root/CHECKIT/checkout/$Program.$host.Current_Output"
echo "Outfile is $OutFile"
```

In this new file, the first couple of lines have been removed. This means that the initial value of $Program is nothing, as is the initial value of $host. In addition, defaults are placed within the parameters. The : - tells the system that if the variable has a null value or is undefined, use the default specified after the : -. Here is the output of that file:

```
$ ./Example52.ksh
Outfile is /root/CHECKIT/checkout/CHECKIT.Moose.com.Current_Output
New program is Test.ksh
Outfile is /root/CHECKIT/checkout/CHECKIT.Moose.com.Current_Output
Outfile is /root/CHECKIT/checkout/Test.ksh..Current_Output
New program is ./Example52.ksh
Outfile is /root/CHECKIT/checkout/Test.ksh..Current_Output
Outfile is /root/CHECKIT/checkout/./Example52.ksh..Current_Output
```

Another strength of parameter expansion is the capability to substitute a different variable. Similar to : -, but with a subtle but powerful difference, is : =. Whereas : - replaces a null or empty string with the word following the : -, : = replaces a null or empty string with the word following it and then performs the parameter expansion with that default word.

For example, in the following code, the value for OutFile has its default value set, a value is then given for the name of the program, and the value for OutFile is then reset. This new file is called Example53.ksh:

EXAMPLE

```
#!/bin/ksh
typeset DEFAULT_OUTFILE="CHECKIT"
echo "Default outfile:\t\t$DEFAULT_OUTFILE"

typeset OutFile="${Program:=$DEFAULT_OUTFILE}"
echo "After typeset:\t\t\t$OutFile"

Program=$0
echo "New program:\t\t\t$Program"
typeset OutFile="${Program:=$DEFAULT_OUTFILE}"
echo "Outfile is :\t\t\t$OutFile"
```

Here is the output of that script:

```
$ ./Example53.ksh
Default outfile:            CHECKIT
After typeset:              CHECKIT
New program:               ./Example53.ksh
Outfile is :               ./Example53.ksh
```

After a value has been given for the file, that value becomes the value for OutFile; until then, the default value is used.

A third strength of the parameter expansion is its capability to display a default error message if the value of the parameter is empty or null. The syntax for this command is :?. In the following example, a message is given to indicate that the value is null. First, here is the source code. Notice it is exactly the same as the previous code, but that the new code (:?*message*) is inserted instead of :=*variable*. This enables the programmer to place error messages within the code that will be displayed. The following example is in a file called Example54.ksh:

EXAMPLE

```
#!/bin/ksh
typeset DEFAULT_OUTFILE="CHECKIT"
echo "Default outfile:\t\t$DEFAULT_OUTFILE"

typeset OutFile="${Program:?"Error, The value of Outfile is Null!"}
echo "After typeset:\t\t\t$OutFile"

Program=$0
echo "New program:\t\t\t$Program"
typeset OutFile="${Program:?"Error, The value of Outfile is Null!"}
echo "Outfile is :\t\t\t$OutFile"
```

Here is the output of that script:

```
$ ./Example54.ksh
Default outfile:             CHECKIT
./Example54.ksh[10]: Program: Error, The value of Outfile is Null!
```

Had that message not been coded into the script, the following would have resulted. First, here is the code without the error message built in:

```
#!/bin/ksh
typeset DEFAULT_OUTFILE="CHECKIT"
echo "Default outfile:\t\t$DEFAULT_OUTFILE"

typeset OutFile="${Program}
echo "After typeset:\t\t\t$OutFile"

Program=$0
echo "New program:\t\t\t$Program"
typeset OutFile="${Program}
echo "Outfile is :\t\t\t$OutFile"
```

Here is the output of the file:

```
$ ./Example54.ksh
Default outfile:              CHECKIT
Outfile is :
echo After
```

Notice that the system did not care that the variable was either null or empty.

Other options can also be used with parameter expansion. The syntax is similar to those shown previously. Table 5.1 shows several other available options.

Table 5.1: Parameter expansion options

Expansion Modifier	Description
`${parameter:-word}`	Substitutes word if parameter is unset or null.
`${parameter:=word}`	Sets parameter to word and substitutes word if parameter is unset or null.
`${parameter:+word}`	Use word if variable is set. Use null otherwise.
`${parameter:?word}`	If parameter is unset or null, display word at standard error and abort script with unsuccessful status (1).
	Note that all four of the previous options can be used with or without the `:`. With the colon, the meaning of null (which is a variable that exists but has a null value) is treated the same as the value of unset (a variable that has been unset does not exist).
`${#parameter}`	Substitutes the number of characters in the contents of parameter.
`${#array[*]}`	Substitutes the number of elements in the array.
`${parameter#pattern}`	If the regular expression pattern given is found at start of the contents of parameter, it deletes the matching characters and substitutes the remainder. The smallest possible match is deleted.
`${parameter##pattern}`	If the regular expression pattern given is found at start of the contents of parameter, it deletes the matching characters and substitutes the remainder. The largest possible match is deleted.
`${parameter%pattern}`	If the regular expression pattern given is found at the end of the contents of parameter, it deletes the matching characters and substitutes the remainder. The smallest possible match is deleted.
`${parameter%%pattern}`	If the regular expression pattern given is found at the end of the contents of parameter, it deletes the matching characters and substitutes the remainder. The largest possible match is deleted.

The following sequence shows examples of many of the parameter expansion options, including a few modifiers:

EXAMPLE

```
$ unset n
$ print ${n-dennis}     # The ':' is optional, without it,
                        # the check is on unset, not null

dennis
$
$ print $n              # Did not set the value of variable n


$
$ print ${n=dennis}
dennis
$ print $n              # Did set the value of variable n
dennis
$
$ print ${n+den}        # Use den if n is set. Use null if unset or null
den
$ print $n
dennis
$
$ print ${z?whoops!}
/bin/ksh: z: whoops!# To standard error
$

$ print ${#n}           # Count of characters in variable n
6
$ ls
names  obr  obrr  obrrr  regextest
$ filenames=(*)         # Creates indexed array named filenames (ksh 93),
                        # use [*] in an earlier ksh
$
$ print ${#filenames[*]}
5                       # Count of array elements
$
$ name=dennis.michael.patrick.obrien   # Set new variable
$
$ print ${name%.*}    # Removes smallest matching right pattern
dennis.michael.patrick
$
$ print ${name%%.*}   # Removes largest matching right pattern
dennis
$
```

```
$ print $name         # Does not change the original variable
dennis.michael.patrick.obrien

$ print ${name#*.*}   # Removes smallest matching left pattern
michael.patrick.obrien

$ print ${name##*.*}  # Removes largest matching left pattern

$
```

Arithmetic Expansion

Command substitution uses the expression $(...), where the output of what is inside the parentheses replaces the expression. Arithmetic expansion uses a similar expression: $((...)).

An easy example demonstrates this. The following is a simple program for performing arithmetic expansion:

EXAMPLE

```
#!/bin/ksh
a=5
b=6
c=$(( a*b ))
echo "$a * $b equals $c"
```

At first glance, the reader is probably unsure what will happen with the echo command. Here is the output of the script (named Example55.ksh):

```
$ ./Example55.ksh
5 * 6 equals 30
```

Notice that the echo command does not expand the math, but gives it literally. A common error here is in removing the double quotes from around the echo command. Here is the program without the double quotes:

```
#!/bin/ksh
a=5
b=6
c=$(( a*b ))
echo $a * $b equals $c
```

And the following is the output:

```
$ ./Example55.ksh
5 C*t CHECKIT Example51.ksh Example52.ksh Example53.ksh Example54.ksh Example55.
ksh array_index assigning integers 6 equals 30
```

It is important to recognize that the program took the metacharacter * and expanded it to equal all the files in the current directory. It then assigned 6 to equal 30. This is obviously not what was intended; more than likely, it is not what the reader expected to happen either.

Arithmetic Expressions

The Korn Shell evaluates arithmetic expressions. A null value evaluates to 0. An easy example taking the previous program and removing the line assigning a value to $b is shown in the following code:

EXAMPLE

```
#!/bin/ksh
a=5
c=$(( a*b ))
echo "$a * $b equals $c"
```

As expected, the value for $b should evaluate to 0. Here is the output of the code:

```
$ ./Example56.ksh
5 *  equals 0
```

The results are as expected. Because $b is undefined, no value is printed in the echo command.

In addition to the standard expressions of plus (+), minus (-), multiply (*), divide (/), and modulus (%), a number of other expressions (normally referred to as *functions*) are allowed. The standard function is denoted by `function (expression)`. Table 5.2 lists some of the mathematical functions available. In this table, functions requiring angles expect the angles to be expressed in radians. Functions are explained in much more depth in Chapter 7, "Data Manipulation."

NOTE

The following list works with some implementations of ksh and not with others. As a general rule, these do not work with the standard implementation of ksh shipped with Linux.

Table 5.2: Functions built into the Korn Shell

Function	Description
abs	Absolute value
acos	Arc cosine of angle in radians
asin	Arc sine
atan	Arc tangent
cos	Cosine
cosh	Hyperbolic cosine
exp	Exponential with base e, where e = 2.718
int	Greatest integer less than or equal to value of expression
log	Logarithm
sin	Sine
sinh	Hyperbolic sine

Table 5.2: continued

Function	Description
sqrt	Square root
tan	Tangent
tanh	Hyperbolic tangent

What's Next

The Freud-accredited quote at the beginning of the chapter has been proven true. There are indeed times when a cigar is just a cigar (and an asterisk is just an asterisk), and when in doubt, quoting helps out. The difference between a single quote and a double quote has been explored. In addition, substitution—both command and arithmetic—has been explored.

Chapter 6, "Flow Control," begins what is for many the real meat of programming—control structures. According to the *X-Files*, the truth *is* out there, and in the coming pages, we will find that truth!

Flow Control

The truth about shell programming is that there is no single way to get a job done. Sometimes a given set of circumstances dictates the best way to accomplish a task, but if the circumstances change, the path down which to travel to arrive at the point of accomplishment becomes less certain. Sometimes logic says we should take the path less traveled.

This chapter introduces control structures, mechanisms by which you can automate decision making as your script runs. These decisions can involve the termination of repetitive activities, the testing of a variable value against a series of cases, testing file existence and characteristics, or simply testing a variable for equality. You will see several syntax options that enable the script's logic to branch, flow and repeat infinitely, flow and repeat a set number of times, or flow and repeat until a condition is met. You also will find ways to break out of a looping construct.

This chapter teaches you the following:

- The syntax of an if test
- How to use ((and [[
- How to use the case statement
- How to use while loops
- How to use until loops
- How to use for loops
- How to use select loops
- How to use the break and continue commands

If Test

To find out the truth, you must ask questions. The *if* test provides a means for the script to query a variable, compare strings, check a loop counter, find out whether a command completed successfully, and perform similar activities.

Basic if-test syntax is as follows:

```
if command
then
command(s)
fi
```

Cute, huh? The logic of the if test is bracketed by the words `if` and `fi`, which is "if" spelled backwards. You will see this same cuteness one other time in this chapter (case/esac). The syntax means that if the command is true, then do the command or commands appearing between the `then` and the `fi`. But how does a command become true or false?

As a command completes, it reports its exit status to the shell. This status is held in a special variable named $? (see Chapter 1, "The Environment"). Therefore, all you have to do is test $? after a command executes and you can decide which road to travel by. That is, do you execute the commands between the `then` and the `fi`, or do you skip them and continue processing with the command that follows the `fi`?

Exit Status

Note that any command, program, or script can exit with an arbitrary exit status, but a status of zero usually represents success.

The following shows a directory with one file in it named tf1:

```
$ ls
tf1
$
```

EXAMPLE The following is the successful execution of an `ls  -l` command. Note that the `print $?` command shows a status of 0 (success):

```
$ ls -l tf1
-rw-r--r--   1 obrien    users      31 Aug 26 15:17 tf1
$
$ print $?
       0
```

The following is the unsuccessful execution of an `ls  -l` command. Note that the `print $?` command shows a non-zero status (failure):

EXAMPLE

```
$ ls -l tf2
ls: tf2 not found
$
$ print $?
   2
$
```

The exit status of the `ls -l` command indicates a failure of some sort. The number to display is determined by the logic of the `ls` program.

You might be wondering why I have spent some energy on describing the return status from a command when I am supposed to be describing the if test. In essence, an if test looks at the return status (0 equals success, and non-zero equals failure) of the command that appears after the if syntax. If the status is 0 (success), the commands between `then` and `fi` are executed. On the other hand, if the status is non-zero (failure), the commands between `then` and `fi` are not executed. Take another look at my general description of the syntax of an if test. It is repeated here for your convenience:

```
if command
then
command(s)
fi
```

Notice that the syntax expects a command after the if. This might not jibe with your recollections of various script snippets you may have seen in other books or at your job site because the syntax seems to imply that you don't need to have a test after the if. You most likely recall syntax such as the following:

```
if (( a == b ))
then
commands_to_do
fi
```

or

```
if [[ $a = $b ]]
then
commands_to_do
fi
```

The ((and [[Commands

Given these two simple examples, and considering the template that has been shown twice, indicating that after the if there should be a command, you must conclude that the ((and the [[are actually commands! Indeed, they are commands, although not exactly what you would call standard commands.

The following example initializes the variable named x to the value of 5 and then executes some ((commands:

EXAMPLE

```
$ x=5                    # Set variable x to 5
$ ((x==5))               # Test contents of x against 5
$ print $?               # Show previous command status
0                        # Success (0), so x must = 5
$ ((x==6))               # Is x = 6?
$ print $?
1                        # Nope
```

Notice that the return status is 0 (success) for the first test and 1 (failure) for the second test. You won't be doing tests using the technique shown in the previous examples. I'm trying to open the hood on the if test so you can peer into the engine of it.

The following example uses more complete and standard syntax to perform a test:

```
$ if ((x==5))
> then
> print "Result is true"
> fi
Result is true
$
```

The ((command is actually a modernization of the let command. You won't find many modern-day scripts performing if tests as follows:

```
$ if let "x==5"
> then
> print "result is true"
> fi
result is true
$
```

This also can open the hood on string comparisons (the ((examples are doing arithmetic comparisons). String tests are surrounded by [[instead of ((. The syntax of the [[command is similar to ((, but it tends to be a bit more picky with respect to whitespace. Make sure that each item within the [[ ]] is separated from the others by at least one space. Note that in the arithmetic comparisons, you could use spaces or not; it made no difference to the shell. It definitely makes a difference with the following string tests:

EXAMPLE

```
$ [[ x = 5 ]]                  # Must precede variable with $
$ print $?
1
$ [[ $x = 5 ]]
$ print $?
0
$
$ [[ $x = 5]]                  # Oops, no space after the 5
>                              # The shell assumes there is more syntax coming
$
$ [[ $x = "5" ]]              # Quotes are ok too
$ print $?
0
$ [[ $x == "5" ]]
$ print $?
0
```

Notice that the test for equality is made using a single =. In ksh93, you should use the == for string equality tests (although the = will still work). If you are using ksh88, the == will cause an error when used for string comparisons.

Other syntax options exist that can appear in older scripts you might be responsible for maintaining. The following example uses some syntax available for numeric tests of string contents (for instance, a string containing the numerals 1 and 7 can be interpreted as the integer 17 or the string containing 1 and 7):

```
$ [[ $x -eq 5 ]]
$ print $?
0
$
```

Syntax Options Used for Testing

The following are conditional tests for numerics using [[ ]]:

- -eq—Tests for equality
- -ne—Not equal
- -gt—Greater than
- -ge—Greater than or equal to
- -lt—Less than
- -le—Less than or equal to

The following are conditional tests for numerics using (( )):

- ==—Equality
- !=—Not equal
- >—Greater than
- >=—Greater than or equal to
- <—Less than
- <=—Less than or equal to

Here are the conditional tests for strings using [[ ]]:

- == (or = ksh88)—Strings are equal.
- !=—Strings are different.
- >—First string is lexically (ASCII precedence) before second.
- <—First string is lexically (ASCII precedence) after second.

A standard if test for string equality might look like the following:

EXAMPLE

```
$ if [[ $x == "5" ]]
> then
> print "Strings are the same"
> fi
Strings are the same
$
```

You are probably wondering what the command underlying the [[is. The [[command is actually the test command in disguise. The test command can still be used to evaluate an expression, but you will seldom see it in an if test. The following is an example of what your if tests could look like:

```
$ test $x == 5                # test command at prompt
$ print $?
0
$
$ if test $x == 5             # test command in an if test
> then
> print "Strings are equal"
> fi
Strings are equal
$
```

This syntax tends to be unwieldy and confusing. Your habit should be to use the [[ ]] for your string tests and the (( )) for your numeric tests.

Commands Within If Tests

The conclusion you should be drawing by now is that an if test expects to be given a command to execute. It evaluates the return status (in variable $?) to see whether the command reports success status. If it was successful, the if logic forces the commands between the then and fi to execute. If the command does not report success status, the commands between then and fi do not execute.

The following examples show simple commands within an if test. The first shows a successful ls command, whereas the second shows a failing ls command:

EXAMPLE

```
$ ls j*                                    # Two junk files exist
junk   junk2
$
$ if ls -l junk2                           # Successful test
> then
> print "ls was successful"
> fi
-rwxr-x---   1 obrien   obrien       1398 Nov 19 13:54 junk2
ls was successful
$
$ if ls -l junk3                           # Unsuccessful test
> then
> print "ls was successful"
> fi
ls: junk3: No such file or directory
$
```

The same result could be attained by an overt test of the contents of $?, but this style would be clumsy and unnecessary:

EXAMPLE

```
$ ls -l junk2
-rwxr-x---   1 obrien   obrien       1398 Nov 19 13:54 junk2
$
$ if [[ $? == 0 ]]
> then
> print "ls was successful"
> fi
ls was successful
$
```

One-Line If Tests Using && or ||

Two operators are available in the Korn Shell to provide a one-line if test. They are the && and || operators. The && means execute the command to the right only if the command on the left was successful. The || means execute the command to the right only if the command on the left was not successful:

EXAMPLE

```
$ ls junk2 && print "Done"
junk2
Done
$
$ ls junk3 && print "Done"
ls: junk3: No such file or directory
$
$ ls junk2 || print "Done"
junk2
$
$ ls junk3 || print "Done"
ls: junk3: No such file or directory
Done
$
```

This can be useful in scripts to quickly test whether a user has presented enough command-line arguments for the script to run, and if not, to prompt the user again. The following example uses the set command to prepare the first three command-line arguments ($1, $2, and $3). Normally, this would be done by the executing shell as a script is started:

```
$ print $#                     # No command-line args currently
0
$
$ set first second third       # Set up first three command-line args
$
$ print $1                     # Display them
first
$
$ print $2
second
$
$ print $3
third
$
$ print $#                     # Count is now three
3
$
$ (($#!=3)) && print "Need three items, dude!"
                               # Use && to decide on reprompt
$
$ shift                        # Remove one argument
$
$ print $#                     # Count is now two
```

```
2
$
$ (($#!=3)) && print "Need three items, dude!"
                                    # Reprompt is necessary now
Need three items, dude!
$
```

An if test can also have one or more elif sections and one else section. If you are sure that the test is binary—meaning it can go one way or the other—then you can use an if/then/else sequence. **If** I had read this book two months ago **then** I would have had an easier time with my job, **else** I just muddle along:

```
$ if ((x==5))
> then
> print "x equals 5"
> else
> print
> print "x does not = 5"
> fi
x equals 5
$
```

If your if test is complex enough, you might have to test for several conditions. The following script uses an elif clause to check for more than one condition in a single if construct:

EXAMPLE

```
$ cat guess
#!/bin/ksh
read guess?"What is your guess? "          # Prompts for number
if [[ $guess -gt 48 ]]
        then
        print "too high"
elif [[ $guess -lt 48 ]]                    # elif statement
        then print "too low"
else
        print "correct"
fi

$
$ guess
What is your guess? 23
too low
$
$ guess
What is your guess? 78
too high
$
```

```
$ guess
What is your guess? 48
correct
$
```

Compound If Tests

If you need to combine more than one test to see whether a condition is met, you can use the syntax from the one-line conditionals (&& and ||) to create compound conditionals. Keep in mind that the && causes the execution of the command to its right only if the command to its left reports success status. Well, suppose the command to its left is an if test? This would result in the left test being performed, and if the test evaluates to true (success), the if test to the right of the && will also execute, and so forth. Essentially, the && functions as a logical and in this case. This means that the entire logical and evaluates to true only if both the if tests evaluate to true.

Likewise, the || functions as a logical or, which means the test to the left of the || or the test to the right must evaluate to true for the result of the entire logical or to be true. The following example tests to see whether the user responds with y or yes, and if so, it tests to see whether the filename found in the first command-line argument ($1) is a regular file. If the user response (prompt is not shown here) is y or yes, the type of file is checked. If it is a regular file, the entire compound if evaluates to true. So whatever commands appeared after the then would be executed:

```
if [[ ($resp=="yes" || $resp=="y") && -f $1 ]]
then
    do_some_commands
fi
```

Be aware that the testing part of a compound if terminates when enough information has been gathered to determine the result of the compound test. For instance, in the previous example, if the user had responded to the prompt with no, the -f $1 test would not have been performed. The reason for this is that the result of the && could be determined after the left part of it evaluated to false. If the left half of the && compound test—which evaluates to true only if both halves are true—evaluates to false, why even bother with the right half? The shell already knows how the movie turns out. It doesn't get the girl and the truck blows up! No. I'm sorry. I got lost in a *Die Hard* plot.

The shell realizes that the entire compound test evaluates to false if the left half of a logical and (&&) evaluates to false, so the testing is "short circuited" at that time and the right part of the compound test is never

executed. Most of the time this is not an issue. I mention it here so you can consider what is really happening during a compound if. Understanding the way a compound if works might get you out of a sticky debugging mess at some point in the future.

Nested If Tests

If tests can be used within other if tests. Be aware that the indentation you might use is meaningless to the shell. The syntax determines the logic of your request. Indentations, however, can be very useful for script readability, which will enhance maintenance efforts in the future.

The following script uses a special file conditional (discussed in Chapter 7, "Data Manipulation") to check whether a file is executable before using the cat command to display its contents. I include it here to show you an example of nested if tests:

EXAMPLE

```
$ ls -l dow1
-rwxrwxr--   1 obrien    obrien          266 Oct 11 14:19 dow1 # Executable file
$
$ ls -l yy
-rw-rw-r--   1 obrien    obrien          111 Nov  6 23:42 yy   # Regular file
$
$ cat showit
#!/bin/ksh
# example of file conditionals
(($# != 1)) && { print "Next time, gimme a file!"; exit 1; }
                                      # Checks for 1 command-line arg
if [[ -f $1 ]]                        # Makes sure file is regular
then
        if [[ -x $1 ]]               # Checks if file is executable
        then
                read response?"$1 is executable still want to see it?"
                if [[ $response == [Yy]* ]]
                                      # Checks for yes response
                        then    cat $1
                else
                        print "Not displaying."
                fi
        else
                cat $1
        fi
```

```
else
        print "$1 is not a regular file.\nNot printing."
fi

$
$ showit
Next time, gimme a file!
$
$ showit yy
  PID TTY          TIME CMD
  614 pts/1     00:04:30 ksh
16911 pts/1     00:00:00 ps
16912 pts/1     00:00:00 tee
$
$ showit dow1
dow1 is executable still want to see it?y   # Asks before displaying executable
#! /bin/ksh

function dow
{
if [[ -z $1 ]]
(...)
$
```

case Conditionals

You might find yourself generating a series of if/elif/elif/elif/else syntax and wondering whether a better way of handling a multiway test exists. The case statement provides a succinct way to express multiway tests. This construct is similar to a switch statement in some programming languages and is vaguely similar to computed go tos. The syntax checks a certain value against several cases. Each case is terminated by ;;, and the value to be tested appears after the case syntax. The syntax is as follows (keywords are bold):

```
case test_variable in
test_pattern1)          command(s)              ;;
test_pattern2)          command(s)              ;;
pattern3|or_pattern4) command(s)             ;;
*)      commands_to_execute_for_default_case    ;;
esac
```

The patterns can include file matching wildcards (?, *, and []). The following example shows a case statement with patterns using the * to represent multiple character match:

EXAMPLE

```
$ date
Mon Nov 20 22:49:15 EST 2000
$
$ date +%B
November
$
$ cat mon
#!/bin/ksh
month=$(date +%B)                                    # get the month name
case $month in
J*)
        print "Current month $month begins with a \"J\"."
        ;;
M*)     print "Current month $month begins with a \"M\"."
        ;;
*)      print "$month starts with letter other than J or M."
        ;;
esac

$
$ mon
November starts with letter other than J or M.
$
```

Looping Constructs

In the next several sections of this chapter, you are introduced to four types of looping mechanisms. A *looping mechanism* is what enables a script writer to repeat a sequence of lines as many times as necessary. Without looping capability, if you wanted to repeat the same three lines of commands five times, you would have to simply type the lines in repetitively in your script. Using a looping mechanism, a repeat sequence is formed and a test is evaluated to determine whether the looping should repeat. As you will see, the positioning of the test and the steps for executing the loop vary slightly for the four flavors of looping.

This clunky technique does work, by the way. But it certainly has no elegance to it. It's like going to the prom in galoshes—you've got shoes on all right, but you sure do look like a jerk.

The next example demonstrates galoshes at the prom:

EXAMPLE

```
$ cat galoshes
#! /bin/ksh
print "left"
print "        right"
print "I'm dancing"
```

```
print "left"
print "          right"
print "I'm dancing"
print "left"
print "          right"
print "I'm dancing"
print "left"
print "          right"
print "I'm dancing"
print "left"
print "          right"
print "I'm dancing"
$
$ galoshes
left
                right
I'm dancing
left
                right
I'm dancing
left
                right
I'm dancing
left
                right
I'm dancing
left
                right
I'm dancing
$
```

Pretty ridiculous, huh? You know a better way must exist, and one does. In fact, several better ways are available. Let's have a look at them.

while Loops

The while loop is useful when you want to repeat a series of lines but aren't quite sure how many times to loop. Your script can set up a test to control whether your logic continues within the loop or jumps out of the loop and executes whichever commands appear after the loop. The general syntax follows:

```
while test
do
command(s)
done
```

The commands between do and done repeat until the test evaluates to false. Be aware, however, that if the test evaluates to false as you enter the loop for the first time, the commands between do and done do not execute at all. The following example has our promgoer dancing slightly more elegantly:

EXAMPLE

```
$ cat galoshes2
#! /bin/ksh
at_prom="yes"
integer count=0
while [[ $at_prom == "yes" ]]              # Dance while at prom
do
print "left"
print "        right"
print "I'm dancing"
count=count+1                              # Keep track of dances
if ((count==5)) then at_prom="no"; fi      # Alter control variable after 5
done
$
$ galoshes2
left
                right
I'm dancing
left
                right
I'm dancing
left
                right
I'm dancing
left
                right
I'm dancing
left
                right
I'm dancing
$
```

The previous example could have used the count variable to control the loop, but it gave me the opportunity to show you a different type of if test and a new loop construct. Once again, keep in mind that the test part of a while loop is at the top of the while loop. If at_prom were set to no at the beginning of the script, our galoshes wearer would not have danced at all!

until Loops

The until loop is similar to the while loop except that the loop continues to execute until the test result changes from false to true. So an until loop

continues until some condition becomes true, whereas a while loop continues until a condition becomes false. The following example continues until
the variable time_to_leave becomes yes:

EXAMPLE

```
$ cat galoshes3
#! /bin/ksh
time_to_leave="no"
integer count=0
until [[ $time_to_leave == "yes" ]]                          # Begin until loop
do
print "left"
print "          right"
print "I'm dancing"
count=count+1
if ((count==5)) then time_to_leave="yes"; fi
done                                                          # End until loop
print "Time to leave"
$
$ galoshes3
left
               right
I'm dancing
left
               right
I'm dancing
left
               right
I'm dancing
left
               right
I'm dancing
left
               right
I'm dancing
Time to leave
$
```

for Loops

The for loop is typically used when the loop count is somewhat predictable.
It also lends itself to repeating the same action on a series of values. The
for loop has two syntax options. If your ksh is not ksh93 or beyond, you
will probably be restricted to the first style of syntax. The following is the
traditional for loop syntax:

```
for control_variable in list_of_values
do
command(s)
done
```

The following example uses our dancing dude to illustrate a for loop. The until loop is not necessary, but I'll leave it there so our dancer knows when to get his galoshes home:

EXAMPLE

```
$ cat galoshes4
#! /bin/ksh
time_to_leave="no"
until [[ $time_to_leave == "yes" ]]
do
for dance in tango lambada twist chacha stroll          # Begin for loop
do
        print "left"
        print "          right"
        print "I'm dancing the $dance!"
done                                                     # End the for loop
time_to_leave="yes"
done
print "Time to leave"
$
$ galoshes4
left
               right
I'm dancing the tango!
left
               right
I'm dancing the lambada!
left
               right
I'm dancing the twist!
left
               right
I'm dancing the chacha!
left
               right
I'm dancing the stroll!
Time to leave
$
```

The newer form of the for loop matches what is available within the C programming language. So if you have some experience with C, you will find this very familiar. If not, I'll get you through it.

Essentially, the newer style of for loop consists of a set of double parentheses within which are three semicolon-separated statements. The three statements are the initializer, which is executed once; the test, which causes the loop body to execute if it evaluates to true; and the iteration, which can be used to increment (or decrement) a variable. The syntax is as follows:

```
for (( initializer_command; test; increment_or_decrement ))
   do
 command(s)
 done
```

The following example uses the newer for loop syntax to keep track of the time so that the dancer knows when to leave the prom:

EXAMPLE

```
$ cat galoshes5
#! /bin/ksh
time_to_leave="no"
integer time=0
set -A dances tango lambada twist chacha stroll  # Array of dances
until [[ $time_to_leave == "yes" ]]
do
for (( hour=8; hour<12; hour++ ))                 # New (ksh93) for loop format
do
time=hour-8
print -n "At $hour o'clock "
               print "left"
               print "         right"
               print "I'm dancing the ${dances[$time]}!\n"
done                                              # End of for loop
time_to_leave="yes"
done
print "Time to leave"
$
$ galoshes5


# Execute script
At 8 o'clock left
               right
I'm dancing the tango!

At 9 o'clock left
               right
I'm dancing the lambada!
```

```
At 10 o'clock left
                right
I'm dancing the twist!

At 11 o'clock left
                right
I'm dancing the chacha!

Time to leave
$
```

select **Loops**

The final looping construct is the select loop. It produces a simple numbered menu with choices for the user. The format of this loop is close to that of the old for loop, except the for is replaced with select and the list consists of menu items. The general syntax is as follows:

```
select control_variable in list_of_menu_items
do
command(s)
done
```

The user is prompted with the string contained in the PS3 variable. The default prompt is #?, but it might be different on your system. If necessary, you can customize a large menu with the LINES and COLUMNS variables. The user's response to the menu should be a number selected from the displayed menu list. The value entered by the user is stored in a variable named REPLY.

The following example provides a menu of dances from which our dancer can choose:

EXAMPLE

```
$ print $PS3                                    # Default prompt for select
#?
$
$ cat galoshes6
#! /bin/ksh
time_to_leave="no"
integer hour=8
PS3="Select a dance :"                          # New select prompt
select dance in tango lambada twist chacha stroll go_home # Menu of dances
do
            print "left"
            print "           right"
case $dance in                                  # Check dance choice
      tango)
            print "At $hour o'clock I'm ${dance}ing\n"
```

```
                              hour=hour+1
                              ;;
                lambada)
                              print "At $hour o'clock I'm ${dance}ing\n"
                              hour=hour+1
                              ;;
                twist)
                              print "At $hour o'clock I'm ${dance}ing\n"
                              hour=hour+1
                              ;;
                chacha)
                              print "At $hour o'clock I'm ${dance}ing\n"
                              hour=hour+1
                              ;;
                stroll)
                              print "At $hour o'clock I'm ${dance}ing\n"
                              hour=hour+1
                              ;;
                *)
                              print "At $hour o'clock I'm outta here."
                              exit
                              ;;
        esac
        done
        $
        $ galoshes6                                    # Execute script
        1) tango
        2) lambada
        3) twist
        4) chacha
        5) stroll
        6) go_home
        Select a dance :3
        left
                        right
        At 8 o'clock I'm twisting

        Select a dance :5
        left
                        right
        At 9 o'clock I'm strolling

        Select a dance :6
        left
                        right
        At 10 o'clock I'm outta here.
        $
```

Loop-Related Commands

The shell provides several loop-related commands to be used in special logic circumstances. For instance, suppose you were executing a while loop and wanted to skip the execution of the rest of the current pass of the loop but continue processing the loop. The continue command provides this capability.

You also might want to exit from a loop prematurely. The break command provides this capability. If you want to exit from the script, you can use the exit command. The exit command can be followed by an exit status, which will be accessible outside the script through $?.

The shift command is a specialized command used to shift the positional parameters (sometimes called command-line arguments) so that one fewer exists than before the shift. The parameter dropped after a shift command is the $1 (first) argument. The following example shows the shift command used in a loop to access the next command-line argument:

EXAMPLE

```
$ cat argshift
#!/bin/ksh
# This script echoes script arguments using
# shift and until
integer next=1
until (($# == 0 ))                          # Checks count, decremented by shift
do
        echo "Parameter $next is $1"
        shift                               # Shifts arguments
        next=next+1
done

$
$ argshift den cheryl chris scott
Parameter 1 is den
Parameter 2 is cheryl
Parameter 3 is chris
Parameter 4 is scott
$
```

Backup Loop Example

The following example might stimulate some thoughts on the power of the looping constructs learned in this chapter. The example takes the output of a df command, isolates the file system names, places them in the list portion of a for construct and performs a dump command on each one of them. The level of the dump command is based on the day of the week (Sunday is level 0, or full dump day). You most likely will have to tweak this script to make it work on your system, but the ideas are powerful and solid.

The script also does some pattern work to isolate the file system name with no slashes (/home becomes home). But this causes a problem with the root file system, so the script handles the special case of the root file system (/) with more pattern work, yielding the backup location for the root file system in /home/backup_root.

The date +%0w command yields the day of the week, with Sunday being day 0. This script would be a good candidate for inclusion as a crontab job so that it could run every night. The dump command is usually restricted to the root user, so this script would have to be run as root:

EXAMPLE

```
$ df | sed -e '1d' -e 's/.* //'     # Generates list of file systems
                                     # Deletes first header line
                                     # Preserves first field in other lines
/
/boot
/home
/usr
$
$ date +%0w                          # Generates numeric day of week
2
$
$ date
Tue Nov 21 02:10:40 EST 2000
$
$ fs_dir=/home                       # Syntax check
$ fs_nam=${fs_dir##/}
$ print $fs_nam
home                                 # Isolates file system name
$
$ fs_dir=/
$ fs_nam=${fs_dir##/}
$ print $fs_nam
                                     # Root (/) will be a special case
$
$ fs_nam=${fs_nam:-root}             # If fs_nam is blank, use "root"
$
$ print $fs_nam
root
$
$
$ cat backemup                       # Script starts
#!/bin/ksh
#####################
```

```
# Script to perform incremental
# backups on a daily basis with Sunday = 0
#######################
PATH=$PATH:/sbin:/usr/sbin
                        # Get the file system directory names
for fs_dir in $(df | sed -e '1d' -e 's/.* //')
do
        ### CHANGE /home/backup to appropriate tape/filename
fs_nam=${fs_dir##/}
        fs_nam=${fs_nam:-root}
        backup_loc=/home/backup_${fs_nam}
        blevel=$(date +%0w)
        print "\n*********************"
        print "Starting level $blevel backup of $fs_dir"
                        # Do incremental backup
        dump -${blevel}uf $backup_loc $fs_dir
        if [[ $? = 0 ]]
        then
                print "Backup of $fs_dir complete."
        else
                print "Error backing up $fs_dir"
        fi
        print "*********************\n"
done

$
$ su -                              # Become root
Password:
[root@linden /root]#
[root@linden /root]#
[root@linden /root]# ./backemup       # No dot in PATH for root

*********************
Starting level 2 backup of /
  DUMP: Date of this level 2 dump: Tue Nov 21 02:16:31 2000
  DUMP: Date of last level 0 dump: the epoch
  DUMP: Dumping /dev/hda8 (/) to /home/backup_root
(...)
Starting level 2 backup of /boot
  DUMP: Date of this level 2 dump: Tue Nov 21 02:17:30 2000
  DUMP: Date of last level 0 dump: the epoch
  DUMP: Dumping /dev/hda1 (/boot) to /home/backup_boot
(...)
Starting level 2 backup of /home
  DUMP: Date of this level 2 dump: Tue Nov 21 02:17:32 2000
  DUMP: Date of last level 0 dump: the epoch
```

```
    DUMP: Dumping /dev/hda6 (/home) to /home/backup_home
(...)
Starting level 2 backup of /usr
  DUMP: Date of this level 2 dump: Tue Nov 21 02:18:09 2000
  DUMP: Date of last level 0 dump: the epoch
  DUMP: Dumping /dev/hda5 (/usr) to /home/backup_usr
(...)

[root@linden /root]# exit              # Back to normal user
logout

$
```

What's Next

Chapter 7 adds to the powerful syntax introduced in this chapter. File tests are introduced to build some sanity checking into your scripts. The use of the filter type of command is discussed, and functions are presented to enable you to build some modularity into your scripts. This chapter and the next chapter should enable you to toss the galoshes and feel pretty confident about your potential for script-writing success.

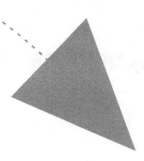

Data Manipulation

Now that you have the power to control the flow of logic in your scripts, you can learn how to manipulate data within a script. Data can be displayed, changed, filtered, tested, compared, declared, or presented to a function. This chapter shows you some examples of the many forms of data manipulation.

Many powerful constructs are shown in this chapter. You will see several examples of filters, as well as numerous test operators for files and strings. Along the way you will see how to manipulate data in functions and use it in computations.

This chapter teaches you the following:

- How to use command-line functions
- How to present arguments to functions
- How to use function return values
- The difference between local and global variables
- How to use object-oriented discipline functions
- How to use a recursive function
- How to autoload a function
- How to use functions to extend the Korn Shell
- The power of filters
- How to use test operators for file and string testing

Functions

As you develop a script, you might find yourself repeating a sequence of lines. An example is a sequence of commands to check for a yes or no response from the user of your script. You might find the same script sequence appearing many times throughout the script.

Let's say the sequence of lines consists of 10 commands. If the sequence needs to be repeated 50 times in a row, it is a candidate to be put in one of the looping constructs discussed in Chapter 6, "Flow Control."

But what if the 50 times that the sequence of 10 commands is to be repeated turn out to be dispersed randomly over the body of your script? Consider the following:

```
Lines
Lines
Lines
(Sequence of 10 commands)
Lines
Lines
(Sequence of 10 commands)
Other lines
Other lines
Lines
(Sequence of 10 commands)
(. . .)
```

This situation is not solved by any of the looping constructs from the previous chapter. You might be thinking that you can handle this by creating a small script containing the sequence of 10 commands and then executing it at the appropriate times. This idea works but involves excess overhead due to the potential for many separate script invocations.

Korn Shell *functions* can contain many commands and do not cause a separate script invocation when used. Functions provide a method to group together commands that might require repetitive, distinct (nonloop) executions. Functions typically execute in the context of the environment in which they are declared. They execute more quickly than dot scripts (scripts run within the current context with the . command—for instance, $. myscript) because they are preread by the shell, they can have local variables, and they preserve positional parameters ($1, $2, and so on).

The two ways to define functions are POSIX-style and Korn Shell-style. The Korn Shell supports both styles, which are differentiated by their syntax. I'm going to present the POSIX-style syntax for reference only. I recommend using the Korn Shell-style functions because they support local variables, unlike the POSIX-style functions, which do not.

POSIX syntax is as follows:

```
function_name()
```

Korn Shell syntax is as follows:

```
function name
```

In the previous code, *function* is a keyword.

Command-Line Functions

The following example declares a Korn Shell-style function called dow, which displays the day of the week and has an option to set the variable WEEKDAY to the current day. This example is typed at the interactive prompt for illustration only. Normally, the following syntax appears at the beginning of a script. Functions created at the command line are removed when the shell exits:

```
$ function dow
> {
> if [[ -z $1 ]]                  # Check for existence of option on command
➥line
> then
>     date +%A                    # If not, display day of week on stdout
>       return 0                  # Return success
> fi
> case $1 in
> -s) WEEKDAY=$(date +%A);;       # If -s is used, set variable WEEKDAY
> *) print "Format is \ndow [-s]" # Anything else is an error
>     return 1;;                  # Return failure
> esac
> }
$
$ dow
Wednesday
$
$ dow -s                          # Sets variable silently
$
$ print $WEEKDAY
Wednesday
$
$ dow -x                          # Invalid option
Format is
dow [-s]
$
```

Viewing Functions

Functions can be viewed with the following typeset options:

- `typeset -f`—Shows function names and definitions

- `typeset +f`—Shows names only

- `typeset -f` *name_of_function*—Shows named function definition only

The following example requests that the shell display the names of functions it currently knows. The dow function is the one just created. The mc function happened to be in existence on my Red Hat UNIX system:

EXAMPLE

```
$ typeset +f                        # Shows names only
dow
mc
$
```

The following example shows the actual contents of the function named mc.

```
$ typeset +f mc              # Linux function found on Red Hat 6.1,
                             # runs Midnight Commander visual shell
mc()
{
        mkdir -p ~/.mc/tmp 2> /dev/null # Make parent directories if needed
        chmod 700 ~/.mc/tmp             # Make sure owner has rwx permissions
MC=~/.mc/tmp/mc$$-"$RANDOM"     # Make a random filename, store in MC
        /usr/bin/mc -P "$@" > "$MC"    # Run the mc program
        cd "'cat $MC'"                 # cd to temp directory
        rm "$MC"                       # Remove temporary file
        unset MC;                      # Clear variable
}
$
```

Function Arguments Versus Command-Line Arguments

The dow function shown previously checks for one argument. If it gets passed no arguments, it assumes you want the output on the screen. If you present it with the -s argument, it assumes you want to set the value of the variable WEEKDAY. Note that command-line arguments presented to a script do not automatically become command-line arguments to a function executing within that script:

The following example creates a function named dow within a script named dow1. The lesson to be learned from the example is that $1 inside of a function refers to the first argument to the function, whereas $1 inside of a script refers to the first positional parameter passed to the script on the command line:

EXAMPLE

```
$ cat dow1
#! /bin/ksh

function dow                          # Defines function within this script
{
if [[ -z $1 ]]                        # $1 is first argument to function
then
     date +%A
     return 0
fi
case $1 in
-s) WEEKDAY=$(date +%A);;
 *) print "Format is \ndow [-s]"
    return 1;;
esac
}
# Script begins execution here #
print "first arg is $1"              # Script gets argument from command line
                                     # into $1

dow                                  # Function call, presents no arguments
print "WEEKDAY contains $WEEKDAY"

$

$ chmod ug+x dow1                    # Make script executable
$
$ ./dow1                             # Execute (not relying on PATH)
first arg is
Wednesday
WEEKDAY contains
$ dow1 -s                            # Execute (relying on PATH)
-ksh: dow1: not found
$
$ echo $PATH                         # No dot (current directory) in PATH
/usr/local/bin:/bin:/usr/bin:/usr/X11R6/bin
$
$ PATH=$PATH:.                       # Add current directory to PATH
$
$ echo $PATH
/usr/local/bin:/bin:/usr/bin:/usr/X11R6/bin:.
$
$ dow1 -s                            # Present argument to script
first arg is -s
```

```
Wednesday
WEEKDAY contains                    # Variable not set
$
```

If you change the script so you call the dow function and present $1 to it, you effectively are giving the script's command-line argument to the function:

```
$ cat dow2
#! /bin/ksh

function dow
}
(...)                               # Same as in dow1
}
# Script begins execution here #
print "first arg is $1"
dow $1                              # Added $1
print "WEEKDAY contains $WEEKDAY"

$
$ dow2 -s
first arg is -s
WEEKDAY contains Wednesday          # WEEKDAY is set
$
```

Function Return Values (Integer)

The function can pass a return value back to the calling script by using the return statement. Typically, this technique is used to pass small (< 255) integer values back to the script. The return value then can be checked by the calling script by examining the contents of $?. The next example adds some return statements to the dow function and checks the returned value:

EXAMPLE

```
$ cat dow3
#! /bin/ksh
function dow
{
(...)
case $1 in
-s) WEEKDAY=$(date +%A)
    return 2;;                      # Added this return statement
                                    #Returns value to dow3 script
 *) print "Format is \ndow [-s]"
    return 1;;                      # Returns value to dow3 script
esac
}
# Script begins execution here #
```

```
print "first arg is $1"
dow $1                              # Call dow
case $? in                          # Check return value from function dow
0) print "Displayed";;
        1) print "Error";;
        2) print "Set";;
        *) print "undefined";;
esac
print "WEEKDAY contains $WEEKDAY"
return 0                            # This value is returned to the shell
$
$ dow3
first arg is
Wednesday
Displayed                           # Function returned 0
WEEKDAY contains
$
$ dow3 -s
first arg is -s
Set                                 # Function returned 2
WEEKDAY contains Wednesday
$
$ dow3 -x
first arg is -x
Format is
dow [-s]
Error                               # Function returned 1
WEEKDAY contains
$
$ print $?0
                                    # Script returned 0 to the shell
```

Function Return Values (String)

If necessary, you can return a string from a script. You simply enclose the function call in a set of parentheses preceded by a dollar sign. In effect, you are capturing the script's output as a string. Typically, you would store the string in a variable. In the next example, I have removed a few lines from the script, but included syntax to enable the function to return a string:

```
$ cat dow4
#! /bin/ksh
function dow
{
(...)                               # Same as previous examples
}
# Script begins execution here #
```

```
retval=$(dow $1)                      # Captures function output
                                      # in variable 'retval'
print "String value returned from the function is $retval."
                                      # Prints returned string
print "WEEKDAY contains $WEEKDAY"
return 0
$
$ dow4
String value returned from the function is Wednesday.
                                      # String returned from function
WEEKDAY contains
$
```

Function Programming Details

The next few subtopics might be a bit on the shaky side for nonprogrammers. But hey, we're here to learn how to write scripts (which are very program-like), so damn the torpedoes, let's dive in! You are about to learn that functions can have local and global variables, present function arguments by value or by reference, be recursive, be autoloaded, be made to execute in an object-oriented way, and even be used to execute home-grown C programming language functions. If you are starting to feel queasy, put a yellow tab in the book at this point and move on to the math section of this chapter. Come back here after you have digested the rest of the information in this very important chapter. If you're still with me, strap in tightly. Here we go!

Local Variables

Earlier in this chapter, I mentioned that a function can declare a *local variable*, which is a variable whose value is meaningful only within the function. Any variable that is explicitly declared within the function is considered local to that function. So, if funcA uses a variable named count and funcB also uses a variable named count, no problems would occur if the variables were local to each function. In the next example, you mess with your trusty dow function and overtly declare your intentions to use the variable WEEKDAY. You do this within the curly braces of the function, which makes WEEKDAY local to the function dow:

EXAMPLE

```
$ cat dow5
#! /bin/ksh
function dow
{
typeset WEEKDAY                      # Declare local variable
if [[ -z $1 ]]
then
```

```
        date +%A
        return 0
fi
case $1 in
-s) WEEKDAY=$(date +%A)
    print "Inside the function, WEEKDAY contains $WEEKDAY."
                                    # Access local variable within function
    return 2;;
 *) print "Format is \ndow [-s]"
    return 1;;
esac
}
# Script begins execution here #
dow $1
print "Outside the function, WEEKDAY contains $WEEKDAY"
                                    # Try to access WEEKDAY outside of function
return 0
$
$ dow5 -s
Inside the function, WEEKDAY contains Wednesday.
Outside the function, WEEKDAY contains
                                    # Not available outside of function
$
```

Global Variables

You might be wondering why accessing variables inside and outside of functions wasn't a problem in the earlier scripts examples. When ksh sees a variable for the first time, it checks to see whether it has been declared; if not, it automatically assumes it is a *global variable*. Global variables are available to all functions within the script. If you feel compelled to declare your variables (or your boss demands it), you can make the variable global by declaring it outside any function boundaries. The following example declares WEEKDAY as a global variable. If a local variable with the same name as the global variable exists, the local variable takes precedence within the function:

EXAMPLE

```
$ cat dow6
#! /bin/ksh
typeset WEEKDAY                     # Global variable
function dow
{
if [[ -z $1 ]]
then
    date +%A
    return 0
fi
```

```
case $1 in
-s) WEEKDAY=$(date +%A)
    print "Inside the function, WEEKDAY contains $WEEKDAY."
                                  # Global variable accessed within function
    return 2;;
 *) print "Format is \ndow [-s]"
    return 1;;
esac
}
# Script begins execution here #
dow $1
print "Outside the function, WEEKDAY contains $WEEKDAY."
                                  # Global variable accessed outside of function
return 0
$
$ dow6 -s
Inside the function, WEEKDAY contains Wednesday.
Outside the function, WEEKDAY contains Wednesday.
$
$ print $WEEKDAY                  # Globals are not set at the shell level

$
```

Argument Passing by Reference

When the dow6 script calls the dow function, you present an *argument* to the function. Don't think of the argument as being a yelling match between the function and the script. Instead, think of it as a reasonable conversation in which points are made and you actually persuade someone to act differently based on your eloquent dissertation. The latter case more accurately describes what happens when arguments are presented to a function. They are items of information the function can process and base subsequent actions on.

Perhaps you'd like your conversation to have a tangible result—meaning you are not happy with someone being persuaded by your argument. Rather, you want him to really see the light and make a change. It's like the difference between convincing someone that it's a good idea to donate to the Salvation Army, and convincing him to put a few bucks in the pot. How can you get your functions to have an effect on the pot (argument) they are handed?

This can be achieved by presenting your argument *by reference*. The programmers know that this means presenting the address of a variable, rather than the current contents of a variable. So far, all the arguments in this chapter have been *by value*, and most of the time, you will use by value style arguments. But here's the news on by-reference argument passing:

Setting up by reference argument passing consists of two parts. First, the calling script must present the argument to the function without preceding it with the dollar sign. (Remember that the $ in front of a variable tells the shell to find the value of the variable.) You don't want to present the value of a variable as an argument; instead, you want to present the variable name itself as an argument.

Second, the function must declare the variable using the nameref keyword. This prepares the function for the responsibility of altering the contents of a variable in the caller's environment:

EXAMPLE

```
$ cat dow7
#! /bin/ksh
function dow
{
nameref optarg=$1              # Use nameref to define optarg
                               # as a by reference variable
if [[ -z $optarg ]]
then
     date +%A
     return 0
fi
case $optarg in
-s) WEEKDAY=$(date +%A)
    optarg="set"               # Alter by_ref_arg indirectly
    return 2;;
 *) print "Format is \ndow [-s]"
    return 1;;
esac
}
# Script begins execution here #
by_ref_arg=$1                   # Create by_ref_arg to pass
print "Before function call, by_ref_arg contains $by_ref_arg."
dow by_ref_arg
print "After function call, by_ref_arg contains $by_ref_arg."
return 0
$
$ dow7 -s
Before function call, by_ref_arg contains -s.
After function call, by_ref_arg contains set.
                               # Note the change after the function is called
$
```

NOTE

The `nameref` keyword is available in ksh93 and beyond. Check your version by pressing the Ctrl+V sequence.

Object-Oriented Discipline Functions

One of the cornerstone concepts of object-oriented programming is to be able to associate certain functions with certain actions on a data object. The Korn Shell provides for three types of functions you can associate with actions on a data object. (Note that discipline functions are available in ksh93 and above.) As you might have guessed, the data object in the Korn Shell is a shell variable. The supported action functions are as follows:

- `get`—Called automatically when the variable is accessed (referred to as an *accessor* method in C++)

- `set`—Called automatically when the variable is assigned a value (referred to as an *assignor* method in C++)

- `unset`—Called automatically when the variable is unset (referred to as a *destructor* method in C++)

Note that all these functions are called automatically—you never call the function explicitly. It's called for you as the variable is used during the run of your script. Sounds pretty different, huh? This concept is a bit of a leap for the Korn Shell (and I suspect it is for you and me, too). Needless to say, some special syntax is required to support this capability. The functions called as described previously are referred to as *discipline functions*. This is probably because they must be disciplined enough to adhere to a strict set of rules dictating when they are to be called.

For variable x, the discipline functions can be defined using the function names of `x.get`, `x.set`, and `x.unset`. Within the discipline functions, special reserved variables are available to access the name of the variable you are manipulating (`.sh.name`), the value of the variable you are manipulating (`.sh.value`), and the name of the subscript if you are examining an array element (`.sh.subscript`). The following example sets up several discipline functions using several reserved variables:

EXAMPLE

```
$ cat dow8
#! /bin/ksh
integer count=0            # Global variable
function data_object.set   # Set discipline function
                           # for variable data_object
{
```

```
print "In the set function."
vararr[count]=${.sh.value}         # Reserved variable
count=count+1
}
function data_object.get            # Get discipline function
                                    # for variable data_object

{
print "In the get function."
vararr[count]=${.sh.name}
count=count+1
}
# Script begins execution here #
data_object=15                      # Data object being disciplined
print "data_object contains $data_object"
for z in ${vararr[*]}               # Prints strings from array filled in
                                    # by discipline functions
do print $z
done
return 0
$
$ dow8
In the set function.
In the get function.
data_object contains 15
15
data_object
$
```

Recursive Functions

You probably won't be needing recursive functions very often. A *recursive function* is one within whose curly braces a call is made to itself. This is a powerful tool, but it can be a bit tricky. Have you ever looked in a mirror on one wall of a barber shop, only to see the reflection of the mirror on the other wall, which has the reflection of the first wall, and so on? If so, then you've experienced a form of recursion gone amok. The following example shows a reasonable use of a recursive function to generate the factorial of an input number (a factorial of 4 = 4*3*2*1):

```
$ cat recurse
#! /bin/ksh
integer res                         # Global variable
function factorial                  # Recursive function
{
```

```
integer ret_val=0
integer factarg=0

if (( $1 <= 1 ))
then
        res=1
        return 0
else
        (( factarg = $1 - 1 ))
        factorial $factarg       # Recursive call
        (( ret_val = $1 * $res ))
        res=$ret_val
        return 0
fi
}
# Script begins execution here #
factorial $1
printf "Factorial of %d is %d\n" $1 $res
return 0
$
$ recurse 3
Factorial of 3 is 6
$ recurse 7
Factorial of 7 is 5040
$
$ recurse 8
Factorial of 8 is 40320
$
$ recurse 12
Factorial of 12 is 479001600
$
```

Using `autoload` on Functions

As you get more comfortable with functions and start to make some corkers,
you should consider sharing them with your fellow workers. Korn Shell provides a method for creating a repository for functions that can be referenced
from script files. The *repository* is nothing more than a directory into which
you place files named after the functions they contain. The directory must
be pointed to using the FPATH reserved variable. In addition, the script must
reference the function with the `autoload` keyword. The following example
removes the `factorial` function from the recurse script and places it in an
autoload directory:

EXAMPLE

```
$ cat recurse1
#! /bin/ksh
integer res
autoload factorial              # Autoload request
# Script begins execution here #
factorial $1
printf "Factorial of %d is %d\n" $1 $res
return 0
$
$ ls autofuncs                  # Autoload directory
factorial
$
$ cat autofuncs/factorial       # Function factorial is in autoload directory
function factorial
{
integer ret_val=0
integer factarg=0

if (( $1 <= 1 ))
then
        res=1
        return 0
else
        (( factarg = $1 - 1 ))
        factorial $factarg
        (( ret_val = $1 * $res ))
        res=$ret_val
        return 0
fi
}
$
$ recurse1 5
recurse1: line 5: function: not found    # Shell must know autoload directory
$
$ print $FPATH

$ FPATH=/home/obrien/scripts/autofuncs    # Set FPATH variable
$
$ recurse1
recurse1: line 5: function: not found    # Must be exported
$ export FPATH
$
$ recurse1 5                             # Works now
Factorial of 5 is 120
$
```

Built-In Extension Functions

If you have a hotshot C programmer handy (or if you are one), you will be interested in this section. The Korn Shell has many built-in functions. Some of them we use repetitively without giving it any thought, such as cd, print, umask, and typeset. A complete list of built-ins is at the end of this section. What exactly are the built-ins built into? They are functions (masquerading as commands) that are built into the ksh code. They do not cause a new process to be created to function (as a command such as ls would). Therefore, built-ins have less overhead, and their use can improve the performance of your script.

Well, suppose you're interested in the improvement of speed, but the functionality you want is not available in a currently existing built-in? In the UNIX tradition, you can roll your own. The next example shows the creation of a home-grown extension to the Korn Shell using the built-in function extension capability. This example makes a built-in named ppid, which displays the PID of the parent process of the one currently executing. It's not the most exciting example, but it will give you the idea:

```
$ cat getppidfunc.c

#include <unistd.h>
#include <stdio.h>
#include <stdlib.h>
int b_ppid(int argc, char *argv[]) # Function name must start with b_
{
printf("Parent PID is %d\n",getppid());
return(EXIT_SUCCESS);
}
$
$ cc -c getppidfunc.c               # Produce an object file
$ ls *.o
getppidfunc.o
$
$ ld -share -o ./libppid.so getppidfunc.o
                                    # Create a shared library
$
$ builtin -f ./libppid.so ppid      # Register the new builtin
$
$ ppid                              # Try it out
Parent PID is 986
$
$ builtin                           # Show all builtins
:
.
[
```

```
alarm
alias
bg
/bin/basename
/bin/cat
/bin/chmod
/bin/cmp
/bin/dirname
/bin/head
/bin/mkdir
/bin/uname
break
builtin
cd
command
continue
disown
echo
eval
exec
exit
export
false
fc
fg
getconf
getopts
hash
hist
jobs
kill
let
login
ppid                              # Hey, that's ours
print
printf
pwd
read
readonly
return
set
shift
sleep
test
trap
true
```

```
type
typeset
ulimit
umask
unalias
unset
/usr/bin/cut
/usr/bin/logname
/usr/bin/wc
vmap
vpath
wait
whence
$
```

Math

One of the more common data manipulation needs involves arithmetic. You saw a few simple math operations in some of the sample scripts in the previous section of this chapter. The Korn Shell provides the standard add, subtract, multiply, and divide capabilities. Additionally, Korn Shell 93 greatly expands the math options available to the script writer by providing floating-point variables and additional canned math functions such as `sin()`, `cos()`, `tan()`, `sqrt()`, and others.

Korn Shell 93 also has provisions for various base number systems. Because the shell provides different base numbering systems, it also provides the tools to use those bases. Not that the average shell script writer will need them very often, but the Korn shell actually provides bitwise operators along with the integer operators.

Two ways exist to indicate to the shell that you want a mathematical operation performed. You can enclose your arithmetic in a set of double parentheses, as in the following:

```
(( count=$count+1 ))
```

Or, you can use the `let` statement:

```
let count=count+1
```

Note that the `let` statement variable (count) is not preceded by a $. This works only if the variable—count in this case—has been previously declared as an integer. Otherwise, the dollar sign is mandatory. Besides addition, Table 7.1 shows the basic Korn Shell arithmetic operators.

Table 7.1: Arithmetic operators

Operator	Operation
+	Addition
-	Subtraction
*	Multiplication
/	Division
%	Modulo
>>	Bit-shift right
<<	Bit-shift left
^	Exclusive or
~	1's complement
&	Bit-wise and
|	Bit-wise or
=	Assignment
op=	+=, -=, ...
++	Increment
--	Decrement

Note that many bit-oriented operations are supported. Several of these are used in the example at the end of this section. If you're going to become a bithead in your scripts, you'll probably want to express values in numbering systems other than good old base 10. A typical base 10 variable declaration might look like this:

EXAMPLE

```
$ typeset -i a=17
$ (( a=a+1 ))
$ print $a
18

$ integer b=12
$ let a=a+b
$ print $a
30
```

To indicate hex (base 16), you would use the following:

```
$ typeset -i16 hexnum=5A          # Shell needs to be told that 5A is hex
-ksh: typeset: 5A: arithmetic syntax error
$
$ typeset -i16 hexnum=16#5A       # Base#value is the correct format
$
$ print $hexnum
16#5a
$
$ printf "%d\n" $hexnum
90                                # Decimal value displayed
```

NOTE

Be aware that different versions of ksh provide varying levels of support for number bases.

You also can represent integer constants of any base using the previous format for hex. Simply replace the 16 with the number representing the base you want to use:

```
$ typeset -i2 binnum=2#110      # Binary 110
$
$ print $binnum
2#110
$
$ typeset -i decnum=0
$
$ let decnum=binnum
$
$ print $decnum
6                               # Is six in decimal
$
```

Script writers have many built-in math functions at their disposal. Most of these are new with Korn Shell 93, so don't be surprised if you can't find these in older ksh implementations. I see most of these as icing on the cake, anyway. If you need to get down to this level, you will probably end up writing a C or FORTRAN program. However, these functions can be useful for prototyping your logic. Table 7.2 lists the math functions.

Table 7.2: Math functions

Function	Operation
abs	Absolute value
acos	Arc cosine
asin	Arc sine
atan	Arc tangent
cos	Cosine
cosh	Hyperbolic cosine
exp	~2.718 raised to a power
int	Integer truncation
log	Logarithm
sin	Sine
sinh	Hyperbolic sine
sqrt	Square root
tan	Tangent
tanh	Hyperbolic tangent

As an example, let's look at the sqrt function. This returns the square root of its argument. Let's see, 9 times 9 is 81, right? So the square root of 81 should be 9. But let's make it a bit more difficult for the sqrt function. Let's ask it to figure out the square root of 82. The answer should be a bit over 9, right? But how will the shell deal with the fractional value? Let's see. This example uses the sqrt math function and also introduces the new floating-point capabilities within ksh:

EXAMPLE

```
$ (( z=sqrt(82) ))
$
$ print $z
9.05538513814
$
```

Pretty slick, huh? You can declare a variable to be floating point using the typeset command or the float command:

```
$ typeset -f fl3=4.5          # Declaring a float
$
$ print $fl3
4.5
$
$ float fl4=5.4               # Alternative float declaration
$
$ print $fl4
5.4
$
$ let tot=fl3+fl4             # Variable tot holds float result
$
$ print $tot
9.9
$
$ (( trunc=int(tot) ))        # Use int function to truncate tot
$
$ print $trunc
9
$
```

The following script uses several base numbering systems (base 8, 2, and 10) and shows some of the mathematical power of the Korn Shell. Along the way, it also provides a chance to revisit the grimy underbelly of the umask command. Don't forget that ~ is the one's complement operator (flip the bits), and & is the bit-wise and operator. Also note that ${defa#*#} is a request for substring removal—the first # removes the smallest matching left pattern. The pattern to be removed is *#, which means any bunch of characters up to and including the first # in the string. In this case, the

string is something like 2#111100000. The goal is to remove the 2#, as
shown in the following example:

```
$ cat mask_magic
#!/bin/ksh
#
# Script which will display default
# permissions in formatted fashion
# based on the current umask setting
#
typeset -i2 defa                    # Make variable defa display in binary
typeset -i onescomp
(( onescomp=~(8#$(umask)) ))        # Get one's complement of current umask
(( defa=(8#666)&onescomp ))         # Calculate default permission mask
default_perm=${defa#*#}             # Strip off leading 2#
print "Default regular file permissions with current umask ($(umask))"
print " u  g  o"
print '_____'
print "rwxrwxrwx"
print $default_perm
print ""
print "Default directory file permissions with current umask ($(umask))"
typeset -i2 ddefa                   # make ddefa display in binary
(( ddefa=(8#777)&onescomp ))        # Calculate default permission mask
                                    # for directory
default_perm=${ddefa#*#}            # strip off leading 2#
print " u  g  o"
print '_____'
print "rwxrwxrwx"
print $default_perm
print ""
print "1s are on, 0s are off"

$
$ umask
0002
$
$ mask_magic
Default regular file permissions with current umask (0002)
 u  g  o
_____
rwxrwxrwx
110110100                           # Represents rw-rw-r--

Default directory file permissions with current umask (0002)
 u  g  o
_____
```

```
rwxrwxrwx
111111101                        # Represents rwxrwxr-x

1s are on, 0s are off
$
$ umask 027                      # Change to a different umask value
$
$ umask
0027
$
$ mask_magic
Default regular file permissions with current umask (0027)
u  g  o


rwxrwxrwx
110100000                        # New default for files is rw-r-----

Default directory file permissions with current umask (0027)
u  g  o


rwxrwxrwx
111101000                        # New default for directories is rwxr-x---

1s are on, 0s are off
$
```

Filters

We are often called on to filter the barrage of visual input we face every day. Depending on your nature, you might have filtered out the view of most of the oddly shaped and sized folks at the public beach last summer. After this filtering, you were left with a few choice items upon which you wanted to spend some processing time.

The Korn Shell provides many mechanisms for filtering data. You probably recognize some of these mechanisms as commands you use everyday. But most likely you don't usually consider the fact that the following are all filters: head, tail, grep, awk, sed, wc, tr, sort, uniq, more, cat, and so on.

What is the common thread that binds the previous list together as filters? They all expect their input from standard input (stdin) and place their output on standard output (stdout). This seemingly innocuous characteristic can become a very powerful tool in the hands of a skilled Korn Shell user or script writer.

Filters are particularly useful in a pipeline of commands. *Pipes* are one of the distinguishing features of UNIX shells. The basic idea is that the output of one command is piped to another command as its standard input. Thus, filter commands are important components of pipelines. Think of a plumbing pipe with threads on each end. UNIX processes get threaded onto each end of the pipe. The image is even better if you tilt the left end of the pipe up a bit, so the information can flow in only one direction. Now you've got the correct picture of a pipe. It is a unidirectional communication channel between two processes in which the left process presents its output to the right process as input.

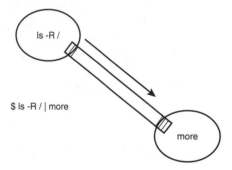

Figure 7.1: *A pipe enables the unidirectional communication of information between one process and another.*

You can have multiple pipes in a command line. This promotes a *toolkit* philosophy of command interface. So you can tinker with pipes and cobble together a single command that accomplishes what would normally take a program or a script to accomplish. Eventually you could assign an alias to your pipeline to reduce your typing and have a convenient name by which to remember it. The following example sorts an ls output based on file size and reports on the five largest files:

EXAMPLE

```
$ ls -1
total 29
drwxrwxr-x   2 obrien   obrien      1024 Oct 12 00:02 autofuncs
-rwxrwxr--   1 obrien   obrien       266 Oct 11 14:19 dow1
-rwxrwxr--   1 obrien   obrien       269 Oct 11 14:35 dow2
-rwxrwxr--   1 obrien   obrien       393 Oct 11 14:59 dow3
-rwxrwxr--   1 obrien   obrien       336 Oct 11 15:15 dow4
-rwxrwxr--   1 obrien   obrien       364 Oct 11 15:55 dow5
-rwxrwxr--   1 obrien   obrien       364 Oct 11 16:03 dow6
-rwxrwxr--   1 obrien   obrien       425 Oct 11 17:08 dow7
-rwxrwxr--   1 obrien   obrien       363 Oct 11 22:26 dow8
-rwxrwxr-x   1 obrien   obrien     11804 Oct 12 00:19 getppid
```

```
-rw-rw-r--   1 obrien    obrien          98 Oct 12 00:19 getppid.c
-rw-rw-r--   1 obrien    obrien         160 Oct 12 00:23 getppidfunc.c
-rw-rw-r--   1 obrien    obrien         984 Oct 12 00:23 getppidfunc.o
-rwxrwxr-x   1 obrien    obrien        2006 Oct 12 00:25 libppid.so
-rwxrwxr--   1 obrien    obrien         923 Oct 12 09:50 mask_magic
-rwxrwxr--   1 obrien    obrien         330 Oct 11 23:41 recurse
-rwxrwxr--   1 obrien    obrien         141 Oct 12 00:03 recurse1
$
$ ls -l | sort +4nr        # Sorts after skipping 4 fields, numeric, reverse
-rwxrwxr-x   1 obrien    obrien       11804 Oct 12 00:19 getppid
-rwxrwxr-x   1 obrien    obrien        2006 Oct 12 00:25 libppid.so
drwxrwxr-x   2 obrien    obrien        1024 Oct 12 00:02 autofuncs
-rw-rw-r--   1 obrien    obrien         984 Oct 12 00:23 getppidfunc.o
-rwxrwxr--   1 obrien    obrien         923 Oct 12 09:50 mask_magic
-rwxrwxr--   1 obrien    obrien         425 Oct 11 17:08 dow7
-rwxrwxr--   1 obrien    obrien         393 Oct 11 14:59 dow3
-rwxrwxr--   1 obrien    obrien         364 Oct 11 15:55 dow5
-rwxrwxr--   1 obrien    obrien         364 Oct 11 16:03 dow6
-rwxrwxr--   1 obrien    obrien         363 Oct 11 22:26 dow8
-rwxrwxr--   1 obrien    obrien         336 Oct 11 15:15 dow4
-rwxrwxr--   1 obrien    obrien         330 Oct 11 23:41 recurse
-rwxrwxr--   1 obrien    obrien         269 Oct 11 14:35 dow2
-rwxrwxr--   1 obrien    obrien         266 Oct 11 14:19 dow1
-rw-rw-r--   1 obrien    obrien         160 Oct 12 00:23 getppidfunc.c
-rwxrwxr--   1 obrien    obrien         141 Oct 12 00:03 recurse1
-rw-rw-r--   1 obrien    obrien          98 Oct 12 00:19 getppid.c
total 29
$
$ ls -l | sort +4nr | head -5                 # Shows top 5 only
-rwxrwxr-x   1 obrien    obrien       11804 Oct 12 00:19 getppid
-rwxrwxr-x   1 obrien    obrien        2006 Oct 12 00:25 libppid.so
drwxrwxr-x   2 obrien    obrien        1024 Oct 12 00:02 autofuncs
-rw-rw-r--   1 obrien    obrien         984 Oct 12 00:23 getppidfunc.o
-rwxrwxr--   1 obrien    obrien         923 Oct 12 09:50 mask_magic
$
$ alias top5='ls -l | sort +4nr | head -5'    # Make an alias
$
$ top5                                        # Use the alias
-rwxrwxr-x   1 obrien    obrien       11804 Oct 12 00:19 getppid
-rwxrwxr-x   1 obrien    obrien        2006 Oct 12 00:25 libppid.so
drwxrwxr-x   2 obrien    obrien        1024 Oct 12 00:02 autofuncs
-rw-rw-r--   1 obrien    obrien         984 Oct 12 00:23 getppidfunc.o
-rwxrwxr--   1 obrien    obrien         923 Oct 12 09:50 mask_magic
$
```

The next example uses many filters, including cat, grep, xargs, sed, awk, sort, uniq, and others. It was created to make a master HTML file that can be read into a browser and provide access to locations in many files conveniently. The idea here is to look at it as an example of pipes and filters. Along the way, it just might be useful for some of you. When you open this file in your browser, it displays alphabetized list of URLs to access with a brief note on what they are about.

First, the script creates a file full of the names and locations of htm and html files. Feel free to give the script a wider scope if you want. I chose the directory in the example so the output wouldn't go on forever. The xargs command executes the grep command on each file it sees coming in the pipe. The cat command opens the file created by the find command and feeds the names to xargs, which kicks in the appropriate grep commands. Without using xargs, the grep would create a command line too large for the shell to swallow, and the script would fail. The curly braces in the grep command function as the placeholders for the filenames xargs is being fed. The /etc/hosts seems spectacularly out of place. I agree. But without it, grep thinks it is searching through only one file, so it doesn't bother displaying the name of the file in which it found the string match. (There's probably a better way.) The -i means ignore case sensitivity.

So, now you have a bunch of lines containing a filename and some form of the string "title". The next sequence of sed removes all the "title" strings and replaces the first : on every line with the @ symbol. Sort that output for sanity, and then present the sort results to awk, which recognizes the @ symbol as the field separator and produces a line containing the <A HREF= notation for HTML. The $1 and $2 in the awk command are not to be confused with the $1 and $2 for command-line parameters. Within awk, the $1 represents input field number 1, and $2 represents field number 2. The final sort ignores blanks (b), folds cases (f, which means it ignores case), considers characters only in keys (i), uses the > as the field separator (-t \>), and skips one field before getting to the key field (+1). Finally, the uniq removes any duplicate lines.

It's not the most friendly script you'll see in this book, but it does serve to emphasize the power of pipes, filters, and scripts. I call it "ouch" because of all the pain it caused when I put it together:

```
$ ls /usr/doc/bzip2-0.9.5c         # Target could be scoped
                                   # more widely if desired
README         manual_2.html  manual_4.html
manual_1.html  manual_3.html  manual_toc.html
$
$ cat ouch1
#!/bin/ksh
# Create the tmp file that holds the html files
find $1 -name "*.htm*" -print > web.tmp # Find all htm and html files
```

```
# ouch command ...
cat web.tmp | xargs -i  grep -i '<title>' {} /etc/hosts| sed -e 's/<TITLE>//'\
 -e 's/<\/TITLE>//' -e 's/<title>//' \
-e 's/<\/title>//' -e 's/:/@/'\
 | sort | awk -F@ '{ printf("<A HREF=\"file:%s\"><LI>%s</LI>\n",$1,$2); }'\
 | sort -bfi -t \> +1 | uniq > jimeee.html
$
$ ouch1 /usr/doc/bzip2-0.9.5c        # Execute the script
$
$ cat jimeee.html                    # Output file for use in browser
<A HREF="file:/usr/doc/bzip2-0.9.5c/manual_2.html"><LI>bzip2 and libbzip2 - How
to use bzip2</LI>
<A HREF="file:/usr/doc/bzip2-0.9.5c/manual_1.html">
<LI>bzip2 and libbzip2 - Introduction</LI>
<A HREF="file:/usr/doc/bzip2-0.9.5c/manual_4.html">
<LI>bzip2 and libbzip2 - Misc
ellanea</LI>
<A HREF="file:/usr/doc/bzip2-0.9.5c/manual_3.html">
<LI>bzip2 and libbzip2 - Prog
ramming with libbzip2</LI>
<A HREF="file:/usr/doc/bzip2-0.9.5c/manual_toc.html">
<LI>bzip2 and libbzip2 - Ta
ble of Contents</LI>
$
```

Testing Files

Before walking on a frozen pond during early winter, don't you test it first? You know, have your little brother go out on it and see whether he falls through. (Kidding!) Likewise, you might want to test files and strings before you march out to the center of the ice and end up falling through.

Sometimes the data to be manipulated is the name of a file. Your script might need to open the file and process the lines in the file. If the file is an executable program or a script, the processing of the file could involve executing it. If it is a directory, you might want to get a listing of the files in the directory. So where does the data manipulation come into the picture?

Before opening a file for reading, you might want to check that the file contains what you expect it to contain. Your script might be expecting a file full of ASCII characters, but the user might have presented a directory file—or worse yet, a compiled and linked executable!

NOTE

Directory files contain a mix of ASCII characters and binary data. The ASCII characters represent filenames, and the binary data represents an inode number (or some other offset into an array of file header metadata).

The result is that you get some readable stuff onscreen, but you probably also get some weird beeps, backward question marks, and other gibberish. The gibberish would be overwhelming if you had tried to access a nonscript executable file.

Therefore, it would be to your advantage to test the filename the user has presented to ensure it will function as your script expects it to function.

For instance, if a script were expecting a directory file, the script could capture the output of an `ls -l filename` command and check the first character to see whether it is a directory (the first character would be a "d"). You also could use a similar technique to check for an executable. In addition, you could use the `file` command to find out whether the file is a script.

These solutions would work. And that's a good thing, right? But the overhead would be exorbitant, and it would just be totally clunky. ("Clunky" is a techno term for not-so-good.)

The Korn Shell provides numerous test operators to efficiently handle situations in which file existence or characteristics should be checked (see Table 7.3).

Table 7.3: Test conditions

Test Condition	True If (Note: Each Category Requires Existence)
-e *file*	File exists (same as -a).
-r *file*	File is readable.
-w *file*	File is writeable.
-x *file*	File is executable.
-f *file*	File exists and is a regular file.
-O *file*	User owns it.
-d *file*	It's a directory file.
-s *file*	File exists and is non-empty.
-c *file*	It is character special.
-b *file*	It is block special.
-p *file*	It is named pipe.
-u *file*	It is setuid bit set.
-g *file*	It is setgid bit set.
-k *file*	It is sticky bit set.
-L *file*	It is a symbolic link.
-G *file*	User is in same group.
-S *file*	It is a socket.

The following example tests to see whether a few files are executable. Note that the [[ ]] notation provides the test capability and that the command if can be used in a script for more reasonable syntax. For you C programmers, note that 0 means yes (or true), whereas non-zero means no (or false). This is the exact opposite of what you are used to within the C programming language, where 0 means false and non-zero means true. Read it and weep:

EXAMPLE

```
$ [[ -x dow5 ]]              # Is dow5 executable?
$ echo $?
0                            # 0 means a successful test (yes)
$ [[ -x web.tmp ]]           # Is web.tmp executable?
$ echo $?
1                            # 1 means a failed test (no)
$
```

Testing Strings

If the data to be manipulated consists of character strings, the Korn Shell provides several special test operators for handling typical string manipulations (see Table 7.4). For instance, you might need to check whether a string variable is empty before presenting it to a function or using it in a test.

Table 7.4: String tests

Test Condition	True If
-z *string*	*string* is zero length
-n *string*	*string* is non-zero length
-o *option*	*option* is on
-t [*unit*]	*unit* is associated with a terminal (default unit 1)

Generally, the command after an if statement can be

- [[*test-expression*]], which allows multiple expressions, grouped with ( ), !, &&, and ||

  For instance

  [[(($a>$b) && ($c<$d)) || !($e<$f)]]

  tests whether either a>b and c<d, or e is not less than f.

- An arithmetic expression using ((...))

- A standard command

Some conditional tests are specific to strings:

- if [[*str1=str2*]]—True if strings are equal
- if [[*str1* != *str2*]]—True if strings are not equal
- if [[*str1* > *str2*]]—True if *str1* is greater than *str2*
- if [[*str1* < *str2*]]—True if *str1* is less than *str2*

Testing Numerals

If a variable holds a series of characters representing a number, specific tests exist that should be used. If a variable has not been declared as an integer or a float, yet it contains numerals, the following syntax can be used for comparisons:

```
[[ exp1 -eq exp2 ]]        # exp1 is equal to exp2
```

You can also use the following instead of -eq:

- -ne—Not equal to
- -gt—Greater than
- -ge—Greater than or equal to
- -lt—Less than
- -le—Less than or equal to

Testing Numbers

If the variables being tested have been declared as integers or floats, the following syntax can be used for comparisons:

```
(( exp1 == exp2 ))         # exp1 is equal to exp2
```

You can also use the following instead of ==:

- !=—Not equal to
- >—Greater than
- >=—Greater than or equal to
- <—Less than
- <=—Less than or equal to

The following three tests are for comparing two files:

```
[[ file1 -nt file2 ]]      # Newer than
[[ file1 -ot file2 ]]      # Older than
[[ file1 -ef file2 ]]      # Is another name for
```

The following script is a simple example of numeric testing using [[ ]]:

EXAMPLE

```
        $ cat you_guess
#!/usr/bin/ksh
    read num?"pick a number? "
  if [[ $num -gt 85 ]]              # Greater than
      then print "too high"
      elif [[ $num -lt 85 ]]        # Less than
        then print "too low"
    else
        print "you got it"
  fi
  $ you_guess
  pick a number? 39
  too low
  $
```

The next example uses a few more test operators:

```
$ saver web.tmp
Happy? y
web.tmp preserved
$
$ cat saver
#!/bin/ksh
if [[ -f ${1} ]]            #checks if file named as first
then                        #command-line arg. exists and
#is not a directory file.
      read ans?"Happy? "
    if [[ ${ans} = "y" ]]
      then
              cp ${1} ${1}${$}
                      # Copies input file to a name trailed by PID
              print  "${1} preserved"
          fi
  fi


$
$ ls web*
web.tmp  web.tmp6177
```

How many times have you used cat to display the contents of a file and had reams of gibberish spew across your screen before you knew it? More than once, I bet. One of the drawbacks of the UNIX file-naming conventions is that no mandated extension exists to identify the type of the file. This can be looked upon as a blessing or a curse. The next example uses some file conditionals to determine whether to display the file:

EXAMPLE

```
$ cat showit
#!/bin/ksh
# example of file conditionals
if [[ -f ${1} ]]
then
        if [[ -x ${1} ]]
        then
                read response?"${1} is executable still want to see it?"
                case ${response} in
                y*)     cat ${1} ;;
                *)      print "Not displaying." ;;
                esac
        else
                cat ${1}
        fi
else
        print "${1} is not a regular file.\nNot printing."
fi

$
$ showit web.tmp                    # Displays regular files
/usr/doc/bzip2-0.9.5c/manual_1.html
/usr/doc/bzip2-0.9.5c/manual_2.html
/usr/doc/bzip2-0.9.5c/manual_3.html
/usr/doc/bzip2-0.9.5c/manual_4.html
/usr/doc/bzip2-0.9.5c/manual_toc.html
$
$ showit ../scripts                 # Not directories
../scripts is not a regular file.
Not printing.
$
$ showit dow2
dow2 is executable still want to see it?y
                                    # Sanity check on request to print executable
#! /bin/ksh

function dow
{
(...)
print "WEEKDAY contains $WEEKDAY"

$
```

Combining Tests

If you need to combine several tests, the Korn Shell provides logical operators: || (or), ! (not), && (and), and != (not equal). Table 7.5 lists some of the operators available to form compound tests.

Table 7.5: Compound test operators

Test	True If
if [[*test_1* || *test_2*]]	Either is true
if [[*test_1* && *test_2*]]	Both are true
[[! *test1*]]	Opposite of test is true

The following is a pseudocode example of a compound test:

EXAMPLE

```
    ...
        read ans?"Sure? "
        if [[ (${ans}="y" || ${ans}="yes") && -f ${1} ]]
                        #if user says yes and
                        #file on command line
                        #exists...
      rm ${1}
     fi
    ...
```

When the condition is satisfied, the processing of the conditional stops. This is sometimes referred to as *short circuiting* a test. You must be aware of this if you use compound tests. Consider a situation in which you need to find out whether a > b AND c > d before executing some commands. If the shell finds that a is not greater than b, why should it bother checking whether c > d? It knows that the result of the compound if will be false. This behavior mimics the C language. It is not an issue unless some side effects are produced by the second (nonperformed) test. For example, if you had set up some discipline functions to trigger when a variable is accessed, you might be surprised by the shell's actions (or nonactions). The variable c would not have been accessed in the test discussed here. Be careful, but don't avoid the compound test because of this minor and occasionally irritating personality trait.

What's Next

What a long and wondrous path you've walked! You started out getting familiar with functions. Then, you found that they bring modularity and conciseness to your scripts. You also saw that they can be used in an object-oriented way and can be used to extend the existing Korn Shell built-ins. You then visited the math functions and associated expressions. Along the way, you also picked up the ability to work with floating-point variables and variables storing values from other number systems. And you now know that ksh can support bit-level operations. I'll wager that you were not expecting that level of capability within the Korn Shell.

Next, you reviewed the power of pipes and filters, and a few powerful scripts were discussed, including an HTML mega-table-of-contents generator. Your trip ended with the ability to test the ice even before you send little brother out there with a rope around his waist. (No, Mom, I never did that.) Finally, you saw the many tests available for string and file condition testing.

I'm sure you are starting to feel pretty empowered at this point. This chapter and the previous chapter have given you many weapons for the shell battles. However, we're not through yet. Chapter 8, "Information Passing," presents command-line arguments, redirection, getting input from the user, and the mysterious coprocess ability.

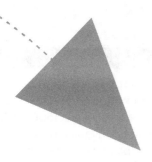

8

Information Passing

Have you ever wished that you could talk back to your TV? I mean actually interact with it? Have an effect on its subsequent displays? Or have you looked for the key to communication with your teenage son or daughter? Have you felt like you were not getting through? That none of your input was being processed properly?

If you can relate to any of the previous paragraph, you are ready to attack this chapter. Now that you have some pretty sophisticated looping and testing mechanisms in your script writing tool kit, let's see how you can give the outside world the capability to communicate with your scripts.

This chapter demonstrates how to present data to the script at runtime. It also examines how the script can alter the typical screen-based presentation of data to the user.

This chapter teaches you the following:

- How to use command-line arguments
- How to get information from the user
- How to redirect information to and from files
- How to interact with a coprocess

Command-Line Arguments

You have already seen several scripts using command-line arguments. As a script is started, the initiating shell searches for extra data on the command line. Anything beyond the script name is treated as a command-line argument and is placed in shell variables. The shell variables used for command-line storage are named $1 (first argument), $2 (second argument), and so on. These are also referred to as *positional parameters* because the position of the argument determines the name of the shell variable into which it is placed. Table 8.1 provides a list of the positional and special parameters available to you within your shell script.

Table 8.1: Positional and special parameters

Parameter	Meaning
0	Name of script, shell, or function.
1, 2, 3, and so on	Value of positional arguments.
@	All parameters delimited by space. If @ is quoted, quoted parameters are set to a single position.
*	Same as @ except quoted arguments are separated by $IFS.
#	Number of command arguments.

The following example displays three positional parameters regardless of whether they are present on the command line. The curly braces ({ }) around the numbers are optional:

EXAMPLE

```
$ cat params
#!/bin/ksh
print "Argument 1 is ${1}"
print "Argument 2 is ${2}"
print "Argument 3 is ${3}"
print "There are $# arguments."

$ params O\'Brien Pitts Ellis
Argument 1 is O'Brien
Argument 2 is Pitts
Argument 3 is Ellis
There are 3 arguments.
$
$ params O\'Brien Pitts Ellis Dyment
Argument 1 is O'Brien
Argument 2 is Pitts
Argument 3 is Ellis
There are 4 arguments.
$
$ params O\'Brien
Argument 1 is O'Brien
```

```
Argument 2 is                       # Parameters are blank if not used
Argument 3 is
There are 1 arguments.
$
```

Positional parameters also can be set using the set command. The following example shows the set command being used at the command prompt to set up positional parameters. The same syntax can be used within a script:

```
$ set Cheryl Den "Bruce Susan"   # Set up 3 positional parameters
$
$ print $2
Den
$
$ print $3
Bruce Susan
$
$ print $#                       # Count of parameters
3
$
$ print $@                       # All parameters
Cheryl Den Bruce Susan
$
$ print $*                       # All separated by IFS (which is a space)
Cheryl Den Bruce Susan
$
```

The following example takes an input value of base 10, 16, 8, or 2 and displays its equivalent in the other bases. It accepts input from the command line:

```
$ cat convertnum
#!/bin/ksh
#######
# Script to convert values to hex, octal, and binary
# Gets input from command line.
#######
integer -i10 value=$1            # Store first parameter as a decimal integer
print "$value \t\t decimal"
typeset -ri16 value
print "$value \t\t hex"
typeset -ri8 value
print "$value \t\t octal"
typeset -ri2 value
print "$value \t binary"

$
$ convertnum 32                  # Input is decimal
```

```
32              decimal
16#20           hex
8#40            octal
2#100000        binary
$
$ convertnum 2#10001            # Input is binary
17              decimal
16#11           hex
8#21            octal
2#10001         binary
$
```

The shell script can be designed to accept options as well as parameters. Options are similar to the command options you use daily. For instance, -l is an option and file1 is a parameter in ls -l file1.

The Korn Shell has a special getopts command to ease the building of command-like scripts. Rather than having to build some special-case code into a script that wants to accept options on the command line, because the Korn Shell is a top-notch shell, it provides a technique for handling them.

A few steps are necessary to handle options. First, the script must recognize that it has been presented with an option, as opposed to a parameter. (The -l is dealt with much differently than the file1 in the ls -l file1 command.) Second, the script needs a place to store the option presently under examination. Third, the script must be capable of handling multiple options (-li or -l -i for instance). Fourth, the script needs a way to handle options that have an argument associated with them, such as -f filename.

The getopts built-in command enables you to process arguments as options, similar to standard UNIX commands. The getopts command expects two fundamental arguments: a list of the options to be supported within your script and a variable name in which to place the next option.

Options in the options list that are followed by a : are expected to accept an argument that will be stored in the variable OPTARG. This handles the previously mentioned situation in which you have an option, such as -f filename.

The getopts command updates a variable called OPTIND each time getopts is executed. In effect, getopts is executed once for each argument you process. Therefore, you most likely will place the getopts command within a loop. OPTIND starts at 1 and is updated with each run of getopts. This variable can be used to shift the arguments beyond the options to get at the nonoption arguments. An item on the command line that does not begin with - indicates the end of the options. Likewise, an argument of -- terminates the options part of your command. In the newer implementations of ksh, the getopts command can also handle + in front of the options, to handle situations in which the option could indicate set or unset. Check your man pages to see whether your getopts has the capability.

In addition, a special syntax within getopts is available that can be used to handle bad options presented by the user. (We all know that never happens!) A leading : in the options list tells getopts to set invalid options to the character ? and to place the bogus argument in OPTARG. It sets the options variable to : if the option has a missing value and the option that is missing the value into the special variable OPTARG.

The next example shows the basics of using getopts to handle command-line arguments and errors. The getopts command is at the top of the while loop. The loop is repeated until getopts reports an unsuccessful status, which occurs when no more options are on the command line. Note that the extra parameters (nonoptions) are not considered by getopts unless they follow the -o or -n options (in the example script).

Let's examine the options list :rwn#o:. The : at the beginning of the options list requests that getopts put bogus arguments into OPTARG and set the variable opt (in this script) to hold a ?. The r and w are normal options, and the n# indicates that the option should be followed by a numeric value. The o:, on the other hand, indicates that the option should be followed by an argument. This is handy for file input options. The opt variable name holds the option being processed currently, so it is perfect for using in a case statement within the getopts loop:

EXAMPLE

```ksh
$ cat getopt1
#!/bin/ksh
######
# Illustration of using getopts, OPTARG, and OPTIND
# to parse a command line
######
while getopts :rwn#o: opt                    # Setting up the expected options
do
case $opt in

r)
        print "Processing for r option ..."  # Could set a flag or call
        ;;                                    # a function
w)
        print "Processing for w option ..."
        ;;
n)
        print "Processing for n option ..."
        num=$OPTARG                           # OPTARG gets the numeric value
        print "Number is $num"                # accompanying -n
```

```
                ;;
        o)
                print "Processing for o option ..."
                ofile=$OPTARG                       # OPTARG gets the argument
                print "Output file: $ofile"         # accompanying -o
                ;;
        :)      print -u2 "OPTION: $OPTARG requires additional info."
                exit 1                              # Variable opt gets : when -o
                ;;                                  # or -n are incomplete
        \?)     print -u2 "$OPTARG is an invalid option to $0."
                exit 2                              # Variable opt gets ? for
                ;;                                  # invalid options
        esac
done
# Shift to arguments after options
shift OPTIND-1                                      # Eliminates options from
print "Processing filenames."                       # command line
for nfile                                           # Access the rest of the
do                                                  # command line
        print $nfile
done

$
$ getopt1 f1                                         # No options used
Processing filenames.
f1
$
$ getopt1 -r f1
Processing for r option ...
Processing filenames.
f1
$
$ getopt1 -rwo denfile f1 f2 f3
Processing for r option ...
Processing for w option ...
Processing for o option ...
Output file: denfile
Processing filenames.
f1
f2
f3
$
$ getopt1 -rwo denfile -n 17 f1 f2 f3
Processing for r option ...
Processing for w option ...
Processing for o option ...
```

```
Output file: denfile                          # From -o option
Processing for n option ...
Number is 17                                  # From -n option
Processing filenames.
f1
f2
f3
$
$ getopt1 -rq                                 # Bogus option
Processing for r option ...
q is an invalid option to getopt1.
$
$ getopt1 -r -o                               # Options can be presented
individually
Processing for r option ...
OPTION: o requires additional info.
$
$ getopt1 -r -o denfile
Processing for r option ...
Processing for o option ...
Output file: denfile
Processing filenames.
$
```

User Input

Getting input through to your teenager may require anything from a gentle tap on the shoulder to a shouted "Wassup?" But either way, the ultimate goal is to alter the behavior based on the input you supply. A shell script may be written such that it requires no input from the user. An example would be the masks_magic script from the previous chapter. A sample run is shown to refresh your memory:

EXAMPLE

```
$ mask_magic
Default regular file permissions with current umask (0002)
u   g   o

rwxrwxrwx
110110100

Default directory file permissions with current umask (0002)
 u   g   o

rwxrwxrwx
111111101

1s are on, 0s are off
$
```

Or it can be written so that it checks the contents of certain environment variables and branches inside of the logic of the script based on what it finds in the variable. Note that this example uses some interesting syntax beyond the simple test of the contents of MASKSDIRS. It uses a function to generate a more readable permission mask. The function is given an argument that is treated as binary and stored in the variable shiftval, which is processed one bit at a time to see whether the associated permission is set or clear. If it is set, the appropriate value in the associative array named perms is placed in the res array for later display:

```
$ cat masks_env
#!/bin/ksh
#
# Script which will display default
# permissions in formatted fashion
# based on the current umask setting
#
function gen_modes
{
integer count=0
typeset -i2 shiftval=2#$1    # Sets up a binary value
perms=( [1]=r [2]=w [3]=x [4]=r [5]=w [6]=x [7]=r [8]=w [9]=x )
                                 # Associative array
while (( count <= 9 ))          # Nine permission bits
do
(( count=count+1 ))
let lment=10-count              # Fill target array from the right to the left
if (( ($shiftval & 1) == 1 ))   # Bitwise-and to check if rightmost bit is set
        then
            res[$lment]="${perms[$lment]}"
                                 # If so, put letter in res array
else
            res[$lment]="-"      # If not, put dash in res array
fi
(( shiftval = shiftval >> 1))   # Get rid of rightmost bit
done
}
######### Script Begins ##########
typeset -i2 defa                # make defa display in binary
typeset -i onescomp
(( onescomp=~(8#$(umask)) ))    # Get ones complement of current umask
(( defa=(8#666)&onescomp ))     # Calculate default permission mask
default_perm=${defa#*#}         # Strip off leading 2#
print "Default REGULAR FILE permissions with current umask ($(umask))"
print "  u     g     o"
#print '_ _ _ _ _ _ _ _ _'
```

```
gen_modes $default_perm           # Call gen_modes function
print ${res[*]}
print "(In binary -- $default_perm)"
print ""
if [[ "$MASKSDIRS" != "YES" ]]    # Check to see if the user would like
                                  # directory information also
then
        exit 0
fi
print "Default DIRECTORY FILE permissions with current umask ($(umask))"
typeset -i2 ddefa                 # make ddefa display in binary
(( ddefa=(8#777)&onescomp ))      # Calculate default permission mask
                                  # for directory
default_perm=${ddefa#*#}          # strip off leading 2#
print "  u    g    o"
#print '_ _ _ _ _ _ _ _ _'
gen_modes $default_perm           # Call gen_modes function
print ${res[*]}
print "(In binary -- $default_perm)"

$
$ print $MASKSDIRS                # Nothing in the MASKSDIRS variable

$
$ masks_env
Default REGULAR FILE permissions with current umask (0002)
u    g    o
r w - r w - r - -                 # Shows regular file default permissions only
(In binary -- 110110100)

$
$ MASKSDIRS="YES"                 # Set MASKSDIRS variable locally
$
$ masks_env                       # Still no directory permission info?
Default REGULAR FILE permissions with current umask (0002)
u    g    o
r w - r w - r - -                 # MASKSDIRS needs to be exported
(In binary -- 110110100)

$
$ export MASKSDIRS                # That should do it
$
$ masks_env
Default REGULAR FILE permissions with current umask (0002)
u    g    o
```

```
r w - r w - r - -
(In binary -- 110110100)

Default DIRECTORY FILE permissions with current umask (0002)
u    g    o
r w x r w x r - x                    # Includes directory permissions also
(In binary -- 111111101)
$
```

It also might just flat out ask the user for some input. This case would require the script to prompt the user for some information and react to the user's response. The next example takes the masks script and allows the user to present a umask value to be analyzed. So far, you have been using the current umask value. To see a different result, you have been altering the umask value at the command line and rerunning the script:

EXAMPLE

```
$ cat masks_ask
#!/bin/ksh
#
# Script which will display default
# permissions in formatted fashion
# based on the requested umask setting
#
function gen_modes
{
(...)                              # Same function as before
######### Script Begins ##########
typeset -i2 defa                  # make defa display in binary
typeset -i8 onescomp
typeset -RZ3 inumask8 inumask     # Three characters, right justified, zero filled
typeset -i8 inumask8              # Display as octal
print -n "What umask would you like to use? "    # Prompt the user
read inumask                      # Read response from stdin into variable inumask
(( inumask8=8#$inumask ))         # Set input to octal
(( onescomp=~(8#$inumask8) ))     # Get ones complement of current umask
(...)
$
$ umask
0002
$
$ masks_ask
What umask would you like to use? 027    # User responds with '027'
Default REGULAR FILE permissions with specified umask 027
u    g    o
r w - r - - - - -
(In binary -- 110100000)
$
```

```
$ masks_ask
What umask would you like to use? 002    # User responds with '002'
Default REGULAR FILE permissions with specified umask 002
u     g     o
r w - r w - r - -
(In binary -- 110110100)

$
```

The `read` statement can be used to read from files other than `stdin`. By default, a script that executes a `read` statement waits until the user responds with some input. Well, how long do you wait after you ask your teenager, "What did you do last night?" Presumably, after a reasonable amount of time, you veer off into another course of action, such as saying, "Earth to teenager!" The point is that the `read` statement can provide a timeout factor (in seconds) by using the `-t secs` option (available in ksh93). You will see examples of reading from data files in the next chapter. The `read` command has many options. If you prefer, you can shorten the prompt and `read` combination as follows:

```
read inumask?"What umask would you like to use? "
```

If you want to include a timeout factor of 10 seconds, use the following command:

```
read -t 10 inumask?"What umask would you like to use? "
```

Although you can use the `echo` command to display information, you might have noticed that the example scripts are now using the `print` command almost exclusively. The `print` command is the preferred method for displaying output under the Korn Shell. It is more portable and faster. Many ksh implementations use a separate program to execute the `echo` command. The following example shows that on Red Hat Linux the `echo` command is a separate program, whereas the `print` command is built into the shell:

```
$ whereis echo
echo: /bin/echo     # The echo command is a separate program
$
$ whereis print
print:              # Not found
$
$ builtin | grep ^p
print               # The print command is a built-in
printf
pwd
```

But does this difference between `print` and `echo` really matter? Take a look at the next example. Two scripts do exactly the same thing, but one uses `echo`, and the other uses `print`. Both programs drop their output into the bit bucket, otherwise known as /dev/null. Note that if your implementation of ksh has an echo built in, you still are better off using the print command because of its portability. The massive speed difference shown in the following is due to the fact that the echolots script forces UNIX to create (and destroy) 5,000 processes to complete the task. The printlots script is executed within one UNIX process.

Be aware that the same performance difference can be seen when a script writer uses sed, grep, and awk, when shell pattern sequences would have done the job. If it is used just once or twice during the running of a script, it won't make much difference. But if you are in a many-pass loop, the difference can be significant:

EXAMPLE

```
$ time echolots
...working...
...working...
...working...
...working...
...working...

real    1m7.54s       # Takes over a minute using echo program
user    0m36.51s
sys     0m30.99s
$
$ time printlots
...working...
...working...
...working...
...working...
...working...

real    0m3.10s                    # Takes 3 seconds using print
user    0m2.48s
sys     0m0.63s
$
$ cat echolots
#!/bin/ksh
x=17
integer count
while (( count < 5000 ))
do
        /bin/echo $x > /dev/null    # Uses the echo program
        (( count=count+1 ))
        (( (count%1000) == 0 )) && print "...working..."
```

```
                                    # Occasional sanity message
done

$
$ cat printlots
#!/bin/ksh
x=17
integer count
while (( count < 5000 ))
do
        print $x > /dev/null        # Uses the print builtin command
        (( count=count+1 ))
        (( (count%1000) == 0 )) && print "...working..."
done
$
```

Following are some of the common options used with the `print` command:

```
print [-Rnprsu[n]] [arg... ]
```

The `-n` option is used for prompting (no trailing newline):

```
print -n "Anybody out there?"
```

For option conflicts, use `-`. Option conflicts can occur when a variable contains a value that starts with a `-`. The `print` command interprets the value as an option that is supposed to alter the `print` command's behavior:

```
$ print - -n
-n
```

The other options to the `print` command are less heavily used. The following is a list of the less common `print` options:

- `-R` or `-r`—Raw output. All characters following this option are displayed.

- `-p`—Can be used to send output to a pipeline connected to a coprocess (discussed later in this chapter).

- `-s`—Sends the output to the history file.

- `-u`—Sends the output to a unit number representing a file you have previously opened.

As you have seen in some of the scripts examined in this chapter, the `read` command is useful for getting input from the user. The `read` command pauses the execution of the script until the user enters some data, or until the specified timeout is reached. If the timeout option is used (`-t secs`), the script writer must check the status in $? after the command completes. If it contains a nonzero value, it means the `read` command completed because of a timeout rather than from the user entering data. The following examples show some simple uses of the read command:

EXAMPLE

```
$ updatenumbers
last name?dyment
phone?555-1234
$
$ updatenumbers
last name?O'Brien
phone?555-3456
$
$ cat updatenumbers
#!/bin/ksh
# writes to friends file
print  -n "last name?"
read last                       # Reads input into variable named last
print -n "phone?"
read phone                      # Reads input into variable named phone
echo "$last $phone" >> friends  # Appends to the file named friends

$
$ cat friends
dyment 555-1234
O'Brien 555-3456
$
```

Alternatively, the program could use the more succinct read-prompt command:

```
$ updatenumbers2
last name?ellis
phone?555-4567
$
$ cat updatenumbers2
#!/bin/ksh
# writes to friends file
read last?"last name?"          # Uses the read with prompt option
read phone?"phone?"
print "$last $phone" >> friends

$
$ cat friends
dyment 555-1234
O'Brien 555-3456
ellis 555-4567
$
```

But what do you do if the user is common-sense impaired and responds with unexpected input? Covering all the bases for these unexpected responses results in making the script bulletproof. A *bulletproof* script is one in which the user's input is thoroughly checked for sanity before being processed. This can require some extensive testing. If the script is for personal use only, you might not want to spend the time bulletproofing your script, but it is a good habit to develop. The following example builds on the umask example, but it checks the user's input to ensure that it is reasonable.

Generally, if a way to break your script exists, users will find it. Either they will specifically search for the holes in your logic, or they will stumble across your script's weaknesses inadvertently. The most obvious example of input that would break your umask script is if the user presented some input that was out of range. The valid values for the umask are between 000 and 777 octal, which means that no numbers higher than seven can exist in any of the three numeral positions. The following example scopes out that potential foul-up:

```
$ masks_ask1
What umask would you like to use? 999
masks_ask1: line 31:  inumask8=8#999 : arithmetic syntax error
```

EXAMPLE

Somehow, you must check the user's response and see whether it makes any sense. If it doesn't, you should help the user to understand her mistake (or you could blow it off and just bomb out of the script). The following example tries to capture aberrant input and react accordingly:

```
$ cat masks_ask2
#!/bin/ksh
#
# Script which will display default
# permissions in formatted fashion
# based on the requested umask setting, checks for bogus input
#
function gen_modes
{
(...)
read inumask?"What umask would you like to use? "
while (( (inumask%10)>7  || (inumask%100)>80 || (inumask%1000)>800 ))
do                      # Checks for numerals > 7
        print "Mask value must be between octal 000 and 777: try again"
        read inumask?"What umask would you like to use? "
done
(...)
$
$ masks_ask2
What umask would you like to use? 029
Mask value must be between octal 000 and 777: try again
```

```
What umask would you like to use? 810
Mask value must be between octal 000 and 777: try again
What umask would you like to use? 817
Mask value must be between octal 000 and 777: try again
What umask would you like to use? 027
Default REGULAR FILE permissions with specified umask 027
u    g    o
r w - r - - - - -
(In binary -- 110100000)
```

That seems to do the trick, don't you think? But consider the fact that a user could insert negative numbers or numbers with more than three numerals, throw some characters at your script, or just hit the carriage return and give you nothing. Now you see that this script has a ways to go before it can be deemed bulletproof.

Redirection

Many times you wish you could play back a tape of a past conversation with your teenager. To do this, you would have to have created an audio tape as the teenager was spouting the output. In the world of scripts, you might want to store the output in a file. You also might prefer to capture all the output, or just some of it. This section examines input and output redirection.

Three streams can be redirected: stdin, stdout, and stderr. By default, all three of these streams are directed to (or from in the case of stdin) your terminal device. A *stream* can be thought of as an open file, despite the fact that we are talking about the terminal device being open. Therefore, the shell deals with stdin, stdout, and stderr as permanently open files for your process.

Each file that is open in a process is represented by a file descriptor. *File descriptors* are small (usually) integer numbers that represent the open file to your process. The file descriptor numbers representing stdin, stdout, and stderr are, 0, 1, and 2, respectively. Some UNIX variants allow a process to have up to 64 open files. I know of one UNIX variant (Compaq's Tru64 UNIX) that allows a process to have up to 65,525 concurrently open files. That ought to do it, huh?

We will focus on redirection involving stdin, stdout, and stderr. Back to your teenager for an analogy. (By the way, if you ARE a teenager, no offense meant in all these examples, but I'm sure you can relate with the situations portrayed.) If your teenager keeps asking you for permission to attend a Metallica concert and repeats the request again and again, you eventually say, "Go ask your mother." (Or father as the case may be.) If you can relate, you understand output redirection. The goal is to take an output stream that is going to its normal place (such as your ear or the terminal) and redirect it so it goes some other place (such as someone else's ear or a file).

Output redirection provides the capability to capture the output of a command or a script in a file. The following examples show some basic output redirection. Note that a > at the end of a command requests stdout redirection, whereas >> also requests stdout redirection but appends the output to an existing file. If a file already exists and you redirect output to the existing file using >, the current contents of the file are lost. This is referred to as *clobbering* an existing file.

When the shell sees a line that has an output redirection indicator at the end of it, one of the first things it does is truncate the existing output file down to zero bytes in size. Then, it places the current output stream in the file. This usually has some uproarious consequences for the novice UNIX user. Incidentally, uproarious is only a hop away from disastrous. Imagine that the file you inadvertently clobbered was your startup company's critical R&D database!

Fortunately, the Korn Shell provides a technique for avoiding clobbers when you don't want to clobber—a shell option called, you guessed it, noclobber. It can be set with the set -o noclobber command. Picture a rookie user trying to sort some database. It makes sense to use a command such as the following:

```
sort infile > infile
```

You have no desire to end up with two copies of the data, so this command seems reasonable. Unfortunately, the shell sees the > before the sort is even started. So, the first thing that happens is the file named infile is truncated down to zero bytes. Then, the shell—feeling all smug and happy because it has done its duty for its good friend sort—kicks in the sort command, which sees an input file named infile that has zero bytes of data to be sorted. The sort command then does its duty, which is to sort nothing, and produces an output file named infile—which contains nothing. Poof, away goes your data, your credibility, your job, and maybe your company goes belly up also. Okay, I'm exaggerating, but did you get my point?

The following are some examples of stdout redirection:

```
$ man ls > ls.man          # man pages sent to file
$ man cat >> ls.man        # appends to ls.man
$ (date; du) > stats       # output of subshell goes to stats file
```

If you can redirect stdout, you must be able to redirect stdin. The symbol for stdin redirection is <. Imagine that every time your teenage son goes out on a date, you preach the same litany of do's and don'ts to him. Your harangue takes about two minutes, during which you get the same grunting sequence of whys and why nots. Rather than waiting for the questions to be asked before you present your answers, you can have the answers on an audio tape so all you have to do is push Play, and your teenager hears your canned responses. Because your teenager is probably listening with about an eighth of his attention, you will be repeating this sequence many times.

Think of the input audio tape with the canned answers for your teenager as an example of stdin redirection. Instead of hearing the answers from the standard place (which is you), you redirect the input to him so that it comes from the tape. Likewise, you can use a file to present input to a program that queries the user repetitively. All you have to do is create the file containing the responses and present it to the command as a substitute (redirection) for stdin. The fictitious payroll program shown in the following would normally query the user for employee name, hourly rate, and hours worked in the current week. Suppose 90% of the employees work the same number of hours each week, their rates don't change that often, and their names don't change. The input file would contain all the normal information for the company's employees, and all that would have to be done each week is change the hours worked if necessary.

The following are examples of stdin redirection:

```
$ payroll < file_containing_employee_hours_and rates
$ mailx obrien < spammail         # mails spammail file contents to obrien
$ tr "OB" "ob" < f1 > f2          # redirects input and output
                                  #changes Os and Bs in f1 to
                                  # os and bs in f2.
```

Sometimes a command you execute during the run of your script can cause error messages to be displayed. Normally, those error messages go to your terminal device, represented by stderr (file descriptor 2). Suppose your script produces a carefully laid out menu interface. If an unexpected error message were to appear in the middle of the run of the script, the carefully planned menu interface could look like a train wreck.

If you want, you can dump the error messages into the bit bucket (/dev/null) so they don't display at all. That solution is fine if you want to take the head-in-the-sand approach, which assumes that if you can't see the errors then all is well.

A better approach is to redirect the error messages to some file, the console device, or some other terminal, rather than letting them appear on your terminal with the neat menu. This approach is certainly more enlightened than the head-in-the-sand approach, which eliminates the possibility of reacting to the error messages. Remember that stderr is associated with file descriptor 2. Therefore, the redirection syntax for stderr is 2>, which means redirect file descriptor 2. You also can use the syntax 1> to indicate stdout redirection, although no script that I have ever seen does that.

The following are examples of stderr redirection:

```
$ payroll < emps1 >pay.out 2> pay.err
                            # payroll program gets input from emps1,
                            # writes output to pay.out,
                            # error messages go to pay.err

$ payroll >pay.out 2>&1      # make 2 (stderr) be the same as 1 (stdout)

$ noerrprog 2> /dev/null     #errors to bit bucket
```

If any of these redirection options end up clobbering a file or two, you might be interested in this next Korn Shell capability. You can prevent clobbering (overwriting of existing files through redirection) by setting the noclobber option using the following syntax:

```
$ set -o noclobber
```

Later on, you might want to override the noclobber option. You can turn it off with the following syntax:

```
$ set +o noclobber
```

Or, you can override the option for a particular command by using the following syntax:

```
$ prog >|bagfile      # writes even if bagfile exists
$ prog >>|bagfile     # writes even if bagfile does not exist
```

Coprocess

Occasionally, a script needs to present input to a program, command, or another script, but not all at once. For instance, you might need to present one item during the beginning of your script, others during the run, and still others at the end. This is generally done by redirecting some input to the appropriate target program. It also can be done through a pipeline. As you saw earlier, a command to the left of the pipe operator presents its output as input to the command to the right of the pipe operator. So, the piping operation is similar to performing redirection, BUT NOT TO A FILE! The redirection is done to the PIPE instead, and the pipe is connected to the next process in the pipeline.

Now consider a situation in which you need to get input to a program through a pipe, but you need to pipe to it many items throughout the run of your script. The implementation is not difficult if you are willing to accept some performance degradation. Remember that in UNIX, every time a command is executed, it is executed in the context of a UNIX process. Each UNIX process has internal support structures and other resources that need to be allocated, and all this takes time.

Without getting into the internals of it, trust me, it would be massively more efficient to run the target program once, and have it stay in existence while you occasionally ask it to process another piece of pipelined input.

Needless to say, you will also want to capture responses from the program running in parallel with yours. A script can achieve this bidirectional pipeline capability through the use of a coprocess and two pipes. Be aware, however, that this is a powerful capability that is not used very heavily because most script writers are only vaguely aware of the coprocess concept and syntax.

I hate to use the teenager analogy again, but what the heck. You're into it now, right? Imagine an off-the-cuff argument with your teenager. Remember all those times when, after it was over, you said to yourself, "I should have said ...," so you went back and said, "... and another thing ...."

The difference between using a coprocess and not using a coprocess is the same as if you had to start the argument from the beginning each time you remembered something else you wanted to say, rather than just saying, "... and another thing ...."

Can you see the waste in starting over for each item of input? It would be like having to start the argument over again from the beginning point, even though you just wanted to add one last little jab. The following example uses a sophisticated utility called dbx, which is used to debug user programs or to look at kernel cells. You'll see this being used without using a coprocess first, and then with a coprocess.(Another example of using a coprocess is shown in Chapter 13, "Pulling It All Together." It creates a coprocess running another instance of ksh to which your script presents commands.)

Figure 8.1 depicts the communication between your script (copro1) and the coprocess running dbx.

You don't need to focus on the dbx utility as you read the example. Instead, focus on the concept of a *coprocess*, which is a process that coexists with another process and communicates through pipelines. The following example uses dbx to examine a kernel cell (lbolt) without using a coprocess.

Figure 8.2 depicts what happens when you don't use a coprocess.

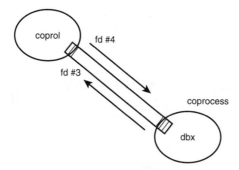

Figure 8.1: *A coprocess communicates with another process through pipelines.*

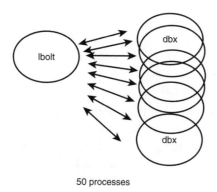

50 processes

Figure 8.2: *Without a coprocess,* dbx *looks at the* lbolt *kernel cell 50 times in a row.*

lbolt doesn't need to be looked at 50 times in a row; it is just a sample kernel cell. If you are curious, though, it holds the system time. Note that the example output also gives a feel for how many UNIX processes had to be created when the script was not using a coprocess:

EXAMPLE

```
# echo $$
725
# ksh
# echo $$
1440                    # Next available PID is approximately 1441
# exit
#
# time ./copro2 /vmunix /dev/mem

real    0m21.06s        # Takes about 21 seconds when not using a coprocess
user    0m19.46s
sys     0m1.21s
#
```

```
# ksh
# echo $$
1596                    # Note how many processes were created (~156)
#
```

The next example does the same thing using a coprocess. Note that the code within the script is a bit more complex, but the payoff is potentially huge, as you can see from the performance comparison:

```
# time ./copro1 /vmunix /dev/mem

real    0m3.90s        # Took about 4 seconds using a coprocess.
user    0m0.00s
sys     0m0.03s
#
#
# ksh
# echo $$
1599                    # Approximately 3 processes were created
                        # to run with a coprocess

#
```

Before you take a look at the script that provided this 7000% increase in the performance of your code, let me show you what an interactive session with dbx looks like. This example uses the live kernel for its target, so you must be root to perform the following command. Note all the preliminary messages before you actually get to present some input to the utility. Interactively, you can ignore this output. But in a script, you must get rid of this data to capture nothing but the data you want. You see two distinct ways of handling this excess output in the following two scripts:

EXAMPLE

```
# dbx -k /vmunix /dev/mem
dbx version 5.1
Type 'help' for help.

stopped at  [thread_block:3074 ,0xfffffc00002d0450]     Source not available

warning: Files compiled -g3: parameter values probably wrong
(dbx) p lbolt
5190922
(dbx) quit
#
```

The first script does not use a coprocess and therefore suffers from some poor performance. Note the succinct check of the command-line arguments. It asks whether the count of arguments is not equal to two, and then executes the command after the &&. The main body of the script falls inside a 50-pass loop in which you repetitively present the output of a print command as the input to the dbx command. It's as if you typed in two

commands at the interactive dbx prompt: p lbolt and quit. The
2>/dev/null syntax removes the display line starting with warning from the
dbx output by redirecting stderr. (And you thought that stderr redirection
would never come in handy, didn't you?) The tail -1 says that all you are
interested in is the last line of output, which you want appended to the file
named times.

If you are thinking that you could use this same technique of piping the
output of a print (or echo) command to just about any interactive utility,
you are right. And I congratulate you for the thought. However, don't run
off and start changing your production scripts yet. Wait until you see the
coprocess example:

```
# cat copro2
#!/bin/ksh

[ $# != 2 ] && {                        # Display message if we don't get two args
print "Usage: $0 vmunix vmzcore"
exit 1
}
# main loop
let ntimes=0;
while (( ntimes < 50 )); do
print 'p lbolt;quit' | dbx -k  $1 $2 2>/dev/null | tail -1>>times2
                               # Creates a process
let ntimes=ntimes+1
done
exit
```

The next example uses a coprocess running dbx to handle the 50 requests
for the current value of the kernel cell named lbolt. An innocuous-looking
but very powerful command is shown after the usage help. It simply says
>times. This looks as if you are trying to redirect the standard output of,
um, nothing, into the file named times. The shell sees the >times, puts on
its truncation hat, and chops the current contents of times to zero bytes,
which is what you wanted. This prevents an uncontrolled growth of the output file for each time the script is run. It also effectively deletes the current
contents of the file and readies it for subsequent processing.

The line that actually starts up the coprocess is dbx -k $1 $2 2>
/dev/null 2> /dev/null |&. The key syntax is the last |&. This special syn-
tax looks like a combination of a pipe request and a background request; in
fact, it uses facets of both activities. When a process is placed in the background, it can coexist with the interactive shell—just as you want in this
example. In addition, when a process uses a pipe, it wants a means of com-
municating with the piped-to process—which also is just what you want

here. So, if you can't remember the syntax for a coprocess in the future, just remember the two parts of it: sorta piping and sorta background |&.

Next, you need a means of opening a communication path to the waiting coprocess. The exec command can be used to execute a new command in the context of the current process. UNIX programmers are familiar with the system-call level of the function. Here, you use it inside your script to indicate that the current process wants to open up file descriptor 3 (exec 3<) as a means to get input (note the direction of the symbol <) from the pipeline that comes from the coprocess &p. Yes, I know the syntax is not intuitive. But it's not as if we have never seen anything nonintuitive in UNIX before!!

Using the same technique, the next command, exec 4>&p, opens up file descriptor number 4 to write output to the coprocess. In summary, writing to file descriptor 4 provides input commands to dbx, and reading from file descriptor 3 gets output from dbx. The while test tries to read from unit 3, and the -r handles reads with a continuation character at the end (\) as part of the line. The semicolon allows the do to be on the same line for readability and style, whereas the variable line is filled with a line of output from dbx running in the coprocess. The case statement looks for and eliminates the lines of introductory information issued by dbx as it starts.

The main loop is executed 50 times. The print command is directed to file descriptor unit number 4 (-u4) and contains a simple dbx command you will send to the coprocess 50 times. In reality, you would be sending a bunch of commands to the utility running in the coprocess. The read gets the next line of output from dbx on unit 3 and dumps it into the variable timebolt. Then, the next print appends the line to the file named times. Subsequently, this repeats 50 times, at which point you finally send the quit command to dbx, which ends the coprocess:

EXAMPLE

```
# cat copro1
#!/bin/ksh

[ $# != 2 ] && {
print "Usage should be: $0 vmunix vmzcore"
exit 1
}
>times                                  # truncates times file
dbx -k $1 $2 2> /dev/null 2> /dev/null |& # start dbx coprocess
exec 3<&p                               # use fd 3 to read from dbx
exec 4>&p                               # use fd 4 to write to dbx
while read -ru3 line; do                # get through dbx banners
case $line in
        "") continue;;                  # skip blank lines
        *dbx*) continue;;               # skip dbx banner
        *Type*) continue;;              # skip dbx banner
        *stopped*) break;;              # exit this loop
```

```
esac
done
# main loop
let ntimes=0;
while (( ntimes < 50 )); do
print -u4 'p lbolt'                          # Send command to coprocess
read -ru3 timebolt                           # Read output from coprocess
print $timebolt >> times
let ntimes=ntimes+1
done
print -u4 'quit'
exit
#
```

What's Next

This chapter presented some powerful options to the script writer. Command-line arguments enable a smoother user interface to the script by allowing the user to provide input without having to be prompted. The getopts command provides a special case to handle shell command-like options on the command line. You also looked at the read command as a means of providing user input to your script. This provides the script writer with yet another means for acquiring data from the user.

After you were presented with the data from the user, you saw several redirection techniques for storing the output from the script in a file. Input redirection was discussed as a means to simplify user input that might repeat, and you also saw examples of redirecting error messages to a destination of your choosing.

The final section of the chapter introduced the high performance coprocessing technique for interacting with a utility repetitively. Special options were shown in scripts using print commands and read commands to communicate with the coprocess. Emphasis was placed on the performance implications of using a coprocess to entice the script writer to take the leap into the brave new world of coprocesses.

Chapter 9, "File and Directory Manipulation," builds on the notions of file descriptors seen in the coprocess example. You'll see how to open and access data files in your scripts. You'll also take a closer look at file attributes, file access techniques, and creating temporary files as your script runs. In addition, you'll revisit filtering relative to open files.

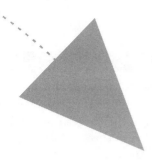

File and Directory Manipulation

When you receive an important document, you probably store it in a file cabinet. Chances are the file cabinet has an organization involving several drawers and various folders and maybe even subfolders. The alternative is to throw all your important documents into a shoebox and stash it under your bed. Note that both methods achieve the goal of storing the document.

The difference is apparent when the time comes to retrieve the document. If you are of the shoebox persuasion, you will probably spend some time pawing through all the unordered papers you had heaped into the shoebox. On the other hand, if the papers are organized into drawers, file folders, and subfolders, retrieving the appropriate paper would be a matter of opening the correct drawer and grabbing the correct folder. The latter approach closely resembles a description of file storage within a directory hierarchy.

All modern file systems provide a directory hierarchy to help organize the storage and retrieval of files. Access to files and directories is a very visible part of the shell's interaction with the system and the user.

This chapter teaches you the following:

- How the PATH variable works
- How files and directories interact
- How file attributes describe files
- The use of device special files
- How to use hard links and symbolic links
- Methods of file access
- The nature of filter commands
- A safe way to create temporary files

Paths

A user or script can request access to a file using an *absolute file specification* or a *relative file specification*. An absolute file specification provides the directory and subdirectory hierarchy path to locate the target file. A relative file specification locates the target file relative to the current working directory. The following example starts by accessing a file using a relative file specification. After changing the default directory, the relative file spec no longer works, but an absolute file spec will always work no matter where your directory default is currently.

The following example successfully uses a relative file specification, changes the default directory, and then fails when attempting to re-execute the same command using the relative file specification. The problem is then solved by using an absolute file specification:

EXAMPLE

```
$ cat params                            # Relative file spec
#!/bin/ksh
print "Argument 1 is ${1}"
print "Argument 2 is ${2}"
print "Argument 3 is ${3}"
print "There are $# arguments."

$
$ pwd
/home/obrien/scripts
$
$ cd /                                  # Change default directory
$
$ cat params                            # Relative spec fails
-ksh: cat: params: cannot open [No such file or directory]
$
$ cat /home/obrien/scripts/params       # Absolute spec works
#!/bin/ksh
print "Argument 1 is ${1}"
print "Argument 2 is ${2}"
print "Argument 3 is ${3}"
print "There are $# arguments."
```

A relative file specification is, at first glance, an incomplete file spec. If you present the command ls -l obrien to the shell, it looks for the obrien file in the current working directory (displayed with the pwd command). If it is a command file being sought by the shell—such as when a command, script, or program is being sought—it looks at the contents of the $PATH variable for a list of locations in which to look for the file.

The shell can determine whether to use the PATH variable or use the current working directory, by the position on the command line. Filenames appearing immediately after the shell prompt ($) are treated as commands, and therefore are sought using the directories listed in the PATH variable.

In the command ls -1 mydata, the ls is sought by looking in the PATH directories, whereas the mydata is sought from the current working directory. Both of these search locations can be overridden by using an absolute file specification, such as /usr/bin/ls -1 /usr/users/obrien/mydata.

The following example displays the current working directory and the contents of the PATH variable. It also documents how to change the PATH variable:

EXAMPLE

```
$ pwd                            # Data files are sought from this directory
/home/obrien
$
$ print $PATH                    # Commands and scripts are
                                 # sought from these directories
/usr/local/bin:/bin:/usr/bin:/usr/X11R6/bin:.
$
$ PATH=$PATH:/usr/opt/networker/bin # Changing PATH variable
$
```

In a script, the habit should be to provide an absolute spec wherever possible. This eliminates the possibility of a user-defined alias replacing the command you had intended to run. This would introduce a level of unpredictability to the script. The next example shows the danger of relying on relative file specs in a script. For illustration purposes, this example is command-line–based. The same principles apply for scripts.

The following example shows the ls command being replaced by an alias:

EXAMPLE

```
$ ls                     #'ls' working properly
getppid.c  getppidfunc.c
$
$ alias ls='cat *'       # Make an alias for 'ls'
$
$ ls                     # Now 'ls' does a 'cat' command
#include <unistd.h>
#include <stdio.h>
int main(void)           #Some file contents
{
printf("Parent PID is %d\n",getppid());
}
#include <unistd.h>
#include <stdio.h>
#include <stdlib.h>
```

```
int b_ppid(int argc, char *argv[])
{
printf("Parent PID is %d\n",getppid());
return(EXIT_SUCCESS);
}
$
$ whereis ls              # Locate the ls program
ls: /bin/ls /usr/man/man1/ls.1
$
$ /bin/ls                 # Execute it presenting its full file specification
getppid.c  getppidfunc.c
$
```

The actual location of a command can usually be found with the whereis command (or the which command or the whence command). If the command is still among the missing, try using the find command. Not all commands will be located by the whereis command, however. The RedHat Linux man page for whereis states, "whereis has a hard-coded path, so may not always find what you're looking for." If I can't find a command that I am quite sure exists, I use the find command to do the grunt work. What the heck, we've got a computer at our fingertips; let's let it do the searching.

Running find as a user can yield many permission denied messages. Be patient, and let it run. If what you are looking for is there, find will find it. If you get annoyed or embarrassed by the error messages, send them to their exile in the bit bucket. You learned stderr redirection in the last chapter, so you should be able to use syntax such as 2> /dev/null to eliminate those pesky messages.

The following example uses the find command to locate the ls program. It also shows the redirection of stderr to eliminate error messages generated by the find command. Note that your system's find command might require the -print option on the end of the command line:

EXAMPLE

```
$ whereis ls
ls: /bin/ls /usr/man/man1/ls.1
$
$ find / -name ls                # Search for the ls program
find: /usr/doc/ppp-2.3.10/scripts/chatchat: Permission denied
find: /proc/1/fd: Permission denied
 (...)
/bin/ls
(...)
$ find / -name ls 2> /dev/null   # Redirect error messages into the
                                 # 'bit bucket'
/bin/ls
```

Either method helps you bulletproof your script if you build in absolute paths for commands. You might feel that this makes the script cumbersome and unwieldy. If so, try hiding the actual locations of the commands in shell variables. Even though this technique might not get rid of the cumbersome feeling, it can prevent errors that might have cropped up if you had to repeat the full file spec for each and every invocation of the ls command.

The following example creates a shell variable to hold the directory location for the ls command and uses it to avoid inadvertent use of aliases:

```
$ lsloc='/bin'              # Create shell variable containing
                            # directory spec for ls command
$
$ $lsloc/ls                 # Use absolute spec through shell variable
getppid.c  getppidfunc.c
```

Descriptors

As discussed in the previous chapter, a *file descriptor* is a small integer value representing an open file. You might recall the three famous (infamous) file descriptors: stdin, stdout, and stderr. These mnemonics represent file descriptors 0, 1, and 2, respectively. They are usually open and typically represent your terminal display device. When you use the redirection symbols on the command line, you are altering file descriptor 0, or 1, or 2 (stdin, stdout, or stderr).

The following example uses the > and >> symbols to redirect output to a file (>), and also to redirect output and append it to an existing file (>>):

EXAMPLE

```
$ date > stats              # Put output of date command into stats file
$ vmstat >> stats           # Append vmstat output into stats file
$
$ cat stats
Mon Oct 16 13:00:15 EDT 2000
   procs                    memory     swap        io     system        cpu
  r  b  w   swpd   free   buff  cache  si  so     bi    bo   in    cs  us  sy  id
  0  0  0   2124    808  13616   7860   0   0      1     0  108     6   0   0 100
```

Other descriptors can be used to represent other files you might want to open in your script. The Korn Shell (and other shells) has so many file manipulation commands built into it that the need to directly open a file and read individual lines is rare. However, for advanced file processing where you might want to have access to data in several files at once, the Korn Shell provides the exec command to open access to a file(s).

The following example script creates a file containing the current date and time, followed by the output of a vmstat command repeated five times. The goal is to produce a log file (named summary in the script) that contains the date and time, and also contains the average number of interrupts occurring per second over the 10-second interval following the recorded date and time. It uses the exec command to open access to files as the script runs. It also shows the read -A command, which enables the reading of a line of data into an array. Note that the -A option might not be available on systems using earlier releases of ksh:

EXAMPLE

```
$ cat openone
#! /bin/ksh
integer tot=0 ave=0
set -A line               # Variable 'line' is an array

date > stats              # Put date in stats file
vmstat 2 5 >> stats       # Put vmstat output in stats file,
                          # repeats every 2 seconds, does it 5 times

exec 3< stats             # Open access to stats on file descriptor number 3
exec 4> summary           # Open write access to summary file on fd number 4

read -u3 line             # Read date into variable line
print -u4 $line           # Write contents of line to fd 4

read -u3; read -u3 ; read -u3 ; read -u3 # Eliminate header lines

while read -A -u3 line # Read second vmstat line into array
do
tot=tot+${line[12]}       # Access interrupt count in field 12
done

ave=tot/4                 # Calculate average
print "Average number of interrupts during the last 10 seconds is $ave ."
                          # To stdout
print -u4 "Average number of interrupts during the last 10 seconds is $ave ."
                          # To fd 4
exit
$
$ openone
Average number of interrupts during the last 10 seconds is 90 .
                          # Script output display
$
$
$ cat summary             # Summary file contents
Thu Nov 2 00:54:00 EST 2000
Average number of interrupts during the last 10 seconds is 90 .
$
$
```

```
$ cat stats              # Stats file FYI
Thu Nov  2 00:54:00 EST 2000
Virtual Memory Statistics: (pagesize = 8192)
  procs       memory        pages                              intr       cpu
  r   w   u  act free wire fault cow zero react  pin pout  in  sy  cs us sy id
  3 154  31  60K 14K 10K   14M  3M  4M  1056   3M    0  83  2K  1K 10  4 86
  2 155  31  60K 14K 10K    1   21   8    0     9    0 122  1K 808  0  1 99
  2 155  31  60K 14K 10K    0    0   0    0     0    0  75 915 719  0  1 99
  2 155  31  60K 14K 10K   379  93  54    0    75    0  86  2K  1K 10  5 85
  2 155  31  60K 14K 10K    0    0   0    0     0    0  78  1K  1K  7  1 91
$
```

Special Files

My first experiences with UNIX were as a C programmer. I was familiar with writing programs for low-level access to devices for reads or writes, or getting or setting device characteristics, but had never done it in UNIX. I had always done this by opening a channel to the device and using functions that run in kernel mode (referred to as *system calls* or *system services*) to get or set what I wanted. I figured I could do the same kind of thing in UNIX, but I didn't know how. I spoke with a new hire who had UNIX experience and asked him how to perform low-level I/Os to a device in UNIX. He thought for a few seconds and said, "Well, that's easy. You just open a file. Everything in UNIX is represented by a file."

I thanked him and backed away thinking to myself, "This guy doesn't have a clue." It turned out it was I who didn't have a clue. Just about everything in UNIX is indeed represented by a file. Files represent all your terminals, printers, disks, virtual memory, physical memory, pseudo-devices, and so on.

Files representing hardware devices are called *device special files*. They can be character special files for terminals, printers, and other character-oriented devices, or they can be block special files for disk devices. Note that these files are actually 0 bytes in size. Take a look at the size field in the following examples (just to the left of the date field). The size field is replaced by two numbers, such as 6 and 27, or 19 and 38.

The leftmost number is the device *major* ID and is used to identify which device driver is to be used to service this device. The other number is the device *minor* ID. It is used to distinguish one device (in a class of devices) from the other. If you had 15 SCSI disks, they would all be served by the same driver, so the major ID in their device special files would be the same for all of them. The minor IDs, however, would all be different to differentiate I/O from each individual device. All the device special files consist of is metadata containing the major and minor IDs, and other typical file attributes such as permissions.

The following example displays the metadata from several device special files (note that all device special files are found under the /dev directory):

```
$ ls -l ttyqb
crw-rw-rw-   2 root      system      6, 27 Feb  7  2000 ttyqb
                                    # Character special file for terminal
$
$ ls -l /dev/rdisk/dsk*c    # Character special files for raw disks
crw-------   1 root      system     19, 38 Dec  6  1999 /dev/rdisk/dsk0c
crw-------   1 root      system     19, 70 Sep 21 20:45 /dev/rdisk/dsk1c
$
$ ls -l /dev/disk/dsk*c     # Block special files for disks
brw-------   1 root      system     19, 37 Dec  6  1999 /dev/disk/dsk0c
brw-------   1 root      system     19, 69 Sep 21 20:27 /dev/disk/dsk1c
```

Links

Do you have a nickname? When you are at work, you might be called Mr. Smith. When at the ball field, you might be Shorty, and when with your mate, you might be Sweetie. These monikers all refer to the same thing: you.

Similarly, files can have multiple names. When you create a file and give it a name, you create a hard link to the file. Note the link count field in the following example. The link count field appears immediately after the permissions. It contains a 1, indicating that currently only one hard link exists to the body of data represented by the file's name:

EXAMPLE

```
$ ls -l stats
-rw-r--r--   1 obrien    guest            629 Nov  2 00:54 stats
```

In addition, the ln command can be used to create more hard links to the same file.

The following example creates a second hard link to an existing file and subsequently drives the link count field from 1 to 2:

```
$ ln stats hardlinktostats                          # Creates a hard link
$
$ ls -l *stats
-rw-r--r--   2 obrien    guest            629 Nov  2 00:54 hardlinktostats
                                                    # Link count is now two
-rw-r--r--   2 obrien    guest            629 Nov  2 00:54 stats
```

All links to the same file can be used to access the file similarly. Unlike your name and nicknames, no distinction exists between the first link to the file and the last. (When signing a check, you typically don't use your nickname, do you?) The hard links to a file are all equal in their capability to represent the file. Additionally, a hard link is represented in its directory by a filename that is associated with the same inode number as an existing file.

The following example shows that two hard-linked filenames will have the same inode number, and therefore will access the same data:

EXAMPLE

```
$ ls -li *stats         # Note same inode number (first field)
75261 -rw-r--r--  2 obrien  guest       629 Nov  2 00:54 hardlinktostats
75261 -rw-r--r--  2 obrien  guest       629 Nov  2 00:54 stats
$
$ cat stats             # Both access the same data
Thu Nov  2 00:54:00 EST 2000
Virtual Memory Statistics: (pagesize = 8192)
  procs      memory       pages                            intr      cpu
  r   w   u  act free wire fault cow zero react pin pout  in  sy  cs us sy id
  3 154  31  60K 14K 10K  14M  3M  4M  1056  3M   0  83 2K 1K 10  4 86
  2 155  31  60K 14K 10K    1  21   8     0   9   0 122 1K 808  0  1 99
  2 155  31  60K 14K 10K    0   0   0     0   0   0  75 915 719  0  1 99
  2 155  31  60K 14K 10K  379  93  54     0  75   0  86 2K 1K 10  5 85
  2 155  31  60K 14K 10K    0   0   0     0   0   0  78 1K 1K  7  1 91
$
$ cat hardlinktostats   # Both access the same data
Thu Nov  2 00:54:00 EST 2000
Virtual Memory Statistics: (pagesize = 8192)
  procs      memory       pages                            intr      cpu
  r   w   u  act free wire fault cow zero react pin pout  in  sy  cs us sy id
  3 154  31  60K 14K 10K  14M  3M  4M  1056  3M   0  83 2K 1K 10  4 86
  2 155  31  60K 14K 10K    1  21   8     0   9   0 122 1K 808  0  1 99
  2 155  31  60K 14K 10K    0   0   0     0   0   0  75 915 719  0  1 99
  2 155  31  60K 14K 10K  379  93  54     0  75   0  86 2K 1K 10  5 85
  2 155  31  60K 14K 10K    0   0   0     0   0   0  78 1K 1K  7  1 91
$
```

Have you ever wondered why UNIX has no delete command? Sure, it has the rm command, but what do the letters "rm" stand for? They stand for "remove," meaning remove a link. The rm command decrements the link count in a file's metadata by one. If the link count is brought down to 0 by the rm command, the storage used by the file is freed.

Hard links do, however, have limitations. They cannot be used to represent a directory, and they can be used only within a file system. Note that a UNIX system can have many file systems. Each file system has its own storage locations and characteristics. You can see your machine's currently available file systems by examining the output of the df command.

The following example attempts to create a hard link to a file in another file system, and attempts to create a hard link to a directory:

```
$ ln /etc/passwd  pass          # Attempt to make a hard link
                                # from my directory to /etc/passwd
ln: /etc/passwd and pass are located on different file systems.
$
$ ln /etc  toetc                # Attempt to make a hard link to a directory
/etc is a directory.
$
```

These limitations are addressed through symbolic links. A *symbolic link* is also a nickname for a file, but the mechanism it uses to represent the file does not revolve around the directory and inode mechanism mentioned earlier. Each symbolic link is a file that contains a string of characters representing the absolute file spec of the target file.

The following example creates a symbolic (sometimes referred to as *soft*) link to a file and displays the symbolic link's attributes. Note the permissive permissions (rwxrwxrwx). A final permission check will occur when the linked-to file is accessed:

```
$ ln -s stats softlinktostats     # Create symbolic (soft) link to stats file
$
$ ls -li *stats
75261 -rw-r--r--  2 obrien   guest    629 Nov  2 00:54 hardlinktostats
50994 lrwxrwxrwx  1 obrien   guest      5 Nov  2 01:17 softlinktostats -> stats
75261 -rw-r--r--  2 obrien   guest    629 Nov  2 00:54 stats
$
```

Using the symbolic link mechanism, a link can be created pointing to a directory or to a file in another file system:

EXAMPLE

```
$ ln -s /etc/passwd pass    # Create symbolic link to /etc/passwd
$
$ ln -s /etc toetc          # Create symbolic link to /etc
$
$ ls -l pass
lrwxrwxrwx  1 obrien   guest           11 Nov  2 01:20 pass -> /etc/passwd
$
$ ls -l toetc               # Symbolic link permissions
lrwxrwxrwx  1 obrien   guest            4 Nov  2 01:20 toetc -> /etc
$
$ ls -lL pass               # Follow symbolic link
-rw-r--r--  1 root     system     1316 Oct 30 15:15 pass
$
$ ls -lL toetc              # Follow symbolic link to access a directory
total 1204
-rwxr-xr-x  1 bin      bin           1 Jul 20  1999 TIMEZONE
```

```
-rwxr-xr-x  1 root     uucp       12008 Apr  5  2000 acucap
drwxrwx--x  4 auth     auth        8192 Jul 21  1999 auth
(...)
drwxr-xr-x  3 root     system      8192 Jun  1 18:54 yp
drwxr-xr-x 20 root     system      8192 Oct 31 00:53 zoneinfo
$
$ cat pass                 # Use symbolic link to access password file
root:ycjCpCjPIrUzI:0:1:system PRIVILEGED account:/:/bin/ksh
nobody:*Nologin:65534:65534:anonymous NFS user:/:
```

If you delete the file to which a symbolic link is pointing, subsequent uses of the symbolic link will fail. You can, however, recreate the file to which a symbolic link points, and the symbolic link will function once again:

EXAMPLE

```
$ pwd
/home/obrien/scripts
$
$ ls -li stats
4036 -rw-rw-r--  1 obrien    obrien       589 Nov  4 15:36 stats
                             # Note size of stats is 589
$
                             # Note inode number is 4036
$ cd ..                      # Change to another directory
$
$ ln -s /home/obrien/scripts/stats   symstats
                             # Create symbolic link symstats
$
$ ls -li symstats
16090 lrwxrwxrwx  1 obrien   obrien        26 Nov  4 15:37
                             # Note linkage and permissions
                        symstats -> /home/obrien/scripts/stats
                             # Note size is 26 (length of file spec)
$
$ ls -lL symstats
                             # -L shows what the link points to
-rw-rw-r--  1 obrien   obrien       589 Nov  4 15:36 symstats
                             # Note size is 589
$
$ rm /home/obrien/scripts/stats
                             # Remove file pointed to by link
$
$ ls -l symstats
lrwxrwxrwx  1 obrien   obrien        26 Nov  4 15:37
                             # Link still exists
                        symstats -> /home/obrien/scripts/stats
$
$ ls -lL symstats
```

```
lrwxrwxrwx   1 obrien   obrien        26 Nov  4 15:37
                                 # -L shows no difference
                          symstats -> /home/obrien/scripts/stats
$
$ cat symstats
                                 # Link use fails
-ksh: cat: symstats: cannot open [No such file or directory]
$
$ cat > /home/obrien/scripts/stats
                                 # Re-create file called stats
New stuff in new stats file.
$
$ cat symstats                   # Link works now
New stuff in new stats file to replace missing stuff.
$
$ ls -li symstats
16090 lrwxrwxrwx   1 obrien   obrien        26 Nov  4 15:37
                          symstats -> /home/obrien/scripts/stats
$
$ ls -lLi symstats
4079 -rw-rw-r--   1 obrien   obrien        52 Nov  4 15:39 symstats
                          # Note size is 52
                            Different inode number
$
```

Directories

Some of our first experiences with a computer involve the organizing of files. Directories are files that provide the capability to catalog files in recognizable logical locations. Rather than having to hunt for an accounting file whose name you have forgotten, you can look in the accounting directory. If you have been lax in your file organization, though, you can still end up hunting. The point is that creating several directories does NOT organize your files. Putting your files in the appropriate directories DOES organize your files.

As I pointed out earlier, directories are files. But they are special files with a special format. They contain a mix of ASCII and binary information. The ASCII information represents a filename, and the binary information represents the file's inode number (or other file system metadata location indicator). *Metadata* is data that describes other data. Many types of file systems are supported by the various UNIX operating systems. For this discussion, we'll stick with the UNIX File System (UFS) because it is common to most UNIX systems.

Most UNIX users labor under the misconception that the information visible from an ls -1 command is held in the directory file. However, most of this information is actually held in the inode that represents the file. Each inode is approximately 128 bytes in size. The first 64 bytes usually holds the file type, permissions, link count, owner, group owner, size, modification date, access date, and metadata modification date.

The inode does not hold the file's name. The filename is held in the directory file. And the directory file associates the filename with an inode number. The inode number is used as an offset into the on-disk inode table to find the metadata for a file. The second 64 bytes of an inode contain location information indicating where on the disk the actual body of the file can be found. Think of the inode as the file's header, and the actual file contents as the file's body.

The following example shows two files in a directory, and then uses an od -Xs command to dump out the raw contents of the directory file in hexadecimal (base 16). (Check the od man page on your system to see which options you can use. The -X option might not be available on all systems.) The -s asks the utility to show any strings that are in the file. The output shows the string dennnn associated with the number 6583 (hex), and the string cheryllll associated with the number 6584 (hex). It then uses the bc command (basic calculator) to display the hex equivalent of the decimal inode numbers 25988 and 25987:

EXAMPLE

```
$ pwd
/usr/users/obrien/subdir
$
$ ls -li
total 8031
25988 -rw-r--r--   1 obrien    users      8192000 Nov  2 16:14 cheryllll
                                     # Note name and inode numbers
25987 -rwxr-xr-x   1 obrien    users        30910 Nov  2 16:14 dennnn
$
$ cd ..
$
$ od -Xs subdir
0000000   00006582 00010014 0000002e 00006582
0000020   00008001 00006367 00020014 00002e2e
0000040   00006367 00008001 00006583 00060018
0000060   6e6e6564 00006e6e 00006583 00008001    # Inode is 6583 (hex)
0000060 dennnn                                    # Note name
0000100   00006584 0009001c 72656863 6c6c6c79
0000120   0000006c 00006584 00008001 00000000    # Inode is 6584 (hex)
0000110 cheryllll                                 # Note name
```

```
0000140  000001a4 00000000 00000000 00000000
      (...)
$ bc
obase=16
ibase=10
25988                                       # 6584 hex = 25988 dec
6584
25989                                       # 6585 hex = 25989 dec
6585
quit
$
```

Hidden Files

Certain files are listed only when you specifically ask to see them. These are called *hidden* files. Your .profile file is an example of a hidden file. Any file whose name begins with a . is treated as hidden. These filenames are not displayed by an unadorned ls command, but are displayed when requested with the -a option (-a means all).

The following example shows an ls -l command with no hidden files displayed, followed by an ls -la command that includes hidden files in its output:

EXAMPLE

```
$ ls -l                                          # Does not display
hidden files
total 4
-rw-r--r--   2 obrien   guest      629 Nov  2 00:54 hardlinktostats
-rwxr-xr--   1 obrien   guest      412 Nov  2 00:53 openone
lrwxrwxrwx   1 obrien   guest       11 Nov  2 01:20 pass -> /etc/passwd
lrwxrwxrwx   1 obrien   guest        5 Nov  2 01:17 softlinktostats -> stats
-rw-r--r--   2 obrien   guest      629 Nov  2 00:54 stats
-rw-r--r--   1 obrien   guest       92 Nov  2 00:54 summary
lrwxrwxrwx   1 obrien   guest        4 Nov  2 01:20 toetc -> /etc
$
$ ls -la                                         # Shows hidden files
total 20
drwxr-xr-x   2 obrien   guest     8192 Nov  2 01:33 .    # Hidden file
drwxr-xr-x   5 obrien   guest     8192 Nov  2 00:10 ..   # Hidden file
-rw-r--r--   1 obrien   guest        0 Nov  2 01:33 .dbxinit
                                                         # Hidden file
-rw-r--r--   2 obrien   guest      629 Nov  2 00:54 hardlinktostats
-rwxr-xr--   1 obrien   guest      412 Nov  2 00:53 openone
lrwxrwxrwx   1 obrien   guest       11 Nov  2 01:20 pass -> /etc/passwd
lrwxrwxrwx   1 obrien   guest        5 Nov  2 01:17 softlinktostats -> stats
-rw-r--r--   2 obrien   guest      629 Nov  2 00:54 stats
```

```
-rw-r--r--   1 obrien    guest          92 Nov  2 00:54 summary
lrwxrwxrwx   1 obrien    guest           4 Nov  2 01:20 toetc -> /etc
$
```

Attributes

Each file has *attributes* associated with it to describe its characteristics. Some attributes are ownership, group ownership, permissions, type of file, and link count. Oh, that's the stuff from the inode! Yes. The inode contains the file's attributes. Some attributes are more shell-oriented than file-oriented, yet they control the behavior of file activities. All of us have had the UNIX file clobber experience. You know, when you inadvertently name a new file the same as an existing file on a redirection. 'Fess up. We've all done that, much to our chagrin.

The following example shows the existence of a 629-byte file named stats, followed by a redirection that clobbers the file and then replaces the file contents with the output of a ps command consisting of 159 bytes:

EXAMPLE

```
$ ls -li stats
75261 -rw-r--r--  2 obrien    guest         629 Nov  2 00:54 stats
$
$ ps > stats
                                    # Oops, I just clobbered the stats file
$
$ ls -li stats
75261 -rw-r--r--  2 obrien    guest         159 Nov  2 01:35 stats
                                    # Note size difference
$
```

This can be controlled by the noclobber shell attribute.

The following example sets the noclobber option and shows that a user will be prevented from clobbering an existing file:

EXAMPLE

```
$ set -o noclobber                          # Protecting myself from myself
$
$ ls -li stats
75261 -rw-r--r--  2 obrien    guest         159 Nov  2 01:35 stats
$
$ vmstat > stats
dtksh: stats: file already exists [File exists]
                                            # No clobbering allowed
$
$ ls -li stats
75261 -rw-r--r--  2 obrien    guest         159 Nov  2 01:35 stats
                                            # Unchanged
$
```

You can override the noclobber option for an individual command by insisting that you want it done with the >| syntax. The following example uses the >| syntax to temporarily override the noclobber option. It also uses the wc -c command to count the characters in the test file named f2:

EXAMPLE

```
$ wc -c f2
      35 f2                               # f2 has 35 characters
$
$ set -o noclobber                       # Turn off clobbering
$
$ set -o | grep clobber
noclobber        on                      # Note noclobber option is on
$
$ ps > f2                                # Prevents clobbering f2
-ksh: f2: file already exists [File exists]
$
$ wc -c f2
      35 f2                               # f2 still has 35 characters
$
$ ps >| f2                               # Override noclobber with >|
$
$ wc -c f2
      83 f2                               # f2 has 83 characters now
$
$ set -o | grep clobber
noclobber        on                      # Noclobber is still on
$
$ ls -l > f2                             # Can't clobber
                                         # unless overridden with >|
-ksh: f2: file already exists [File exists]
$
```

You can turn clobbering back on by using the set +o noclobber command:

EXAMPLE

```
$ set +o noclobber                       # Turn noclobber off
$
$ set -o | grep clobber
noclobber        off
$
$ ls -l > f2                             # Clobber away!
$
$ wc -c f2
     826 f2
$
```

File ownership and permissions are some of the more visible file attributes. These can be viewed with the ls -l command. A file is owned by its creator. The user account from which the command to create the file was issued is recorded in the inode as the owner of the file. Once again, the ownership, permissions, and other attributes of a file are NOT stored in the directory file. That information is held in the metadata (typically the inode) that supports every file that currently exists in your file system.

The following example shows the typical file ownership and related file attributes:

```
$ ls -l stats
-rw-r--r--  2 obrien   guest          159 Nov  2 01:35 stats
$
```

The file is also imprinted with a group-level ownership. Most Berkeley-flavored UNIX variants record the group ownership of a newly created file as the group ownership of the directory in which the file was created. This is not intuitively obvious, so I suggest you take note here. Check to see whether your UNIX exhibits this behavior.

The following example shows that the group ownership of a new file matches the group ownership of the directory file in which it is created. It creates a file in the /usr/users/obrien directory and then creates another file in the /tmp directory:

EXAMPLE

```
$ ls -ld ..
drwxr-xr-x  5 obrien   guest         8192 Nov  2 00:10 ..
                          # Directory's group is guest
$
$ touch test1
$
$ ls -l test1
-rw-r--r--  1 obrien   guest            0 Nov  2 01:41 test1
                          # New file's group is guest
$
$ ls -lLd /tmp
drwxrwxrwt  9 root     system        8192 Nov  2 01:05 /tmp
                          # Directory's group is system
$
$ touch /tmp/test2
$
$ ls -l /tmp/test2
-rw-r--r--  1 obrien   system           0 Nov  2 01:42 /tmp/test2
                          # New file's group is system
$
```

Most System V–flavored UNIX variants assign group ownership based on the primary group of the user creating the file. Be aware that your UNIX might be capable of switching between the two behaviors (Compaq's Tru64 UNIX can do this, as shown in the following).

The following example shows the typical Berkeley-style behavior for assigning group ownership of a new file, and then it shows what happens when the system administrator switches to the System V style of group ownership (typically done by changing a kernel attribute):

EXAMPLE

```
$ id
uid=201(obrien) gid=15(users)
                          # User obrien is in the 'users' group
$
$ cd /tmp
$
$ ls -lLd
drwxrwxrwt   4 root      system      8192 Nov  2 16:47 .
                          # Note group ownership of directory is system
$
$ touch den1              # Make a new file
$
$ ls -l den1
-rw-r--r--   1 obrien    users          0 Nov  2 16:52 den1
                          # Note group ownership is 'users'
$
$ #Change the system's behavior to its default which is BSD style.
  # (SysAdmin will have to do this.)
$
$ touch den2              # Make another new file
$
$ ls -l den2
-rw-r--r--   1 obrien    system         0 Nov  2 16:53 den2
                          # Note group ownership is 'system'
$
```

NOTE

These group ownership issues are related to the UNIX operating system you are running and are not directly the result of running a particular shell.

Permissions

Permissions determine the access allowed to a file. In an earlier chapter, you looked at permission basics. We proposed that the umask value could be subtracted from octal 777 for directories and octal 666 for nondirectory files. The truth is a bit more complicated, and because you've made it this far in the book, you might as well know the truth. If you consider that the umask value can be set to octal 777—which is an extreme and unusual value, but legitimate nonetheless—you can deduce that the subtraction technique presented earlier, while useful, is flawed. With a umask of 777, the subtraction technique yields -1,-1,-1, which makes no sense.

The one's complement of the umask is derived and then bitwise ANDed with the raw permission value (666 for files; 777 for directories). The resulting permissions for a nondirectory file when the umask is set to 677 would be -- ------.

The following example sets an unusual umask value (677) and then creates a file to demonstrate the application of the umask:

EXAMPLE

```
$ umask 677                                    # Set umask value
$
$ touch test4                                  # Create file
$
$ ls -l test4
----------  1 obrien   guest       0 Nov  2 01:51 test4 # Note permissions
$
```

Acceptable Filenames

The single most visible attribute of a file is its name. As mentioned in an earlier section, filenames are cataloged in a directory file. The Korn Shell accepts files with names containing letters, numbers, the period, and the underscore. It also accepts characters drawn from the following set: *, &, ?, [,], -, <, >, $, !, ', and `. However, I would recommend against using them. Believe it or not, it is also legitimate to use a space in a filename. Note that some unusual and unexpected characters are in this set. Using some of the special characters in filenames can lead to difficulty in deleting or accessing files. Common sense is suggested here.

The following example shows potential problems with using characters with special meaning to the shell in filenames. This example uses the asterisk (*). Most problems with special characters in filenames can be overcome through the use of apostrophes or quotes:

EXAMPLE

```
$ cat > "a*b"     # Create file with asterisk in its name
junk in file
$
$ cat a*b         # Seems to work ok
junk in file
$
$ cat > axxxb     # Create another file that begins with 'a' and ends with 'b'
more junk
$
$ ls a*b          # Asterisk expands.  Not what we wanted
```

```
a*b     axxxb
$
$ ls 'a*b'          # Apostrophes remove special meaning of *
a*b
$
```

Accessing Files

Files can be created through editors, commands, redirection, or programs. The mechanism you choose to create a file should be based on your needs and abilities. Needless to say, you wouldn't create a file with the emacs editor if you were unfamiliar with emacs! An empty file can be created with the touch command.

The following example demonstrates several techniques for creating files:

EXAMPLE

```
$ touch sm3 sm4     # Create two empty files
$
$ ls -l sm*
-rw-r--r--  1 obrien   guest           0 Nov  3 00:22 sm3
-rw-r--r--  1 obrien   guest           0 Nov  3 00:22 sm4
$
$ ls > sm5          # Create a small file through output redirection
$
$ >sm6              # Shell creates an empty file whenever it sees >
$
$ ls -l sm*
-rw-r--r--  1 obrien   guest           0 Nov  3 00:22 sm3
-rw-r--r--  1 obrien   guest           0 Nov  3 00:22 sm4
-rw-r--r--  1 obrien   guest          99 Nov  3 00:22 sm5
-rw-r--r--  1 obrien   guest           0 Nov  3 00:23 sm6
$
```

Many commands create files as part of their function (for example, cc and script). The script command captures all commands and output until the user types exit.

The following example uses the script command to capture some screens from the terminal and place them in a file:

EXAMPLE

```
$ script outstuff              # Start gathering
Script started, file is outstuff
$ ls -l sm*
-rw-r--r--  1 obrien   guest           0 Nov  3 00:22 sm3
-rw-r--r--  1 obrien   guest           0 Nov  3 00:22 sm4
-rw-r--r--  1 obrien   guest          99 Nov  3 00:22 sm5
-rw-r--r--  1 obrien   guest           0 Nov  3 00:23 sm6
$ ps
```

```
        PID TTY      S           TIME CMD
204646 pts/2    S          0:00.23 dtksh
204657 pts/2    I          0:00.07 -ksh (ksh)
204703 pts/2    S    +     0:00.02 script outstuff
204719 pts/2    S    +     0:00.00 script outstuff
204716 pts/6    S          0:00.03 sh -is
$ pwd
/usr/staff/g1/obrien/denscrs
$ exit
Script done, file is outstuff    # End the script session

$ ls -l ou*
-rw-r--r--   1 obrien    guest          648 Nov  3 00:26 outstuff
$
$ cat outstuff                   # File outstuff contains screen dumps
Script started on Fri Nov  3 00:25:58 2000
$ ls -l sm*
-rw-r--r--   1 obrien    guest            0 Nov  3 00:22 sm3
-rw-r--r--   1 obrien    guest            0 Nov  3 00:22 sm4
-rw-r--r--   1 obrien    guest           99 Nov  3 00:22 sm5
-rw-r--r--   1 obrien    guest            0 Nov  3 00:23 sm6
$ ps
        PID TTY      S           TIME CMD
204646 pts/2    S          0:00.23 dtksh
204657 pts/2    I          0:00.07 -ksh (ksh)
204703 pts/2    S    +     0:00.02 script outstuff
204719 pts/2    S    +     0:00.00 script outstuff
204716 pts/6    S          0:00.03 sh -is
$ pwd
/usr/staff/g1/obrien/denscrs
$ exit

script done on Fri Nov  3 00:26:24 2000
$                                # End of contents of file named outstuff
```

Simply redirecting the output of a command also creates a file:

```
$ ls -l sm* > smfiles
$
$ cat smfiles
-rw-r--r--   1 obrien    guest            0 Nov  3 00:22 sm3
-rw-r--r--   1 obrien    guest            0 Nov  3 00:22 sm4
-rw-r--r--   1 obrien    guest           99 Nov  3 00:22 sm5
-rw-r--r--   1 obrien    guest            0 Nov  3 00:23 sm6
$
```

EXAMPLE

Use an editor if you need to craft a file (see Appendix B, "vi Tutorial," for more information):

```
$ vi letter
"letter" [New file]
Dear Boss,
        I deserve a raise.
Regards,
        Den
:wq
$
```

Files can be joined through the use of the append redirection operator (>>):

```
$ ls -l o*
-rwxr-xr--  1 obrien   guest        412 Nov  2 00:53 openone
-rw-r--r--  1 obrien   guest        648 Nov  3 00:26 outstuff   # Note size 648
$
$ cat openone >> outstuff                                      # Append file
$
$ ls -l o*
-rwxr-xr--  1 obrien   guest        412 Nov  2 00:53 openone
-rw-r--r--  1 obrien   guest       1060 Nov  3 00:35 outstuff   # Note size 1060
$
```

Files can be copied with the cp command:

EXAMPLE

```
$ cp openone openother
$
$ ls -l op*
-rwxr-xr--  1 obrien   guest        412 Nov  2 00:53 openone
-rwxr-xr--  1 obrien   guest        412 Nov  3 00:38 openother
$
```

Files also can be deleted using rm. Note that rm removes a hard link to a file. As such, you might not be freeing up any disk space in the case where a file has several hard links. The rm command would simply subtract one from the hard link count in that case. It would check to see whether the result of the subtraction yields a result of zero. If so, the file's body would truly be deleted and disk space would be regained. I emphasize that this behavior is exhibited by hard links only. Symbolic links are essentially files whose contents are a file specification to locate another file.

The following example shows two filenames that are links to the same data. It then shows how the link count changes when one of the file links is removed:

```
$ ls -l *stats
-rw-r--r--   2 obrien    guest         159 Nov  2 01:35 hardlinktostats
                         # Note link count
lrwxrwxrwx   1 obrien    guest           5 Nov  2 01:17 softlinktostats -> stats
-rw-r--r--   2 obrien    guest         159 Nov  2 01:35 stats
$
$ rm stats                # Remove a link
$
$ ls -l *stats
-rw-r--r--   1 obrien    guest         159 Nov  2 01:35 hardlinktostats
                         # Note link count
lrwxrwxrwx   1 obrien    guest           5 Nov  2 01:17 softlinktostats -> stats
$
```

A file can be moved from one directory to another. On the way, the file can have its name changed. Thus, the mv command functions as a rename command.

TIP

mv can be used to move a file beyond the border of its file system. The mv command also can be used to rename a file without moving it to another directory.

The following example shows the mv command functioning as a rename command:

EXAMPLE

```
$ ls /tmp/ha*              # No file starting with ha in /tmp
ls: /tmp/ha* not found
$
$ mv hardlinktostats /tmp  # Move it (rename) to a different directory
$
$ ls /tmp/ha*              # Successfully moved
/tmp/hardlinktostats
$
```

File contents can be read with several commands (cat, page, lpr, any editor, view, and so on). While in a script, you might want to open a file for reading and then access the data line by line. A combination of the exec command and the read command provides this capability. Several files can be open at once.

The following example uses the exec command to open access to a file; it then processes the lines of the file one at a time using the read command:

```
$ cat /tmp/hardlinktostats            # Display file contents
   PID TTY      S          TIME CMD
200691 pts/6    S       0:01.11 dtksh
200731 pts/6    I       0:00.19 -ksh (ksh)
```

```
200774 pts/6     I        0:00.17 dtksh
$
$ exec 5< /tmp/hardlinktostats          # Open access to file through fd 5
$
$ read -u5 line                         # Read a line from fd 5
$
$ print $line                           # Display line
PID TTY S TIME CMD
$
$  read -u5 line                        # Read next line
$
$ print $line                           # Print line
200691 pts/6 S 0:01.11 dtksh
$
$ read -u5 line
$
$ print $line
200731 pts/6 I 0:00.19 -ksh (ksh)
$
```

Suppose you need to empty the contents of a file, but not delete the file. Clipping off the end of a file is sometimes referred to as *file truncation.* Redirection to an existing file causes file truncation down to a size of 0 bytes.

Each time the shell is asked to perform redirection of output, it makes several checks. It checks to see whether the target of the redirection is an existing file. If so, it checks to see whether noclobber is set. If not, the file is truncated down to 0 bytes in size, and then the redirected output is used to repopulate the file. This behavior can be seen in a rookie's use of the sort command, where the same file is used for input and output.

The following example requests output redirection to a file that is used as input for the command. One of the first things the shell does when it interprets a line is to look for redirection syntax (>, <, >>, and so on). If it finds output redirection, it immediately truncates the target file down to 0 bytes in size. In the example, the file to be sorted is truncated before the sort command gets its hands on the file. sort sees an empty file, so it doesn't do anything:

EXAMPLE

```
$ cat sortfile                          # Unsorted file
pears
oranges
apples
beer
$
```

```
$ sort sortfile                    # Sorted output onscreen
apples
beer
oranges
pears
$
$ sort sortfile > sortfile         # Redirect output to same file as input
$
$ cat sortfile                     # Empty!
$
$ wc -c sortfile
      0 sortfile                    # Empty!
$
```

Filtering

Many filter style programs provide the capability to manipulate the contents of files (for example, the commands, grep, tail, head, wc, sed, awk, xargs, and so on). Several of these are so powerful that they are the subject of separate books. Generally, a filter can accept input from stdin and pushes output to stdout. Become proficient with filter commands, and the need for using scripts to open individual files is diminished. Your creations will become more succinct and powerful. Many of these commands could easily take up a chapter on their own, but in this book, I'll introduce them and entice you to check them out on your own.

head

If you need to display the beginning lines of a file, use the head command. The head command outputs the first 10 lines of a file by default. You also can specify a count of lines to display.

The following example uses the head command to display the first 2 lines of a file:

EXAMPLE

```
$ cat sortfile2
pears
oranges
apples
beer
$
$ head -n 2 sortfile2
pears
oranges
$
```

tail

Sometimes you might need to access the tail end of a file. The `tail` command displays the last 10 lines of a file by default.

The following example displays the last 2 lines of the `sortfile2` file:

```
$ tail -n 2 sortfile2
apples
beer
$
```

EXAMPLE

wc

The `wc` command displays the count of bytes, whitespace separated words, and lines found in a file.

The following example shows a `wc` command reporting three counts; a second use counts lines only:

```
$ wc sortfile2
      4       4      26 sortfile2
$
$ wc -l sortfile2
      4 sortfile2
$
```

cat

The `cat` command is used to display the full contents of a file. The name "cat" comes from the little-used English word *catenate*, which is a synonym for concatenate. Basically, it concatenates the contents of the input file to the bottom of the output display (or output file).

The following are some of the `cat` command's options:

- `-b`—Displays the number of nonblank output lines
- `-E`—Displays $ at the end of each line
- `-n`—Displays the number of all output lines
- `-s`—Squeeze; if multiple blank lines separate nonblank lines, never show more than one blank line in the output
- `-T`—Displays Tab characters as `^I`
- `-v`—Show nonprinting characters

The following example shows a vanilla-flavored `cat` command, followed by a `cat` command using the `-n` option, which causes the display to include line numbers:

EXAMPLE

```
$ cat sortfile2
pears
oranges
apples
beer
$
$ cat -n sortfile2          Number of the output lines
1   pears
      2   oranges
      3   apples
      4   beer
$
```

tee

The `tee` command writes whatever is presented as its standard input and writes to standard output, but it also writes to any other files placed on its command line. It provides an opportunity to redirect the output of a command into many locations, including the `stdin` for the process.

The following are some of the `tee` command's options:

- `-a`—Appends to the given files, but does not overwrite

- `-i`—Ignores interrupt signals

The following example shows the `tee` command being used to redirect the output of a `ps` command into two files, named `newfile` and `newfile2`. The `tee` command does not prevent the output from appearing onscreen, as a typical redirect of `stdout` would. Therefore, the output of the `ps` command has gone to three places: `stdout`, `newfile`, and `newfile1`:

EXAMPLE

```
$ ps | tee newfile newfile2
                  # Show output of ps onscreen, and place in two files
  PID TTY         TIME CMD
  614 pts/1   00:00:00 ksh
  727 pts/1   00:00:00 ps
  728 pts/1   00:00:00 tee
$
$ cat newfile
  PID TTY         TIME CMD
  614 pts/1   00:00:00 ksh
  727 pts/1   00:00:00 ps
  728 pts/1   00:00:00 tee
$
```

```
$ cat newfile2
  PID TTY          TIME CMD
  614 pts/1    00:00:00 ksh
  727 pts/1    00:00:00 ps
  728 pts/1    00:00:00 tee
$
```

sort

The sort command places sorted input onto standard output. It performs an ASCII sort (see the man page on ascii). If no input file is presented, it looks for the data to be sorted from stdin. By default, the command sorts using whitespace-separated key fields, starting with the leftmost field. Older scripts using sort might indicate a different sort key field using the +field_num syntax. That syntax is now obsolete. A sort command, such as sort +5 -6 +2 -3 *file_to_be_sorted*, requests that the first key field be found after the fifth field and stop at the sixth field, and the tiebreaker key be found after the second field and stop at the third field. That syntax should be replaced with the following:

sort -k 6 -k 3,4 *file_to_be_sorted*

NOTE

The second key field could have been shown as -k 3. The syntax shown is useful if the sort key encompasses more than one field. Also, the -k option represents the first field as field number 1. (The obsolescent syntax represented the first field as field number 0.) Obviously, the UNIX gods were totally uninterested in keeping any form of consistency with this command!

Some of the options for the sort command are as follows:

- -b—Ignores leading blanks in sort fields or keys

- -c—Checks whether given files are already sorted; does not sort

- -d—Considers only [a–z, A–Z, and 0–9] characters in keys

- -f—Folds lowercase to uppercase characters in keys

- -g—Compares according to general numerical value (might not be available on all UNIX variants)

- -k POS1[,POS2]—Starts a key at POS1 and ends it at POS2

- -m—Merges already sorted files; does not sort

- -n—Compares according to string numerical value

- -o FILE—Writes the result on FILE instead of standard output

- -r—Reverses the result of comparisons

- -u—Outputs only the first of an equal sequence (unique)

The following example shows a simple sort using field 4 (the CMD column) as the key field. It performs the same sort job using the new syntax and then the obsolescent syntax:

EXAMPLE

```
$ cat newfile2
  PID TTY          TIME CMD
  614 pts/1    00:00:00 ksh
  727 pts/1    00:00:00 ps
  728 pts/1    00:00:00 tee
$
$ sort -rk 4 newfile2                    # Reverse sort based on key field number 4
  728 pts/1    00:00:00 tee
  727 pts/1    00:00:00 ps
  614 pts/1    00:00:00 ksh
  PID TTY          TIME CMD
$
$ sort -r +3 -4 newfile2                 # Same but using old syntax
  728 pts/1    00:00:00 tee
  727 pts/1    00:00:00 ps
  614 pts/1    00:00:00 ksh
  PID TTY          TIME CMD
$
```

grep

The grep command uses regular expressions to search for a pattern of characters. The letters stand for *global regular expression print*. The grep command searches through the contents of files for the requested patterns; it does not search for filenames. If you need to search for filenames, use the find command.

Some of the options for the grep command are as follows (check your man pages to see whether your UNIX supports all these options):

- -A NUM—Prints NUM lines of trailing context after matching lines

- -B NUM—Prints NUM lines of leading context before matching lines

- -b—Prints the byte offset within the input file before each line of output

- -c—Prints a count of matching lines for each input file

- -f FILE—Obtains patterns from FILE, one per line

- -h—Suppresses the prefixing of filenames on output when multiple files are searched

- -i—Ignores case distinctions in both the pattern and input files

- -n—Prefixes each line of output with the line number within its input file

- -r—Reads all files under each directory, recursively

- -v—Inverts the sense of matching, to select nonmatching lines

The following examples show the grep command being used to locate selected strings within files. The examples use several regular expressions to represent aggregates of string information:

EXAMPLE

```
$ cat sortfile2
pears
oranges
apples
beer
$
$ grep app sortfile2      # Search for expression app in sortfile2
apples
$
$ grep s$ sortfile2       # Search for lines ending with the letter 's'
pears
oranges
apples
$
$ grep ^b sortfile2       # Search for lines beginning with the letter 'b'
beer
$
$ ls -l | grep ^d         # Search the output of an ls -l command for directories
drwx------   2 obrien   obrien      1024 Oct 12 19:30 Mail
drwxrwxr-x   3 obrien   obrien      1024 Nov  4 15:39 scripts
drwxrwxr-x   2 obrien   obrien      1024 Oct 16 12:59 temp
$
```

sed

The sed command is a noninteractive editor. You can present your edit requests on the command line or in a sed script file. The command applies the edits to the data it reads from the input file and writes the altered data and the unaltered data to the standard output device unless redirected. The edit syntax is derived from the ex editor (see man ex). Note that sed does not alter the data in the input file. See the sequence at the end of the sed examples for some ideas on getting sed to make changes in many files.

Some of the options to the sed command are

- -n—Does not produce output lines unless requested by the p command
- -e edits—Provides a mechanism to present multiple edits to the data
- -f script-file—Presents a file full of sed edits to the command

The following example uses the sed command to replace any occurrences of the string appl with snapple. Note that the output displays all lines in the file, including unchanged lines. Remember that sed is an editor, not a string search command like grep:

EXAMPLE

```
$ cat sortfile2
pears
oranges
apples
beer
$
$
$ sed 's/appl/snappl/' sortfile2    # Replace appl with snappl
pears
oranges
snapples
beer
$
```

The following examples show how to limit the lines displayed by sed:

```
$ sed '2q' sortfile2              # Display two lines and then quit
pears
oranges
$
$ sed '2d' sortfile2              # Delete line 2 from the display
pears
apples
beer
$
$ sed '1,2d' sortfile2           # Delete first two lines from the display
apples
beer
$
```

The following example combines the sed command with a Korn Shell loop to make changes to the contents of files:

```
$ cat sedtest1                   # Contents of first test file
Welcome to the world of Donald Davis.
$
$ cat sedtest2                   # Contents of second test file
```

```
Donald Davis knows how to quack jokes.
$
$ cat sedtest3                        # Contents of third test file
Goodbye to the world of Donald Davis.
$
$ for f in sedtest?                   # Use a for loop to make global changes
> do
> mv $f old$f                         # Rename files
> sed 's/Davis/Duck/' old$f > $f      # Recreate original files applying edits
> done
$
$ cat sedtest1
Welcome to the world of Donald Duck.
$
$ cat sedtest2
Donald Duck knows how to quack jokes.
$
$ cat sedtest3
Goodbye to the world of Donald Duck.
$
```

xargs

The xargs command builds a command line consisting of the argument you present to it and the standard input the command is given. It is most commonly used in a pipeline. The term *xargs* comes from execute arguments. The key thing to remember about xargs is that it will form multiple commands if necessary to handle the size of input data presented from the pipe.

Some options to xargs are as follows (check your xargs man page to see whether your system supports all these options):

- -0—Input filenames are terminated by a null character instead of by whitespace.

- -i[replace-str]—Replaces occurrences of replace-str in the initial arguments with names read from standard input.

- -l[max-lines]—Uses at most max-lines nonblank input lines per command line.

- -n max-args—Uses at most max-args arguments per command line.

- -p—Prompts the user about whether to run each command line and read a line from the terminal.

- -t—Prints the command line on the standard error output before executing it.

- -P max-procs—Runs up to max-procs processes at a time.

The following example uses a while loop to create 19,000 files. The loop is stopped by a Ctrl+C. The files are then deleted by piping the output of a find command into an xargs using rm. The find command is used because an attempt to use rm * at the command line would cause a line too long error on most flavors of UNIX.

Another option is to use the find command's -exec option. However, it requires a process creation per file. In addition, it is not as efficient as xargs, which makes each process execute an rm command with as many file-names as it can fit on a single command line. This therefore leads to fewer processes being created during the delete operation:

EXAMPLE

```
$ integer count=1
$
$ while >file$count                    # Create files using the redirect operator
> do
> count=count+1
> done
$                                       # Terminate loop with a Ctrl+C
$
$ ls -l | wc -l                         # Count how many files we have created
    19168
$
$ pwd
/home/obrien/lotsofiles
$
$ find . -name 'file*' | xargs rm      # Use find and xargs to remove
$
$ ls -l | wc -l
      2
$
```

awk

The awk command is a pattern scanning and processing language. It is a programmable filter. The name "awk" comes from the initials of the three creators of the program: Aho, Weinberger, and Kernighan. It searches for a pattern and performs an action upon pattern match. The actions to be per-formed are surrounded by curly braces ({ }). awk can be used to extend the features of the sed command.

Some options to the awk command are as follows:

- `-F fs field-separator`—Indicates that a nondefault field separator is being used. The default field separator is whitespace (blank(s), tabs).

- `-v var=val`—Assigns the value, val, to the variable, var, before execution of the program begins.

- `-f file`—Reads the awk program source from the file, instead of from the first command-line argument.

The following example uses the awk filter command to process the data in the stats file:

EXAMPLE

```
$ cat stats
    PID TTY     S          TIME CMD
200691 pts/6   S       0:01.11 dtksh
200731 pts/6   I       0:00.19 -ksh (ksh)
200774 pts/6   I       0:00.17 dtksh
$
$ awk '{print $4}' stats                  # Prints field four in the stats file
TIME
0:01.11
0:00.19
0:00.17
$
```

The following example uses awk to process data from the /etc/passwd file. It also uses the -F option, which identifies a nondefault field specifier, the colon (:).

EXAMPLE

```
$ sed 3q /etc/passwd | awk -F: '{print $1}'
                        # Shows field 1 of the first 3 records in /etc/passwd
root
bin
daemon
$
$ awk -F: '{print $1}' /etc/passwd
                        # Shows all usernames from /etc/passwd
root
bin
daemon
adm
(...)
obrien
$
```

The following example uses awk as a formatter:

EXAMPLE

```
$ cat firstlastamount
Dennis O'Brien 234.56                          # Unformatted data
Cheryl Dyment 12345.67
Al Smith 66.33
Juana D'Ance 22.11
$                                              # Awk being used as a formatter
$ awk '{printf "%4d %-10s %-10s %10.2f\n", NR, $1, $2, $3 }' firstlastamount
   1 Dennis    O'Brien        234.56
   2 Cheryl    Dyment       12345.67
   3 Al        Smith           66.33
   4 Juana     D'Ance          22.11
$
```

The following example uses an awk script to search through the password file looking for records with an empty password field (second field). This is a major security break because it would allow anyone to log in without needing to present a password:

EXAMPLE

```
$ cat breakers                                 # An awk script
BEGIN   {                                      # BEGIN section executed first
        print "Investigate these accounts:";
        }
        {                                      # Pattern search and action section
        if ($2 == "") { print "Account name is ", $1,"\nUser is", $5 };
        }
END     {print "Done. \n"}                     # END section done last
$
$ awk -F: -f breakers /tmp/passwd
                                        # Present awk script file to awk command
Investigate these accounts:
Account name is  hacker
User is Bertha D. Blooze
Done.

$
$ grep hacker /tmp/passwd
hacker::13:30:Bertha D. Blooze:/usr/lib/hacker:/bin/ksh
$
```

Using Temporary Files

As presented earlier in this chapter, many options exist when it comes to filenames. Often, scripts might need to create a temporary file in an unpredictable directory, or in the /tmp directory. The script should be designed so that it will not clobber the script user's existing files and will not inadvertently clobber another user's files in the shared /tmp directory. But how can this be achieved without cumbersome file existence and name-checking code?

If you name your temporary file with the shell variable $$ at the end, you will be creating a filename with your process identification number (PID) tacked on the end. Because the system guarantees that two processes with the same PID will never be in existence at the same time, you are all but guaranteed a unique filename. The $$ will be expanded into the PID of the current process.

The following example creates a file with a PID on the end of the name:

EXAMPLE

```
$ print $$              # Shows current PID
204646
$
$ touch denfile$$       # Create file using current PID to make it unique
$
$ ls -l den*
-rw-r--r--  1 obrien   guest         0 Nov  3 01:03 denfile204646
                        # Note number in name
$
```

What's Next

Now that you have buffed up your file and directory knowledge, your next job is to try for more sophistication in the output you generate from your scripts. Chapter 10, "Output Control," distinguishes the echo, print, and printf commands. It also introduces some additional redirection options, including here documents.

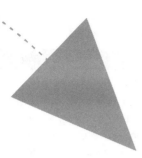

10

Output Control

The vocabulary you have at this point in your life is not the same as it was many years ago. The style and content of your speech has matured. Likewise, the way you produce output in your scripts has matured since the start of this book. You began by using the echo command almost exclusively. As you continued to mature as a script writer, you began using the more sophisticated, portable, and efficient print statement.

You also went from the vanilla style of placing output on your terminal to using various forms of redirection to better achieve the goals of your scripts. Have you reached full maturation? Is there no further improvement possible on the styles and techniques you already have seen?

This chapter examines the Korn Shell's printf command as a logical extension of the print command. You'll also see several twists on output redirection, including a method for selectively redirecting output from loops. This chapter ends by taking a look at the often misunderstood here document capability that enables input redirection to be pointed toward lines within the currently executing script.

This chapter teaches you the following:

- The difference between the echo and print commands
- How to use the printf command
- Output redirection from loops and subshells
- The difference between pipes and redirection
- How to redirect stderr
- How to use here documents

Echoing Output

One of the first commands a rookie UNIX wizard learns is the echo command. It is a simple program that places the input parameters from the command line on stdout. It's easy enough for anyone to wrap his mind around. The echo command can be used in a pipeline to present input to a utility (as seen in the next example). In scripts, the echo command can be used for prompt display duty, as well as producing standard script output.

The following example uses the echo command to produce the input command stream to the ex editor. The following script uses ex to search for any lines in the file containing a ?. All such lines are deleted when found. This eliminates all processes that are not associated with a terminal (the TTY column contains a ?). A count of remaining lines is created using wc -l and is then displayed using substring removal of the largest right pattern (${*count*%% /*}). The pattern removal request eliminates all characters from the first / to the end of the line. Without using the substring removal syntax, the count variable would contain a number followed by /tmp/newstats1234.

EXAMPLE

```
$ ps laxw                              # Generate long ps output
  F   UID    PID  PPID PRI  NI    VSZ  RSS WCHAN  STAT TTY       TIME COMMAND
100     0      1     0   0   0   1104  368 do_sel S    ?         0:04 init [5]
040     0      2     1   0   0      0    0 bdflus SW   ?         0:00 [kflushd]
(...)
100   500    614   613  12   0   2084 1284 wait4  S    pts/1     4:28 -ksh
000   500  15954   614  19   0   2496  828 -      R    pts/1     0:00 ps laxw
$
$ ps laxw | wc -l
      34                               # Note Line count
$
$ cat noquestions                      # Korn shell script
#!/bin/ksh

ps laxw > /tmp/newstats$$              # Redirect output to temp file
echo 'g/?/d\nwq' | ex /tmp/newstats$$
                                       # Use echo to create input to ex command
noques=$(wc -l /tmp/newstats$$)
print "Count of processes using terminals is "${noques%% /*}
                                       # Substring removal
rm /tmp/newstats$$                     # Remove temporary file
$
$ noquestions
Count of processes using terminals is   13
$
```

The echo command has several options, including the heavily used -n, which means do not produce a newline after producing the prompt. This enables a script writer to produce a prompt and have the cursor remain at the end of the prompt string, rather than appearing on the next line. The slight difference in the behavior of echo provided by the -n option is built into many scripts. Here comes the bad news: Not all implementations of the echo command understand the -n option!

You might ask, "But aren't all Korn Shell implementations the same?" Most of them are, but Korn Shell portability is not the issue. Suppose your UNIX has an administrative command called disklabel. Does that mean all UNIX variants will have the same command available? Of course not. Well, this is also true for the echo command. What I'm trying to do is emphasize that the echo command can be implemented as a separate program, and as such will be executed in a separate process. Therefore, it has little to do with the Korn Shell proper.

Having said that, you will probably find that many ksh implementations do indeed have a built-in echo command, but you can't rely on it being there. And if it's not built in, it will be run as a separate program. The details of its behavior and option support is up to the UNIX implementation.

The following example shows that using the echo command can be a perilous choice. It shows that the echo executable program interprets the -n option to mean produce no trailing newline, whereas the built-in echo just sees it as more characters to echo to stdout.

EXAMPLE

```
$ find / -name echo 2>/dev/null
/bin/echo                        # Echo executable program
$
$ whence -v echo                 # Shell has a built-in version
echo is a shell builtin
$
$ echo -n Say what?              # Built-in does not interpret -n
-n Say what?
$
$ /bin/echo -n Say what?         # Program does interpret -n
Say what?$
$
```

How do you create your scripts such that when they produce output, they have a chance of being portable? I recommend getting into the habit of using the print command. This command is built in to the Korn Shell and has reliable syntax. You have seen many examples of the print command in the last few chapters, but here is a refresher example of the print command.

Use the `-n` option to prompt with no trailing newline:

```
print -n "Anybody out there?"
```

Use the `-` option if the output should consist of strings that can be mistaken as command options:

```
$ print - -n
-n
```

Use the following escape sequences in your `print` commands to achieve various formatting needs (the `-R` option ignores these options). The following list documents optional syntax that can be used within the print string to achieve non-printable (generally) output:

- `\a`—Bell
- `\n`—Newline
- `\f`—Formfeed
- `\r`—Return
- `\t`—Tab
- `\v`—Vertical tab
- `\\`—Backslash
- `\0n`—ASCII character with octal value *n*
- `\c`—Same as the `-n` option, except it skips the remaining characters

The following example uses the `\a` sequence in a print string to make a bell ring after the output is displayed. It provides an audio cue to pay attention to the output:

```
$ print "A bell has rung!  \a"
A bell has rung!                        ← Makes a 'bing' sound.
$
```

Many times the item to be displayed needs to be doctored up a bit before you send it on its way to `stdout`. The following examples show some options available by coupling the `print` command with variable substitution and escape sequences.

The following series of examples uses the `print` command to display various parameter expansion options. All escape sequences are also available to the print statement.

```
$ x="Freddie is a dreamer. "          # Set contents of variable x
$
$ print $x                            # Display contents using print
Freddie is a dreamer.
$
```

```
$ print ${x}                          # Braces are optional
Freddie is a dreamer.
$
$ print $xand a bird.                 # Looks for $xand, which is null
a bird.
$
$ print ${x}and a bird.               # Looks for $x and appends
Freddie is a dreamer. and a bird.
$
$ print ${x#*a}                       # Remove small left pattern matching *a
dreamer.
$
$ print ${x##*a}                      # Remove large left pattern
mer.
$
$ print ${x%a*}                       # Remove small right pattern
Freddie is a dre
$
$ print ${x%%a*}                      # Remove large right pattern
Freddie is
$
$ print ${x:4:3}                      # Skip 4 bytes, grab the next 3
die                                   # (Must be fully ksh93 to use)
$
$ print ${x:4}                        # Eliminate 4 bytes
die is a dreamer.
$
$ print ${x/Fredd/Denn}               # Replace Fredd with Denn
Dennie is a dreamer.
$
$ print ${x/#Fr/T}                    # Replace string at beginning of line
Teddie is a dreamer.
$
$ print ${x/%e*r*/ump.}               # Replace string at end of line
Frump.
$
$ print ${x//e/o}                     # Replace all instances of e with o
Froddio is a droamor.
$
$ print ${x//e}                       # Eliminate all instances of e
Frddi is a dramr.                     # (Must be fully ksh93 to use)
$
$ print ${#x}                         # Report string length
22
$
```

printf

If your output vocabulary and style needs another level of maturation, the Korn Shell provides the `printf` command. The "f" in `printf` stands for "formatted." So, this command provides some formatting options for your output. It can handle floating-point displays, integer displays, and string displays. If this is starting to sound familiar to you C language programmers out there, it should. The `printf` command is based on the `printf` function available in the standard C library.

Its syntax includes a quoted format section followed by the variables to be placed in the formatted specification. The format string can contain zero or more control variables, which will be replaced by the respective variables at the end of the command line.

The control variables are designated by the % symbol. The following command produces an output line of -. The total is 245. followed by a newline (\n). The value 245 is the contents of the shell variable `tot`:

```
printf "The total is %d.\n" $tot
```

NOTE

`printf` does not include the newline unless you request it. In contrast, the `print` command automatically includes the newline.

Table 10.1 documents the `printf` format specifiers.

Table 10.1: **printf** *Format Specifiers*

Specifier	Description
%d	Decimal integer
%e	Float (scientific notation)
%f	Float (decimal)
%o	Octal integer
%P	R.E. to shell exp
%s	String
%x	Hexadecimal integer

Table 10.2 displays some twists on the format specifiers.

Table 10.2: **printf** *Format Specifier Wrinkles*

Specifier	Description
%+d	Positive integer with + sign.
%8d	Right justify, eight places, int.
%*d	* specifies width variable.
%q	Surround output with quotes.

Table 10.2: continued

Specifier	Description
%#x	Hex number with 0x.
%.2f	Two characters after the period.
%9s	String nine places.

The following examples use many of the printf statement's format specifiers.

The first example uses %d, %x, and %o to request that an integer variable be displayed in different number system bases (decimal, hex, and octal). The example emphasizes that any format specifiers not matched with a shell variable will be displayed as a zero:

EXAMPLE

```
$ integer x=82                                    # Decimal examples
$
$ printf "x contains %d decimal, %x hex, %o octal\n" $x
x contains 82 decimal, 0 hex, 0 octal
```

The following example uses three format specifiers and three shell variables ($x three times):

```
$ printf "x contains %d decimal, %x hex, %o octal\n" $x $x $x
x contains 82 decimal, 52 hex, 122 octal
$
```

The following example shows how printf interprets a mismatch in the number of format specifiers (one in this case) and the number of shell variables to be substituted (three in this case). Note that if you present more variables than specifiers, printf uses the last format specifier repeatedly for the trailing shell variables. This is another instance in which the behavior of the printf command differs from the printf function in the C programming language standard library:

```
$ integer x=82
$
$ printf "x contains %d decimal\n" $x $x $x
x contains 82 decimal
x contains 82 decimal
x contains 82 decimal
$
```

The following example uses the plus sign in front of a format letter to indicate that a sign is desired in the output:

```
$ printf "x contains %+d decimal, %x hex, %o octal\n" $x $x $x
x contains +82 decimal, 52 hex, 122 octal
$
```

The next example precedes each format letter with a number (5) to request a minimum of five spaces be allocated to display the number. Note that if more than five spaces are needed, it expands as necessary:

```
$ printf "x contains %5d decimal, %5x hex, %5o octal\n" $x $x $x
x contains    82 decimal,    52 hex,    122 octal
$
```

EXAMPLE

This example also requests five spaces for each formatted display value, but it includes a dash (-) in front of the size number, which requests that the display be left justified:

```
$ printf "x contains %-5d decimal, %-5x hex, %-5o octal\n" $x $x $x
x contains 82    decimal, 52    hex, 122    octal
$
```

The next series of examples switches to floating point. The first example establishes a shell variable named ave and initializes it to 18.654. Note that the command float is new in ksh93 and might not be available in your version of ksh. It then displays the contents of ave in float format (%f), in scientific notation (%e), and formatted within a 10-space field with only two characters after the decimal point (%10.2f):

```
$ float ave=18.654                            # Floating point examples
$
$ printf "ave contains %f, %e, %10.2f. \n"  $ave $ave $ave
ave contains 18.654000, 1.865400e+01,      18.65.
$
```

The next example asks for the floating point variable to be displayed with three characters after the decimal point and then one character after the decimal point. Note that the %.1f format request resulted in the value being displayed rounded off (not truncated):

```
$ printf "ave contains %.3f, %.1f. \n"  $ave $ave
ave contains 18.654, 18.7.
$
```

Many script writers are unaware of the advantage of declaring a shell variable as type float. Remember that float is an alias for typeset -E. Most scripts produce correct output whether or not the shell variable is declared as type float. The following example uses a few loops to perform some floating-point calculations repetitively:

```
$ cat floater1
#! /bin/ksh
x=17.56                          # x is of type string, not float
integer y=0
```

```
for (( y=0; y<5; y++ ))
do
        while (( x<20000.0 )) # Repeat as long as x is less than 20,000.0
        do
        (( x=x+1.2 ))           # x must be converted to float each time
        done
done
print $x
print $y
$

$ time floater1
20001.16                        # Correct output
5

real    0m4.56s                 # Took about 4.5 seconds to run
user    0m4.49s
sys     0m0.04s
$
```

Now let's see what happens if you take the time to properly prepare the variable that is the focus of all this floating-point activity (x). The following example emphasizes that the shell is forced to convert a string into a float in order to perform a floating-point calculation or display. This example does some simple addition repetitively. The time spent performing the conversions causes the previous script to run more than twice as slowly as the script in the next example:

EXAMPLE

```
$ cat floater
#! /bin/ksh
float x=17.56             # Declare x as a float
integer y=0
for (( y=0; y<5; y++ ))
do
        while (( x<20000.0 ))
        do
        (( x=x+1.2 ))            # Calculation using float
        done
done
print $x
print $y
$
$ time floater
20001.16                        # Correct result (same as floater1)
5
```

```
real    0m1.96s              # Much faster
user    0m1.93s
sys     0m0.02s
$
```

The next example creates a shell variable named s and initializes it to the string "Dennis". The printf command uses several string-oriented format specifiers:

- %s—Format as string

- %.2s—Format as string showing the first two characters

- %q—Format as string but surround output with quotes if the string to be substituted is surrounded by apostrophes and contains at least one space

- %12s—Format as string in a field 12 spaces wide

- %-12s—Format as string left justified in a field 12 spaces wide

- %12.5s—Format as string in a field 12 spaces wide, displaying the first five characters

Note that %q is not interpreted correctly in some Korn Shell implementations. Here is the code:

EXAMPLE

```
$ s=Dennis                                       # String examples
$
$ printf "s contains %s, %.2s, %q, %12s, %-12s, %12.5s.\n" $s $s 'Dennis OB'
$s $s $s
s contains Dennis, De, 'Dennis OB',      Dennis, Dennis       ,        Denni.
$
```

The printf command can also handle escape sequences by placing them within the control string. The following example makes the bell sound and then applies three tabs before displaying the string.

```
$ printf "s contains \a\t\t\t %s\n" $s
s contains                 Dennis
$
```

Output Redirection

In the last chapter, we discussed the redirection of stdin, stdout, and stderr. By far the most commonly used is output redirection. You have seen that output can be redirected into a file, using the >, or appended to an existing file, using >>. Output can be redirected for the entire script, for the output of a subshell, for the output of a command, or for the output of a loop. The subshell and loop options are not intuitive, so we'll take a look at them next.

Subshell Output Redirection

You can run commands or scripts within a subshell by surrounding them with a set of parentheses on the command line. This forces the creation of a new process running a new copy of the Korn Shell program. Therefore, any changes made to aliases, environment variables, or the default directory will have no effect on the original shell. Remember the teenager analogy? Well, if your teenager gets a nose ring, does that mean you have to get one, too? No, because the teenager, in effect, is running in a subshell. The subshell is obviously, and maybe unfortunately, related to the originating shell, but there is not an immediate impact on the originating shell upon an alteration to the subshell. Am I stretching it here? Forgive me, I'm just trying to get the point across.

The following example creates a subshell that changes the default directory and performs a few other commands. The output of the subshell is redirected into a file. Note that the current working directory of the parent shell is not altered by the actions within the subshell.

EXAMPLE

```
$ pwd
/home/obrien/scripts
$
$ (cd /tmp; pwd; date; ls -l) > subshellout    # Redirect output of subshell
$
$ pwd
/home/obrien/scripts
$
$ cat subshellout
/tmp
Mon Nov  6 23:22:44 EST 2000
total 32
-rw-rw-r--  1 obrien  obrien   143 Nov  6 01:06 breakers
-rw-rw-r--  1 obrien  obrien     0 Nov  4 16:21 denn
-rw-rw-r--  1 obrien  obrien    79 Nov  6 00:39 firstlastamount
-rw-rw-r--  1 obrien  obrien  1105 Nov  6 11:12 newstats15924
-rw-rw-r--  1 obrien  obrien  1105 Nov  6 11:14 newstats15929
-rw-rw-r--  1 obrien  obrien  1105 Nov  6 11:19 newstats15935
-rw-rw-r--  1 obrien  obrien  1105 Nov  6 11:21 newstats15943
drwx------  2 root    root    4096 Nov  5 00:38 orbit-root
-rw-rw-r--  1 obrien  obrien   704 Nov  6 01:03 passwd
$
```

Loop Output Redirection

If capturing all the output from your script gathers too much information, and capturing the output of a command gathers too little, you might be a interested in redirecting the output of a loop. The technique is the same as you have learned for subshell and script redirection: Simply place a > or a >> after the last syntax of the loop.

The following example produces some output during a five-pass loop. The output produced outside the loop is not of interest. The done statement at the end of the loop construct has a redirect at the end of it indicating that all output produced during the loop is to be placed in a file. Note that the output produced by the date command in the loop is not displayed, it is redirected into a file:

EXAMPLE

```
$ cat counter
#! /bin/ksh

integer count=0

print "lots of other lines"

while (( count < 5 ))
do
date
print $count
count=count+1
sleep 1
done > loopout                          # Note redirect at end of loop

print "lots of other lines"

$
$ counter
lots of other lines
lots of other lines
$
$ cat loopout
Mon Nov  6 23:37:03 EST 2000
0
Mon Nov  6 23:37:04 EST 2000
1
Mon Nov  6 23:37:05 EST 2000
2
Mon Nov  6 23:37:06 EST 2000
3
Mon Nov  6 23:37:07 EST 2000
4
$
```

Multiple Output Redirection

Sometimes you might prefer that the output from your command be placed in a file *and* be placed on stdout. The tee command provides this functionality. If you dwell on the name of the program—tee—you can almost visualize what the command does. Picture the output travelling up the vertical part of the letter "T". When it reaches the top of the T, it splits the stream and the output goes in both directions (left and right). By default, the output will go to stdout *and* to the file whose name you specify at the end of the command syntax. The tee command can be used to redirect output to many places at once (not just two, as the name implies).

The following example directs the output of a ps command to files named xx and yy, as well as to the terminal:

EXAMPLE

```
$ ps
   PID TTY          TIME CMD
   614 pts/1     00:04:30 ksh
16910 pts/1     00:00:00 ps
$
$
$ ps | tee xx yy                # Directs output to stdout, file xx, and file yy
   PID TTY          TIME CMD
   614 pts/1     00:04:30 ksh
16911 pts/1     00:00:00 ps
16912 pts/1     00:00:00 tee
$
$ cat xx
   PID TTY          TIME CMD
   614 pts/1     00:04:30 ksh
16911 pts/1     00:00:00 ps
16912 pts/1     00:00:00 tee
$
$ cat yy
   PID TTY          TIME CMD
   614 pts/1     00:04:30 ksh
16911 pts/1     00:00:00 ps
16912 pts/1     00:00:00 tee
$
```

Pipes Versus Redirection

The pipe operator (|) indicates that the output of the command on the left is presented to the command on the right as its stdin. As such, it is related to the redirection operators. However, writing to a pipe, although close in concept, is radically different in action and implementation. The concept is close because both involve taking the stdout from a program and doing something different with it. However, the pipe sends the output to another command for processing, whereas the redirect (>) sends the stdout to a file.

This concept can get confusing if you are not used to it. Just remember that the item to the right of a pipe is a command (usually a filter of some kind), whereas the item to the right of a redirect is a file. Consider this example:

```
$ ps | wc                        # ps command output piped to the wc command
      3      12      83
$
$ ps > wc                        # ps command output redirected to a file named wc
$
$ cat wc                         # Examine contents of the wc file
  PID TTY          TIME CMD
  614 pts/1     00:04:30 ksh
16914 pts/1     00:00:00 ps
$
```

stderr Redirection

If you are starting to feel comfortable with stdout redirection after our second visit, let's build further on that by briefly revisiting stderr redirection. Just as you might want a file full of the stdout produced by your script, or produced by a command, you also might want a file full of the error messages produced by your script. Not that you are going to want to print it out and hang it on the refrigerator, but you might want to produce a log of bad input records, erratic processing, or other exceptional events.

Don't worry, in Chapter 12, "Traps," you learn ways to control the default action of the Korn Shell when it experiences certain errors or is sent certain signals. Consider the following example.

EXAMPLE

```
$ find / -name 'den*' 2> illegal   # Direct error messages to file named illegal
/proc/sys/fs/dentry-state
/tmp/denn
$
$ cat illegal                       # Messages in file
find: /usr/doc/ppp-2.3.10/scripts/chatchat: Permission denied
find: /proc/1/fd: Permission denied
(...)
find: /var/lib/slocate: Permission denied
find: /var/spool/cron: Permission denied
find: /var/spool/at: Permission denied
find: /var/gdm: Permission denied
find: /tmp/orbit-root: Permission denied
find: /etc/X11/xdm/authdir: Permission denied
```

```
find: /etc/default: Permission denied
find: /etc/uucp: Permission denied
find: /root: Permission denied
find: /.gnome: Permission denied
find: /.gnome_private: Permission denied
$
```

Here Documents

No, this is not an example of what you do when you have a dog named documents and you want him to come to you. I have found that the concept of the *here document* has caused much weeping and gnashing of teeth among script writers. More specifically, this capability has caused heads to be scratched when trying to make changes or additions to production- or admin-level scripts.

I think the reason for all the uproar is that the syntax is not intuitive and the name "here document" doesn't bring a picture to mind. Let's review. The > symbol redirects output, and the >> symbol redirects output but appends to the target file rather than clobbering the target. The < symbol redirects input so that it comes from the file appearing after the symbol. Well, that leaves the << symbol, doesn't it?

Prior to seeing the << symbol, you're probably feeling pretty good about your shell- and script-writing knowledge. You are using loops, patterns, functions, tests, and redirections and having a spectacular time. So, you decide to accept the assignment of making several changes to an aging admin script written years ago by some guru who is long gone. You probably blast along, enjoying the semivoyeuristic experience of getting into somebody else's mind and trying to re-discover what he had in mind for the various sections of his script.

Remember what it was like to hit a speed bump when you weren't expecting it? That's probably how you felt when first confronted with the << syntax. What the heck is this? Two requests to redirect stdin? Then you probably reviewed what the difference is between >> and > and wondered if there was some kind of append-related difference to equate with the < and << symbols.

Try as you might, you just couldn't get your aching brain around it. Does this story sound like it stems from first-hand experience? Well, it does. And I wish I could say that it wasn't me who was suffering from confusion and delusion. It was.

I looked in the man page for ksh and found what I needed. The << is followed by a string of characters that indicate the beginning of a stream of input lines. The characters after the << are arbitrary (you can choose any series of characters). The shell knows that if you issue a command followed by the << and some characters, it is to interpret each line of input from that point on as input to be presented to the command. But when does the stream of input lines end?

The input lines end when the exact same sequence of characters that was placed after the << appears as an input line. So, the string of characters acts as a bracketing mechanism. It says between this point here in the document (the string of characters after the <<) and this point here in the document (the same string of characters appearing at the beginning of a line in the script) is the input to be presented to the command in front of the <<. Ahh, so the input information is right "here" in the "document." Thus the name *here document*.

This mechanism works at the command line as well, but it tends to be much more useful within the body of a script.

The following example uses a here document to present the data through which the grep command should search:

EXAMPLE

```
Example
$ cat dates
#! /bin/ksh
print "\nToday's date is $(date). \n\n"
grep -i "$1" <<abcde                      # Begin the here document
Dennis          Sept. 16
Cheryl          Sept. 3
Mark            Sept. 19
Cliff           May   17
Clint           May   17
abcde                                      # End the here document
if (( $? != 0 ))
then
        print "No info here in the document for $1."
fi
$
$ dates cliff

Today's date is Tue Nov  7 00:20:33 EST 2000.


Cliff           May   17
$
$ dates harry
```

```
Today's date is Tue Nov  7 00:20:38 EST 2000.


No info here in the document for harry.
$
```

The here document capability enables a script writer to avoid the creation of extraneous files and the overhead of opening and processing their contents using a series of disk I/Os.

What's Next

Needless to say, as you gather more shell tools to help customize your scripts, and you introduce more complexity and sophistication into your creations, the potential for errors is increased. Chapter 11, "Diagnostics," provides a quick look at the options available within the Korn Shell for debugging scripts.

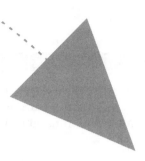

Diagnostics

Now that you have a grip on the bulk of a script writer's tools, you are ready to march off into the world of Korn Shell scripts, write your masterpieces and never make any mistakes or get confused by the shell's peccadilloes! If that's what you are thinking, it's time to eat a reality cookie. Reality cookies are what I eat (or feed my readers) when laboring under false assumptions.

The reality is that script writing is a creative process. And in any creative process there will be some false starts, errors, and even some disasters. Do you think Picasso's trash bin was forever empty? This chapter provides some tools to help debug your masterpieces. Oh, and they will help with any nonmasterpiece scripts you create as well.

Any program-oriented effort involves several phases: First, you are presented with a problem to solve; second, you dream up a possible method of attack on the problem; third, you create a prototype to test your suppositions; and fourth, you create the bulletproof version you will present to your boss or co-workers. I'm leaving out the all-important step 3.5, which is when you try to debug the script.

As you will see, a few very enlightening shell options can help to illuminate the shell's processing of your lines. These provide insight when your regular expressions and wildcards are not doing what you expect them to do. That's the thing about computers—they do what you tell them to do, not what you want them to do.

This chapter teaches you the following:

- How to check your syntax
- The shell's command interpretation sequence
- How to run the shell in verbose mode
- How to get an execution trace
- How to use other debugging hooks

Syntax Checking

Before you take a look at some of the debugging options, let's review the three primary ways to execute a script. Scripts can be run in a subshell, run in the context of the current shell, or a separate ksh command can be issued to customize the debugging environment.

From a debugging perspective, you can present options to the ksh command specifying debugging options such as -v or -x. This technique creates a new process running ksh, and that shell creates another process running ksh with your script as stdin.

The trick is that the ksh command can be used as a standalone command requesting the creation of a process running ksh. This might be used in the case of a hapless C shell user who is stuck in a company steeped in the culture of the C shell. The administrator sets up the user's account such that it starts up csh upon login. The user might choose to execute the ksh program to perform his interactive work in the comfort of a ksh environment.

The following example shows the ksh command executing a script named your_script. Note that if you type the ksh command without the additional script name syntax, the current shell starts a new, interactive instance of the ksh program. Remember also that if you type the ls command, it starts a new process running the ls program. Similarly, if you type the ksh command, it starts a new process running the ksh program.

```
$ ksh your_script
```

EXAMPLE

Any shell variables and aliases created in the script are lost when the script ends. A new process is created running the ksh program. The script is actually executed within a process different from the parent ksh from which the command is actually issued.

The following example starts a script that sleeps to enable you to get a look at the processes supporting its run.

```
$ cat sleeper
#! /bin/ksh
if [[ -z $1 ]]
then
        length=30
else
        length=$1
fi
print "About to sleep for $length seconds"
sleep $length
print "Awake again"
$
```

```
$ print $$
17000                               # Current pid
$


$
$ sleeper 5 &                       # Start script
[1]     17316
About to sleep for 5 seconds
$
$ ps laxw | grep 17000
                                # Next line shows parent process stats
100    500 17000 16999    9    0  1860 1040 wait4  S    pts/1  0:00 -ksh
                                # Next line shows child process stats
000    500 17316 17000   11    4  1884 1008 do_pol SN   pts/1  0:00 ksh sleeper 5
000    500 17317 17000   14    0  2496  828 -      R    pts/1  0:00 ps laxw
000    500 17318 17000   10    0  1240  492 pipe_r S    pts/1  0:00 grep 17000
$
$ Awake again
$
[1] +  Done                     sleeper 5 &
$
```

You can execute your script within your current process by issuing the dot command:

```
$ . your_script
```

This option is useful when executing your .profile file after adding a few lines to it. Rather than logging out and then logging back in to get .profile to execute, you can execute it as a dot script. If you want the changes to be in effect after the script finishes executing, this is the technique to use. Be aware, however, that any variables altered within the script have an effect on the environment of the shell from which the script was executed.

The most common way to execute a script is to make the script file executable and type the script name at the shell prompt. This causes the script to execute as a command would. A process is created within which to execute the script. From a debugging perspective, all shell attributes are inherited by the script you are executing. This is the technique you have been using throughout the book so far:

```
$ chmod ugo+x my_script
$ my_script
```

The man page on ksh details several options for debugging. An important point to keep in mind is that you don't have to perform all your script testing through a script file—syntax can be checked at the command line. This option provides a simple and efficient way to check for errors in the syntax of your shell scripts.

Command Interpretation Sequence

Understanding the way the shell interprets a command is an important debugging tool. The following sequence describes the order in which the shell interprets a line of your script:

1. Process the following reserved words:

{ }	esac	select
case	fi	then
do	for	time
done	function	until
elif	if	while
else	in	[[ ]]

2. Process built-in commands:

alias	exit	bg
export	return	fg
readonly	trap	kill
typeset	echo	wait
unalias	print	:
unset	read	fc
set	cd	getopts
shift	pwd	let
break	times	newgrp
continue	ulimit	test
eval	umask	whence
exec	jobs	

3. Search for functions on the command line.

4. Search for aliases on the command line.

5. Use the PATH variable to identify directories in which to look up programs/ scripts. These programs and scripts must have execute access enabled. The directories in the PATH variable are delimited with a :.

Now that you have reviewed the ways to request the execution of a script, and now that you know the order in which a command line is interpreted, you can execute your script and react to the errors, incorrect output, or non-output it produces. You might even be able to bask in the satisfaction of having created something that works, is useful, and is the product of your own feverish brain.

Before actually attempting to execute the script, you can give it a dry run. Using the ksh noexec option (-n), you can ask the shell to check your commands for any syntax errors. It's sort of like asking the boss's secretary, "How do I look?" before going in for your promotion interview. If she says, "Straighten that tie before you go in," you've been saved the embarrassment of being told later that you lost the job because you looked disheveled. I highly recommend this pre-emptive syntax check before executing any semicomplex ksh script.

The following example uses ksh -n to check syntax in a script file. It reports one error, which is subsequently corrected.

EXAMPLE

```
$ ksh -n masks_env_bad                       # ksh -n complains about line 50
masks_env_bad: syntax error at line 50: 'newline' unexpected
$
$ sed -n '50p' masks_env_bad                 # Use sed to display line 50
print ${res[*]                               # Oops.  Forgot the trailing }
$
$ print "50s/]/]}/\nwq" | ex masks_env_bad   # Alter line 50 using ex editor
$
$ sed -n '50p' masks_env_bad
print ${res[*]}                              # Looks good to me
$
$ ksh -n masks_env_bad                       # ksh -n agrees
$
```

Verbose Mode

Have you ever wished you could follow the logic of your teenager to better understand some conclusion he or she has drawn? (If you are a teenager, you can reverse the roles. You might wonder about the series of logic steps taken by your parents to arrive at a conclusion.) The next Korn Shell debugging option does just that. It provides the bread crumbs to follow through the dark woods of your script's execution.

One of the ksh options for debugging is the verbose option. It displays each shell command before it executes it.

The verbose shell option can be turned on in several ways. You can start a new shell with the -v option using ksh -v. You can put a -v at the end of the #! line at the beginning of your script, or you can type in **set -o verbose** either at the command line or within your script. Each of these options has the same result, which is to display each line of the script as it is about to be executed. Consider the following example:

EXAMPLE

```
$ masks_env                           # Normal run of script
Default REGULAR FILE permissions with current umask (0002)
u    g    o
r w - r w - r - -
(In binary -- 110110100)


$ head masks_env
#!/bin/ksh -v                         # Turn on verbose mode
#
# Script which will display default
# permissions in formatted fashion
# based on the current umask setting
#
function gen_modes
{
integer count=0
typeset -i2 shiftval=2#$1
$


$ masks_env                           # Execute request shows lines of script
#!/bin/ksh -v
#
# Script which will display default
# permissions in formatted fashion
# based on the current umask setting
#
function gen_modes
{
integer count=0
typeset -i2 shiftval=2#$1
perms=( [1]=r [2]=w [3]=x [4]=r [5]=w [6]=x [7]=r [8]=w [9]=x )
while (( count <= 9 ))
do
(( count=count+1 ))
let lment=10-count
if (( ($shiftval & 1) == 1 ))
        then
        res[$lment]="${perms[$lment]}"
```

```
else
        res[$lment]="-"
fi
(( shiftval = shiftval >> 1))
done
}
######### Script Begins ##########
typeset -i2 defa                   # make defa display in binary
typeset -i onescomp
(( onescomp=~($(umask)) ))         # Get ones complement of current umask
(( defa=(8#666)&onescomp ))        # Calculate default permission mask
default_perm=${defa#*#}            # Strip off leading 2#
print "Default REGULAR FILE permissions with current umask ($(umask))"
Default REGULAR FILE permissions with current umask (0002) # Normal output line
print " u      g     o"
  u      g     o                                          # Normal output line
#print '_ _ _ _ _ _ _ _ _'
gen_modes $default_perm
print ${res[*]}
r w - r w - r - -                                         # Normal output line
print "(In binary -- $default_perm)"
(In binary -- 110110100)                                  # Normal output line
print ""

if [[ "$MASKSDIRS" != "YES" ]]                  # Logic sequence is followed
then
        exit 0
fi
```

Execution Trace

I find that the verbose option makes it difficult to locate the normal output lines because they are lost within all the extra displays. Come to think of it, I did ask for "verbose" output, didn't I?

The next debugging option not only leaves the bread crumbs through the woods, but it also leaves the type of bread, the baker, the expiration date, and the names of any animals that might have given it a nibble. (Another one over the top, no?) The idea is that it displays more information than just the command sequence.

Besides displaying the command before executing the command, you also might ask the Korn Shell to expand any wildcards and variables before displaying the command to be executed. This gives you the chance to understand how the Shell is interpreting your input. If a line has an asterisk on it, you can find out whether the asterisk is expanded, and if so, how broadly. All shell variable contents are displayed as well.

The output produced by this option can be distinguished from the regular output of the script because it is preceded by the + sign.

In fact, the PS4 environment variable is being used to produce this character. You can set it to any value that will help you with your debugging; however, the default value is the +. This prompting can be turned on at several levels. You have now seen all four levels of prompting available in the Korn Shell:

- **PS1**—Interactive shell prompt

- **PS2**—Line continuation prompt

- **PS3**—Menu selection prompt in a `select` loop

- **PS4**—Verbose debugging output indicator

The following example executes the masks_env script with the xtrace option enabled:

EXAMPLE

```
$ head -2 masks_env
#!/bin/ksh -x                              # Xtrace debug option is on
#
$
```

```
$ masks_env                                # Run the script
+ typeset -i2 defa
+ typeset -i onescomp
+ umask
+ (( onescomp=~(0002) ))
+ (( defa=(8#666)&onescomp ))
+ default_perm=110110100
+ umask
+ print 'Default REGULAR FILE permissions with current umask (0002)'
Default REGULAR FILE permissions with current umask (0002) # Normal output
+ print '  u    g    o'
   u    g    o                             # Normal output
+ gen_modes 110110100
+ print - r w - r w - r - -
r w - r w - r - -                          # Normal output
+ print '(In binary -- 110110100)'
(In binary -- 110110100)                   # Normal output
+ print ''

+ [[ '' != YES ]]                          # Note test
+ exit 0
$
```

For your maximum debugging pleasure, may I suggest using both the verbose option and the xtrace option.

EXAMPLE

```
$ head -2 masks_env
#!/bin/ksh -xv                          # Set xtrace and verbose
#
$


$ masks_env
#!/bin/ksh -xv
#
# Script which will display default
# permissions in formatted fashion
# based on the current umask setting
#
function gen_modes
{
integer count=0
typeset -i2 shiftval=2#$1
perms=( [1]=r [2]=w [3]=x [4]=r [5]=w [6]=x [7]=r [8]=w [9]=x )
while (( count <= 9 ))
do
(( count=count+1 ))
let lment=10-count
if (( ($shiftval & 1) == 1 ))
        then
        res[$lment]="${perms[$lment]}"
else
        res[$lment]="-"
fi
(( shiftval = shiftval >> 1))
done
}
######### Script Begins ##########
typeset -i2 defa               # make defa display in binary
+ typeset -i2 defa
typeset -i onescomp
+ typeset -i onescomp
(( onescomp=~($(umask)) ))     # Get ones complement of current umask
+ umask
+ (( onescomp=~(0002) ))
(( defa=(8#666)&onescomp ))    # Calculate default permission mask
+ (( defa=(8#666)&onescomp ))
default_perm=${defa#*#}         # Strip off leading 2#    # Verbose line
+ default_perm=110110100                                  # Xtrace line
print "Default REGULAR FILE permissions with current umask ($(umask))"
```

```
+ umask
+ print 'Default REGULAR FILE permissions with current umask (0002)'
Default REGULAR FILE permissions with current umask (0002)
print " u    g    o"
+ print ' u    g    o'
  u    g    o
#print '_ _ _ _ _ _ _ _ _'
gen_modes $default_perm
+ gen_modes 110110100
print ${res[*]}                                          # Verbose line
+ print - r w - r w - r - -                              # Xtrace line
r w - r w - r - -                                        # Output line
print "(In binary -- $default_perm)"
+ print '(In binary -- 110110100)'
(In binary -- 110110100)
print ""
+ print ''

if [[ "$MASKSDIRS" != "YES" ]]
then
        exit 0
fi
+ [[ '' != YES ]]
+ exit 0
$
```

Debugging Hooks

One of the easiest and most effective ways to debug a script is to judiciously place print statements in it to display the current contents of troublesome variables. This technique is not smooth or sexy, but it is very effective.

If your script development is ongoing, you might want to insert some debugging hooks in the script that indicate whether to display the variable contents. If you choose, you can remove the extra print statements after the script is debugged. However, I suggest leaving them in the script because the overhead of leaving them in will probably be minimal. This option is more directed than the ksh -xv technique and produces less busy output.

As you start the script, you can give it an extra command line option, such as -debug, which can be checked by the script as it runs. If it is defined, display the variable contents for debugging purposes. If it is not defined, skip the print commands.

EXAMPLE

```
$ cat masks_env
#!/bin/ksh
#
(...)
######### Script Begins ##########
typeset -i2 defa                    # make defa display in binary
typeset -i onescomp
(( onescomp=~($(umask)) ))          # Get ones complement of current umask
(( defa=(8#666)&onescomp ))         # Calculate default permission mask
default_perm=${defa#*#}             # Strip off leading 2#
print "Default REGULAR FILE permissions with current umask ($(umask))"
print "  u     g     o"
#print '_ _ _ _ _ _ _ _ _'
        if [[ "x$1" == "x-debug" ]]              # Check for debug switch
        then
        print "DEBUG -- default_perm contains $default_perm"
        fi
gen_modes $default_perm
print ${res[*]}
(...)
```

```
$
$ masks_env                                 # Normal run
Default REGULAR FILE permissions with current umask (0002)
  u     g     o
r w - r w - r - -
(In binary -- 110110100)
```

```
$
$ masks_env -debug                          # Run with debug option
Default REGULAR FILE permissions with current umask (0002)
  u     g     o
DEBUG -- default_perm contains 110110100    # Extra output line
r w - r w - r - -
(In binary -- 110110100)
```

```
$
```

A similar effect can be achieved by surrounding the troublesome portion of the script to be debugged with set -o xtrace and set +o xtrace. Effectively, you would be turning on the xtrace option for the area of concern only, rather than for the whole script, as was done in the previous examples.

You can also set up a DEBUG trap, but because we don't talk about traps until the next chapter, we'll hold off on that one.

What's Next

The debugging options are useful for handling the script writer's logic errors. But is there anything that can be done about user errors? If your script is to be used by users other than yourself, Chapter 12, "Traps," will help prevent those other users from interacting badly with your script. This is what I refer to as *bulletproofing* a script. (Some would prefer to call it *idiot-proofing*.)

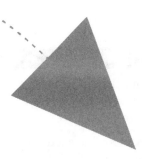

Traps

Rather than waiting to hear through the grapevine about your teenager's latest hi-jinks and then ranting and raving long after the fact, wouldn't it be wonderful if every untoward action generated an "admonishment from parent," which echoed in his head as if it were between two stereo speakers and you controlled the volume and content? Or how about a mechanism where every time he leaves the house there is an automatic litany of do's and dont's that bray into his mind? If either of these mechanisms sounds enticing, you will find the Korn Shell's capability to trap events to be of interest.

Consider two of the most common events that occur during the execution of a script: errors and exits. The errors referred to here are not the syntax and script creation time errors. This chapter's focus is on runtime errors.

This chapter teaches you the following:

- How to define and use script traps
- The importance of comments in scripts
- How to build help within a script
- How to bulletproof your script

Defining and Using Traps

As you will see, your script can trap for errors and the exit condition. These are probably the most commonly trapped-for events. Can other things be trapped? Let's answer that by examining the meaning of a trap.

Traps are typically described as asynchronous events. The event is *asynchronous* because of its unpredictability. An example is a Ctrl+C being pressed while your script is running. The event of the Ctrl+C is totally unpredictable from the perspective of your script. During one run, it might occur after 20 seconds; during another run, it might occur after 2 hours. And during a third run, it might not occur at all.

You may be thinking that a Ctrl+C causes an interrupt, not a trap. The trap is the action of reacting to the interrupt. The interrupt is massaged into a UNIX signal. So ultimately, the Ctrl+C key sequence causes an interrupt, which is transformed into a UNIX signal that is trappable by the process. Most UNIX signals can be trapped (signal number 9, however, cannot be trapped).

If a signal is not trapped by the script writer, the typical default action is to terminate the script. I propose that we break the categories of traps into groups based on function.

The first is the EXIT trap. This typically is used to perform some cleanup processing at the end of a script. It's useful if the logic of your script could take several paths, any of which would end by exiting.

Next is the ERR trap. This trap is triggered any time a command executed during your script returns a nonsuccessful status (a non-zero number in $?). The alternative to this trap is to place an if test after every command to check the return status of the command for a non-zero value. When this event is trapped, you could try to correct the problem or perhaps write a message to a log file, send some email to the person in charge of the application, or ignore the error and continue processing.

Another trap is the SIGNAL trap. Note that no keyword SIGNAL is recognized by the trap command. I am suggesting it as a functional category. This includes all the traps seen in the output of a kill -l command.

Next are the SPECIAL CASE traps, including

- DEBUG—ksh executes your trap response after each command.

- CHLD—ksh uses this trap to inform you that a background command has finished.

- KEYBD—ksh executes your response each time a character is typed interactively.

The following example uses a SIGNAL trap. It traps the signal sent when the user presses Ctrl+\ and reports how many files have been created at this point in the run. It also traps the Ctrl+C signal and reports the total number of files created before it exits the script. Note that this is the only way the script is designed to exit.

The keywords QUIT and INT can be replaced with the numbers 3 (for QUIT) and 2 (for INT). See kill -l output for other signals.

EXAMPLE

```
$ cat makem
#! /bin/ksh

integer count=0

trap 'print "Made $count files."'                      QUIT # Trap Ctrl+\
trap 'print "Exiting...";\
       sleep 2;print "total files made is $count"; exit'  INT # Trap Ctrl+C

while :                                    # Infinite while loop
do
> file$count                               # Create file1, file2, ...
count=count+1
done

$
$ pwd
/home/obrien/lotsofiles
$
$ makem
Made 3083 files.                                          # Ctrl+\
Made 4661 files.                                          # Ctrl+\
Exiting...                                                # Ctrl+C
total files made is 5311
$
$ ls | wc -l
    5314
$                                                         # Count of files
```

The following example uses an EXIT trap. This is the same makem script used earlier, but with an EXIT trap included. The trap calculates a number representing half of the count of files just created. It then presents that number as a parameter to a dot script called removem. The result is that it creates a bunch of files and then deletes the lower-numbered half of them.

```
$ cat makem
#! /bin/ksh

integer count=0
```

```
trap 'count=count/2; . removem $count ' EXIT  # Exit trap, calls another script
trap 'print "Made $count files."'       QUIT
trap 'print "Exiting...";\
        sleep 2;print "total files made is $count"; exit' INT

while :
do
> file$count
count=count+1
done


$
$ cat removem
#! /bin/ksh

integer dels=$(ls | sed 's/....//' | grep '^[0-9]' | sort -n | head -1)
                                        # Calculates lowest number file
if [[ -z $1 ]]
then
        read count?"How many?"
else
        count=$1+$dels
fi

print "Removing $count files, please wait"
while (( dels <= $count ))
do
rm file$dels
dels=dels+1
done
$
$ makem
Made 2172 files.                        # CTRL+\
Made 3094 files.                        # CTRL+\
Exiting...                              # CTRL+C
total files made is 3693
Removing 1846 files, please wait
$
$ ls | wc -l
    1849
$
```

The following example uses an ERR trap. The trap response appends any error messages to a file named errlog. It also appends the date after the name of the file that caused the error. The exec 2> /dev/null eliminates the shell's error displays so that the script can take full control of error reporting and processing.

EXAMPLE

```
$ cat removem
#! /bin/ksh

exec 2> /dev/null                               Get rid of shell errors
trap 'exec 3>> errlog; print -u3 "error file$dels -- $(date)"' ERR# Trap errors

integer dels=$(ls | sed 's/....//' | grep '^[0-9]' | sort -n | head -n 1)

if [[ -z $1 ]]
then
        read count?"How many?"
else
        count=$1
fi

print "Removing $count files, please wait"
(( count=count+$dels ))
while (( dels <= $count ))
do
/bin/rm file$dels                           # Supply location of your rm command
                                            # Eliminates aliases for rm

dels=dels+1
done
$
$ ls errlog                                 # Error log does not exist yet
ls: errlog: No such file or directory
$
$ makem                                     # Make a bunch of files
Exiting...
total files made is 1296
Removing 648 files, please wait
$
$ rm file680 file690                        # Remove a few by hand
$
$ removem 650                               # Remove 650 files
Removing 650 files, please wait
$
$ cat errlog
error file680 -- Tue Nov  7 18:26:01 EST 2000   # Couldn't find these files
error file690 -- Tue Nov  7 18:26:02 EST 2000
error file1296 -- Tue Nov  7 18:26:10 EST 2000
error file1297 -- Tue Nov  7 18:26:10 EST 2000
error file1298 -- Tue Nov  7 18:26:10 EST 2000
error file1299 -- Tue Nov  7 18:26:10 EST 2000
$
```

The following example uses a SPECIAL CASE trap. It sets up the DEBUG trap to display the contents of the variable named de1s. Even though it is not necessary to do so, the script also requests that the default behavior be reinstated using trap - DEBUG. The DEBUG trap can be turned on for a select portion of the script and turned off when not needed, enabling you to bracket the troublesome area of your script.

EXAMPLE

```
$ cat removem
#! /bin/ksh

exec 2> /dev/null
trap 'exec 3>> errlog; print -u3 "error file$dels -- $(date)"' ERR

integer dels=$(ls | sed 's/....//' | grep '^[0-9]' | sort -n | head -n 1)

if [[ -z $1 ]]
then
        read count?"How many?"
else
        count=$1
fi

trap 'print "dels contains $dels."' DEBUG       # Set up DEBUG trap
print "Removing $count files, please wait"
(( count=count+$dels ))
while (( dels <= $count ))
do
/bin/rm file$dels
dels=dels+1
done
trap - DEBUG                                     # Revert to default behavior
$
$ removem 385
dels contains 383.
Removing 385 files, please wait
dels contains 383.
dels contains 383.
dels contains 383.                               # Each line executed causes
dels contains 383.                               # the DEBUG trap to trigger
dels contains 384.
dels contains 384.
dels contains 384.
(...)
```

Documentation Support

Back when I was a cub programmer in the olden days (early 70s), I would feed lustily off the thrill of creating a well-functioning piece of software. The creative thinking and teamwork were eagerly welcomed.

However, another responsibility was put on the programmer's shoulders that was not quite so attractive. Our boss wanted us to carefully document our work so that maintenance programming could be efficiently performed in the future if necessary. Needless to say, the FUTURE, as far as I was concerned at that point in my life, was…maybe dinnertime. As a young man, everything happened RIGHT NOW. There was no time to think about the future.

So my approach to this wasteful busywork was to scribble some nonsense in the document, to meet the letter of the law, but not really put any effort into it. I had no mental energy to devote to this menial and boring task.

Approximately a year and a half after I had participated in my first large software project, some changes had to be performed on the code I had created. Because I was still doing the same job as I had been (you can see that my career was skyrocketing), my boss (same guy—his career was skyrocketing also) came to me and plopped a bunch of printouts and specs on my desk and described the essence of the changes that needed to be made.

On the top of the pile of materials was the documentation book. Yup, the same one that I had not bothered to fill with much useful information a year and a half ago. I cracked it open when I needed some help in figuring out the algorithms I had used 540 days ago. Unfortunately, it contained nothing but my amateurish attempts at whitewashing the fact that I saw no use in documentation.

The bottom line was that a project that should have taken me two days took me two weeks—all because I had taken a shortcut with my documentation. Instead of taking a few hours while the thrill of the software hunt was still fresh in my brain, I chose to write 10-minutes worth of gibberish so I could rush on to the next creative endeavor.

I learned a major lesson at that time. I have since seen evidence that further emphasizes that documentation is worth its weight in stock options. Any pie chart that shows where the software bucks are being spent indicates that more than 80% of the budget goes to maintaining existing code, not the creation of new code.

Not that I expect you to write a separate document that describes all the fine points of your script. I do, however, recommend that you use comments within your script to describe any sticky points in your logic or anything else that might be of use to a maintenance person. Realize that the maintenance person might be you!

Self-Help Scripts

As my mind gets more cluttered with UNIX commands and other technical flotsam, my ability to remember the expected syntax of a particular command or script becomes limited.

One of the techniques I use to quickly recall which options are legitimate and what the order of the parameters is supposed to be is to type the command with no other syntax. Usually this is incorrect for the command or script in question. If the script has been designed with self-help in mind, it displays a little syntax reminder onscreen. This functions as a mini man page, as you can see in the following example.

You can alternatively set up your script to react to a parameter of ? or -help.

EXAMPLE

```
$ gcdksh
Usage: gcdksh {integer_1} {integer_2} ...
$
```

Bulletproofing

The ultimate bulletproofing of a script comes by combining many of the thoughts presented in this chapter. The goal is to make the script impervious to any kind of input the user might throw at it (or that it might read from a file). This special-case "what-if" code can be so detailed and cumbersome to write that it takes up more lines in your script than the main production logic flow. Therefore, I suggest that you implement these ideas in your nonpersonal scripts.

The following example shows an example of bulletproofing.

EXAMPLE

```
$ cat gcdksh
#! /bin/ksh

function gcd {                    # Function to generate gcd between two numbers
        integer u v r

        u=$1
        v=$2
        while ((v))               # Key gcd loop
        do
                r=u%v
```

```
                    u=v
                    v=r
            done
            print $u                # Returns value to caller of function if function
            }                       # called using $(gcd ...) syntax

function syntax {                   # Function to report incorrect syntax
        print -u2 Usage: "${comname##*/} {integer_1} {integer_2} ..."
        exit 1                      # Remove large left pattern up to last /
        }

comname=$0
(($# < 2)) && syntax                # Check if count of args < 2, call syntax
G=0
for f                               # Loop using command args
do
        G=$(gcd  G $f)              # Call gcd function with current G contents
                                    # and next command-line param as args
done
print "Greatest common denominator is $G"
$
$ gcdksh 4 8
Greatest common denominator is 4
$
$ gcdksh 8 4
Greatest common denominator is 4
$
$ gcdksh 8 0
Greatest common denominator is 8
$
$ gcdksh 8                              # Incorrect syntax
Usage: gcdksh {integer_1} {integer_2} ...
$
```

How do you protect against out-of-range input? The following example adds another function to the gcdksh script, providing protection against out-of-range input values.

EXAMPLE

```
$ cat gcdksh
#! /bin/ksh

integer BITS=32         # Assume 32-bit machine
integer len max

max="(1 << BITS-1) - 1" # Generate maximum value for this system
len=${#max}             # How many bytes is it
```

```
function gcd {
        integer u v r

        u=$1
        v=$2
        while ((v))     # Continue while v != 0
        do
                r=u%v   # Main calculation for gcd
                u=v
                v=r
        done
        print $u        # Return value to caller if function
        }               # called using G=$(gcd ...)

function syntax {       # Main syntax error report function
        print -u2 Usage: "${comname##*/} {integer_1} {integer_2} ..."
        exit 1                  # Remove large left pattern up to last /
        }

function inrange {      # Function to determine if value is in range
        typeset str str_len str_quot
                        # Variables local to this function
        str=$1
        str_len=${#str}
        ((str_len < len)) && return 0
        ((str_len > len)) && return 1
        return 1
        }

comname=$0
(($# < 2)) && syntax            # Check if count of args < 2, call syntax
G=0
for f                           # Loop using command args
do
        ! inrange $f && { print -u2 - "$f: out of range"; syntax; }
        G=$(gcd  G $f)          # Call gcd function with current G contents
                                # and next command-line param as args
done
print "Greatest common denominator is $G"
$
$ gcdksh 9 999999999
Greatest common denominator is 9
$
$ gcdksh 9 99999999999
99999999999: out of range
Usage: gcdksh {integer_1} {integer_2} ...
$
```

But what happens if you pick a number between 999999999 and 99999999999? It reports an incorrect result! So you have more work to do. The problem is that when checking for out-of-range values, you need to somehow perform math involving a value that is too large to express. How can you do that?

The solution is to eliminate the rightmost numeral from your test numbers, and then check the range (the numbers must be stored in strings at first). If the outcome is still in doubt, you must isolate the rightmost numeral and check that against the rightmost numeral in the maximum supported value.

Are we over the top here? Maybe. But I think you are getting the point that if you want to make a bulletproof script, it takes some serious work.

The following example prepares for some of the extremes in range testing. It should prevent user input beyond the supported integer range on the system (it assumes a 32-bit system).

EXAMPLE

```ksh
$ cat gcdksh
#! /bin/ksh

integer BITS=32
integer len max quot

max="(1 << BITS-1) - 1"  # Generate maximum value for this system
len=${#max}              # How long is the value
len=len-1                # Decrease by 1 for sign
quot=${max%?}            # Maximum value with rightmost numeral eliminated
typeset -R1 rem=$max     # Isolate the rightmost numeral, store in rem


function gcd {
        integer u v r

        u=$1
        v=$2
        while ((v))      # Continue while v != 0
        do
                r=u%v    # Main calculation for gcd
                u=v
                v=r
        done
        print $u         # Return value to caller if function
        }                # called using G=$(gcd ...)

function syntax {        # Main syntax error report function
        print -u2 Usage: "${comname##*/} {integer_1} {integer_2} ..."
```

```
                exit 1           # Remove large left pattern up to last /
                }

        function inrange {
                typeset str str_len str_quot
                                # Local variables

                str=$1
                str_len=${#str} # Get length of parameter
                                # Check against maximum allowable length
                ((str_len < len)) && return 0
                                # If less, return success
                ((str_len > len)) && return 1
                                # If more, return failure

                str_quot=${str%?}
                                # Remove rightmost numeral from test value
                typeset -R1 str_rem=$str
                                # Isolate rightmost numeral in test value
                                # Check against max value's left numerals
                ((str_quot < quot)) && return 0
                                # If less return success
                ((str_quot > quot)) && return 1
                                # If more return failure
                                # Still undecided, compare right numerals
                ((str_rem <= rem)) && return 0
                return 1
                }

        comname=$0
        (($# < 2)) && syntax            # Check if count of args < 2, call syntax
        G=0
        for f                           # Loop using command args
        do
                ! inrange $f && { print -u2 - "$f: out of range"; syntax; }
                G=$(gcd  $G $f)         # Call gcd function with current G contents
                                        # and next command-line param as args
        done
        print "Greatest common denominator is $G"
        $
        $
        $ gcdksh 9 9999999999
        9999999999: out of range
        Usage: gcdksh {integer_1} {integer_2} ...
        $
        $ gcdksh 9 999999999
        Greatest common denominator is 9
        $
```

What's Next

You are now pretty much tooled up for the task of script writing. You will surely bump across some new twist that was not covered in the materials, but you have more than enough tools to write some serious scripts.

Chapter 13, "Pulling It All Together," presents a final example of a script that uses many of the tools and techniques you have learned in this book.

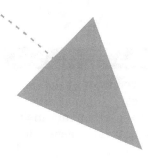

Pulling It All Together

Every now and then, it all comes together. The sun shines. The wind is at your back. The air is crisp. You feel like you can do anything and do it well. Your strength and confidence comes from having learned from all your past experiences and having synthesized that information into a pool of knowledge from which you can draw when necessary. That summarizes where we are in the book.

You certainly don't know everything (nobody does). Just as life can throw some unexpected curve balls at us, our script writing can draw us into situations for which we are less than fully prepared. You are, however, ready to confront a computing need, and address that need with a fairly sophisticated script. I sincerely hope that the lessons learned throughout this book will serve as a springboard for further growth and insights into the world of script writing.

This chapter presents a script that uses many of the techniques discussed in the book. The script executes many system admin level commands and checks their output against a baseline file. If anything has changed since the baseline was taken, a report is displayed. The user has the option of re-executing selected commands or just viewing the differences.

Many interesting shell constructs are used throughout the example, including the following:

- Functions
- Coprocess
- Looping constructs (`for` and `while`)
- Filters and pipes
- Traps
- Here documents
- Arrays

The sys_check Script

The following script is shown in a vi session with the number option set. (In a vi session, the last line-mode command, :set number, displays line numbers at the beginning of each line.) First, a few of the command-line options built into the sys_check script are used; then, several sample runs are shown after the script is introduced. The following example also provides some preliminary insight into the run of the script. The baseline file (and other files) will be stored in /root/checkit/checkout. The baseline file contains the output of the first effective run of the script. You will see that the script reacts differently if no baseline file exists (it creates it). I will provide commentary on many of the lines in the script later in the chapter.

Command Options -h

The following example shows the -h option requesting help concerning the user interface to the script:

EXAMPLE

```
# ./sys_check -h
Usage: syntax [-n] [-h]
        -n: Print list of commands to be executed, do not execute.
        -h: Print help message.
#
```

Command Options (Invalid)

The following example shows how the script reacts to an invalid option on the command line. The script has no special error checking for command-line arguments (as opposed to options, which it does handle); it simply ignores them:

EXAMPLE

```
#
# ./sys_check -a
sys_check: unrecognized option \'a\'
Usage: syntax [-n] [-h]
        -n: Print list of commands to be executed, do not execute.
        -h: Print help message.
#
```

Command Options -n

The following example shows the -n option requesting that a list of the commands to be executed be displayed. The -n option does not request that the commands actually be executed. The default action is that the script executes the commands and checks for differences:

EXAMPLE

```
# ./sys_check -n


Printing Commands (not executing)


#1  /bin/date 2>&1
#2  /bin/date "+%Z" 2>&1
#3  /bin/hostname 2>&1
#4  /bin/uname -a 2>&1
#5  /bin/echo ${PATH} 2>&1
#6  /bin/cat /etc/hosts 2>&1
#7  /bin/cat /etc/fstab 2>&1
#8  /bin/cat /etc/passwd 2>&1
#9  /bin/cat /etc/group 2>&1
#10 /bin/cat /.rhosts 2>&1
#11 /bin/cat /etc/dhcpd.conf 2>&1
#12 /bin/cat /etc/inetd.conf 2>&1
#13 /bin/cat /etc/initlog.conf 2>&1
#14 /bin/cat /etc/lilo.conf 2>&1
#15 /bin/cat /etc/named.conf 2>&1
#16 /bin/cat /etc/resolv.conf 2>&1
#17 /bin/cat /etc/smb.conf 2>&1
#18 /bin/cat /etc/yp.conf 2>&1
#19 /bin/cat /etc/ypserv.conf 2>&1
#20 /bin/cat /etc/aliases 2>&1
#21 /bin/netstat -nr | grep -v "Kernel IP routing table" | awk '{ printf "%s %s
%s %s %s\n", $1,$2,$3,$4,$8 }' 2>&1
#22 /bin/cat /etc/inittab 2>&1
#23 /bin/mount 2>&1
#24 /bin/df -k 2>&1
#25 /bin/netstat -rn   | awk '{printf "%s %s %s %s\n", $1,$2,$3,$6}' 2>&1
#26 /bin/netstat -in 2>&1
#27 for i in $(/usr/bin/lsdev | grep eth | awk '{printf "%s\n",$1}') ; do echo "
XXXXXXXXXXXXX ifconfig for $i XXXXXXXXXXXXXXXXX"; /sbin/ifconfig $i; done 2>&1
#28 /bin/ls /etc/rc.d/init.d 2>&1
#29 for i in $(/bin/ls /var/spool/cron) ; do echo "XXXXXXXXXXXXXXXX cron file $i
XXXXXXXXXXXXXXXXXXXXXX"; cat /var/spool/cron/$i; done 2>&1
#30 /sbin/chkconfig --list 2>&1
#31 /usr/bin/lsdev 2>&1


 Exiting


#
```

First sys_check Run

The following example shows a first-time run of the script. Notice that the target directory (/root/checkit/checkout) is currently empty. After the first run, it has the baseline file in it. After the second run, it has a current file and a differences file, along with the baseline file:

EXAMPLE

```
# ls /root/checkit/checkout                           # No baseline file
#

# ./sys_check

#=========================================================================
1 ====COMMAND=======: # /bin/date 2>&1
#=========================================================================


#1 Sat Nov 25 14:27:45 EST 2000


#=========================================================================
2 ====COMMAND=======: # /bin/date "+%Z" 2>&1
#=========================================================================


#2 EST


#=========================================================================
3 ====COMMAND=======: # /bin/hostname 2>&1
#=========================================================================


#3 linden


#=========================================================================
4 ====COMMAND=======: # /bin/uname -a 2>&1
#=========================================================================


#4 Linux linden 2.2.12-20 #1 Mon Sep 27 10:25:54 EDT 1999 i586


#=========================================================================
5 ====COMMAND=======: # /bin/echo ${PATH} 2>&1
#=========================================================================


#5 /bin:/sbin:/usr/bin:/usr/sbin:/usr/local/bin:/usr/local/sbin:/usr/bin/X11:/us
r/X11R6/bin:/root/bin


#=========================================================================
6 ====COMMAND=======: # /bin/cat /etc/hosts 2>&1
#=========================================================================
```

```
#6 127.0.0.1     localhost.localdomain    localhost
#6 192.206.126.84      linden
#6 192.206.126.26      lapman


#=======================================================================
7 ====COMMAND=======: # /bin/cat /etc/fstab 2>&1
#=======================================================================


#7 /dev/hda8            /                       ext2     defaults      1 1
#7 /dev/hda1            /boot                   ext2     defaults      1 2
#7 /dev/hda6            /home                   ext2     defaults      1 2
#7 /dev/cdrom           /mnt/cdrom              iso9660  noauto,owner,ro 0 0
#7 /dev/hda5            /usr                    ext2     defaults      1 2
#7 /dev/hda7            swap                    swap     defaults      0 0
#7 /dev/fd0             /mnt/floppy             ext2     noauto,owner   0 0
#7 none                 /proc                   proc     defaults      0 0
#7 none                 /dev/pts                devpts   gid=5,mode=620 0 0


#=======================================================================
8 ====COMMAND=======: # /bin/cat /etc/passwd 2>&1
#=======================================================================


#8 root:x:0:0:root:/root:/bin/ksh
#8 bin:x:1:1:bin:/bin:
#8 daemon:x:2:2:daemon:/sbin:
#8 adm:x:3:4:adm:/var/adm:
#8 lp:x:4:7:lp:/var/spool/lpd:
#8 sync:x:5:0:sync:/sbin:/bin/sync
#8 shutdown:x:6:0:shutdown:/sbin:/sbin/shutdown
#8 halt:x:7:0:halt:/sbin:/sbin/halt
#8 mail:x:8:12:mail:/var/spool/mail:
#8 news:x:9:13:news:/var/spool/news:
#8 uucp:x:10:14:uucp:/var/spool/uucp:
#8 operator:x:11:0:operator:/root:
#8 games:x:12:100:games:/usr/games:
#8 gopher:x:13:30:gopher:/usr/lib/gopher-data:
#8 ftp:x:14:50:FTP User:/home/ftp:
#8 nobody:x:99:99:Nobody:/:
#8 xfs:x:100:101:X Font Server:/etc/X11/fs:/bin/false
#8 gdm:x:42:42::/home/gdm:/bin/bash
#8 obrien:x:500:500:Dennis O'Brien:/home/obrien:/bin/ksh


#=======================================================================
9 ====COMMAND=======: # /bin/cat /etc/group 2>&1
#=======================================================================
```

```
#9 root:x:0:root
#9 bin:x:1:root,bin,daemon
#9 daemon:x:2:root,bin,daemon
#9 sys:x:3:root,bin,adm
#9 adm:x:4:root,adm,daemon
#9 tty:x:5:
#9 disk:x:6:root
#9 lp:x:7:daemon,lp
#9 mem:x:8:
#9 kmem:x:9:
#9 wheel:x:10:root
#9 mail:x:12:mail
#9 news:x:13:news
#9 uucp:x:14:uucp
#9 man:x:15:
#9 games:x:20:
#9 gopher:x:30:
#9 dip:x:40:
#9 ftp:x:50:
#9 nobody:x:99:
#9 users:x:100:
#9 floppy:x:19:
#9 utmp:x:22:
#9 xfs:x:101:
#9 console:x:102:
#9 gdm:x:42:
#9 pppusers:x:230:
#9 popusers:x:231:
#9 slipusers:x:232:
#9 slocate:x:21:
#9 obrien:x:500:


#========================================================================
10 ====COMMAND=======: # /bin/cat /.rhosts 2>&1
#========================================================================


#10 ksh[20]: cat: /.rhosts: cannot open [No such file or directory]


#========================================================================
11 ====COMMAND=======: # /bin/cat /etc/dhcpd.conf 2>&1
#========================================================================


#11 ksh[22]: cat: /etc/dhcpd.conf: cannot open [No such file or directory]
```

```
#=========================================================================
12 ====COMMAND=======: # /bin/cat /etc/inetd.conf 2>&1
#=========================================================================


#12 #
#12 # inetd.conf        This file describes the services that will be available
#12 #             through the INETD TCP/IP super server.  To reconfigure
#12 #             the running INETD process, edit this file, then send the
#12 #             INETD process a SIGHUP signal.
#12 #
#12 # Version:  @(#)/etc/inetd.conf    3.10    05/27/93
#12 #
#12 # Authors:  Original taken from BSD UNIX 4.3/TAHOE.
#12 #           Fred N. van Kempen, <waltje@uwalt.nl.mugnet.org>
#12 #
#12 # Modified for Debian Linux by Ian A. Murdock <imurdock@shell.portal.com>
#12 #
#12 # Modified for RHS Linux by Marc Ewing <marc@redhat.com>
#12 #
#12 # <service_name> <sock_type> <proto> <flags> <user> <server_path> <args>
#12 #
#12 # Echo, discard, daytime, and chargen are used primarily for testing.
#12 #
#12 # To re-read this file after changes, just do a 'killall -HUP inetd'
#12 #
#12 #echo       stream  tcp     nowait  root    internal
#12 #echo       dgram   udp     wait    root    internal
#12 #discard    stream  tcp     nowait  root    internal
#12 #discard    dgram   udp     wait    root    internal
#12 #daytime    stream  tcp     nowait  root    internal
#12 #daytime    dgram   udp     wait    root    internal
#12 #chargen    stream  tcp     nowait  root    internal
#12 #chargen    dgram   udp     wait    root    internal
#12 #time       stream  tcp     nowait  root    internal
#12 #time       dgram   udp     wait    root    internal
#12 #
#12 # These are standard services.
#12 #
#12 ftp stream  tcp     nowait  root    /usr/sbin/tcpd  in.ftpd -l -a
#12 telnet      stream  tcp     nowait  root    /usr/sbin/tcpd  in.telnetd
#12 #
#12 # Shell, login, exec, comsat and talk are BSD protocols.
#12 #
#12 shell       stream  tcp     nowait  root    /usr/sbin/tcpd  in.rshd
#12 login       stream  tcp     nowait  root    /usr/sbin/tcpd  in.rlogind
#12 #exec       stream  tcp     nowait  root    /usr/sbin/tcpd  in.rexecd
```

```
#12 #comsat      dgram   udp     wait    root    /usr/sbin/tcpd  in.comsat
#12 talk         dgram   udp     wait    nobody.tty      /usr/sbin/tcpd  in.talkd
#12 ntalk        dgram   udp     wait    nobody.tty      /usr/sbin/tcpd  in.ntalk
d
#12 #dtalk       stream  tcp     wait    nobody.tty      /usr/sbin/tcpd  in.dtalk
d
#12 #
#12 # Pop and imap mail services et al
#12 #
#12 #pop-2   stream   tcp    nowait  root   /usr/sbin/tcpd     ipop2d
#12 #pop-3   stream   tcp    nowait  root   /usr/sbin/tcpd     ipop3d
#12 #imap    stream   tcp    nowait  root   /usr/sbin/tcpd     imapd
#12 #
#12 # The Internet UUCP service.
#12 #
#12 #uucp       stream  tcp     nowait  uucp    /usr/sbin/tcpd  /usr/lib/uucp/uu
cico   -l
#12 #
#12 # Tftp service is provided primarily for booting.  Most sites
#12 # run this only on machines acting as "boot servers." Do not uncomment
#12 # this unless you *need* it.
#12 #
#12 #tftp       dgram   udp     wait    root    /usr/sbin/tcpd  in.tftpd
#12 #bootps     dgram   udp     wait    root    /usr/sbin/tcpd  bootpd
#12 #
#12 # Finger, systat and netstat give out user information which may be
#12 # valuable to potential "system crackers."  Many sites choose to disable
#12 # some or all of these services to improve security.
#12 #
#12 finger       stream  tcp     nowait  nobody  /usr/sbin/tcpd  in.fingerd
#12 #cfinger stream      tcp     nowait  root    /usr/sbin/tcpd  in.cfingerd
#12 #systat      stream  tcp     nowait  guest   /usr/sbin/tcpd  /bin/ps -auwwx
#12 #netstat stream  tcp nowait  guest /usr/sbin/tcpd  /bin/netstat -f inet
#12 #
#12 # Authentication
#12 #
#12 auth    stream  tcp  wait  root /usr/sbin/in.identd in.identd -e -o
#12 #
#12 # End of inetd.conf
#12
#12 linuxconf stream tcp wait root /bin/linuxconf linuxconf --http


#========================================================================
13 ====COMMAND=======: # /bin/cat /etc/initlog.conf 2>&1
#========================================================================
```

```
#13 # /etc/initlog.conf
#13 #
#13 # initlog configuration file
#13 #
#13 # lines preceded by a '#' are comments
#13 #
#13 # anything not recognized is ignored. :)
#13
#13 # This sets the default logging facility. (can override with command-line
     arguments)
#13 facility local7
#13
#13 # This sets the default logging priority. (
        can override with command-line arguments)
#13 priority notice
#13
#13 # ignore foo
#13 # means to discard any output from a command that matches regexp foo
#13
#13 # This regexp is useful if you use fsck's -C option.
#13 ignore [^:]+: |[=]+
#13 # This regexp is useful for quotacheck
#13 ignore ^[-\|/]$


#=======================================================================
14 ====COMMAND=======: # /bin/cat /etc/lilo.conf 2>&1
#=======================================================================


#14 boot=/dev/hda
#14 map=/boot/map
#14 install=/boot/boot.b
#14 prompt
#14 timeout=50
#14 default=linux
#14
#14 image=/boot/vmlinuz-2.2.12-20
#14 label=linux
#14 initrd=/boot/initrd-2.2.12-20.img
#14 read-only
#14 root=/dev/hda8


#=======================================================================
15 ====COMMAND=======: # /bin/cat /etc/named.conf 2>&1
#=======================================================================
```

```
#15 ksh[30]: cat: /etc/named.conf: cannot open [No such file or directory]


#=======================================================================
16 ====COMMAND=======: # /bin/cat /etc/resolv.conf 2>&1
#=======================================================================


#16 search
#16 nameserver


#=======================================================================
17 ====COMMAND=======: # /bin/cat /etc/smb.conf 2>&1
#=======================================================================


#17 # This is the main Samba configuration file. You should read the
#17 # smb.conf(5) manual page in order to understand the options listed
#17 # here. Samba has a huge number of configurable options (perhaps too
#17 # many!) most of which are not shown in this example
#17 #
#17 # Any line which starts with a ; (semicolon) or a # (hash)
#17 # is a comment and is ignored. In this example we will use a #
#17 # for commentry and a ; for parts of the config file that you
#17 # may wish to enable
#17 #
#17 # NOTE: Whenever you modify this file you should run the command "testparm"
#17 # to check that you have not made any basic syntax errors.
#17 #
    (...)


#=======================================================================
18 ====COMMAND=======: # /bin/cat /etc/yp.conf 2>&1
#=======================================================================


#18 # /etc/yp.conf - ypbind configuration file
#18 # Valid entries are
#18 #
#18 #domain NISDOMAIN server HOSTNAME
#18 #    Use server HOSTNAME for the domain NISDOMAIN.
#18 #
#18 #domain NISDOMAIN broadcast
#18 #    Use  broadcast  on  the local net for domain NISDOMAIN
#18 #
#18 #ypserver HOSTNAME
#18 #    Use server HOSTNAME for the  local  domain.  The
#18 #    IP-address of server must be listed in /etc/hosts.
#18 #
```

```
#========================================================================
19 ====COMMAND=======: # /bin/cat /etc/ypserv.conf 2>&1
#========================================================================


#19 ksh[38]: cat: /etc/ypserv.conf: cannot open [No such file or directory]


#========================================================================
20 ====COMMAND=======: # /bin/cat /etc/aliases 2>&1
#========================================================================


#20 #
#20 #   @(#)aliases      8.2 (Berkeley) 3/5/94
#20 #
#20 #  Aliases in this file will NOT be expanded in the header from
#20 #  Mail, but WILL be visible over networks or from /bin/mail.
#20 #
#20 #  >>>>>>>>>>       The program "newaliases" must be run after
#20 #  >> NOTE >>       this file is updated for any changes to
#20 #  >>>>>>>>>>       show through to sendmail.
#20 #
#20
#20 # Basic system aliases -- these MUST be present.
#20 MAILER-DAEMON:      postmaster
#20 postmaster: root
#20
#20 # General redirections for pseudo accounts.
#20 bin:                root
#20 daemon:             root
#20 games:              root
#20 ingres:             root
#20 nobody:             root
#20 system:             root
#20 toor:               root
#20 uucp:               root
#20
#20 # Well-known aliases.
#20 manager:    root
#20 dumper:             root
#20 operator:   root
#20
#20 # trap decode to catch security attacks
#20 decode:             root
#20
#20 # Person who should get root's mail
```

```
#20 #root:              marc
#20


#======================================================================
21 ====COMMAND=======: # /bin/netstat -nr | grep -v "Kernel IP routing table" |
awk '{ printf "%s %s %s %s %s\n", $1,$2,$3,$4,$8 }' 2>&1
#======================================================================


#21 Destination Gateway Genmask Flags Iface
#21 192.206.126.84 0.0.0.0 255.255.255.255 UH eth0
#21 192.206.126.0 0.0.0.0 255.255.255.0 U eth0
#21 127.0.0.0 0.0.0.0 255.0.0.0 U lo
#21 0.0.0.0 192.206.126.82 0.0.0.0 UG eth0


#======================================================================
22 ====COMMAND=======: # /bin/cat /etc/inittab 2>&1
#======================================================================


#22 #
#22 # inittab       This file describes how the INIT process should set up
#22 #               the system in a certain runlevel.
#22 #
#22 # Author:       Miquel van Smoorenburg, <miquels@drinkel.nl.mugnet.org>
#22 #               Modified for RHS Linux by Marc Ewing and Donnie Barnes
#22 #
#22
#22 # Default runlevel. The runlevels used by RHS are:
#22 #   0 - halt (Do NOT set initdefault to this)
#22 #   1 - Single-user mode
#22 #   2 - Multiuser,
    # without NFS (The same as 3, if you do not have networking)
#22 #   3 - Full multiuser mode
#22 #   4 - unused
#22 #   5 - X11
#22 #   6 - reboot (Do NOT set initdefault to this)
#22 #
#22 id:5:initdefault:
#22
#22 # System initialization.
#22 si::sysinit:/etc/rc.d/rc.sysinit
#22
#22 l0:0:wait:/etc/rc.d/rc 0
#22 l1:1:wait:/etc/rc.d/rc 1
#22 l2:2:wait:/etc/rc.d/rc 2
#22 l3:3:wait:/etc/rc.d/rc 3
#22 l4:4:wait:/etc/rc.d/rc 4
```

```
#22 l5:5:wait:/etc/rc.d/rc 5
#22 l6:6:wait:/etc/rc.d/rc 6
#22
#22 # Things to run in every runlevel.
#22 ud::once:/sbin/update
#22
#22 # Trap CTRL-ALT-DELETE
#22 ca::ctrlaltdel:/sbin/shutdown -t3 -r now
#22
#22 # When our UPS tells us power has failed, assume we have a few minutes
#22 # of power left.  Schedule a shutdown for 2 minutes from now.
#22 # This does, of course, assume you have powerd installed and your
#22 # UPS connected and working correctly.
#22 pf::powerfail:/sbin/shutdown -f -h +2 "Power Failure; System Shutting Down"
#22
#22 # If power was restored before the shutdown kicked in, cancel it.
#22 pr:12345:powerokwait:/sbin/shutdown -c "Power Restored; Shutdown Cancelled"
#22
#22
#22 # Run gettys in standard runlevels
#22 1:2345:respawn:/sbin/mingetty tty1
#22 2:2345:respawn:/sbin/mingetty tty2
#22 3:2345:respawn:/sbin/mingetty tty3
#22 4:2345:respawn:/sbin/mingetty tty4
#22 5:2345:respawn:/sbin/mingetty tty5
#22 6:2345:respawn:/sbin/mingetty tty6
#22
#22 # Run xdm in runlevel 5
#22 # xdm is now a separate service
#22 x:5:respawn:/etc/X11/prefdm -nodaemon


#========================================================================
23 ====COMMAND=======: # /bin/mount 2>&1
#========================================================================


#23 /dev/hda8 on / type ext2 (rw)
#23 none on /proc type proc (rw)
#23 /dev/hda1 on /boot type ext2 (rw)
#23 /dev/hda6 on /home type ext2 (rw)
#23 /dev/hda5 on /usr type ext2 (rw)
#23 none on /dev/pts type devpts (rw,gid=5,mode=620)


#========================================================================
24 ====COMMAND=======: # /bin/df -k 2>&1
#========================================================================
```

```
#24 Filesystem            1k-blocks      Used Available Use% Mounted on
#24 /dev/hda8              1612808      46436   1484444   3% /
#24 /dev/hda1                23302       2647     19452  12% /boot
#24 /dev/hda6               202220     118914     72866  62% /home
#24 /dev/hda5              2197888     659880   1426360  32% /usr


#==========================================================================
25 ====COMMAND=======:
# /bin/netstat -rn | awk '{printf "%s %s %s %s\n", $1,$2,
#==========================================================================


#25 Kernel IP routing
#25 Destination Gateway Genmask Window
#25 192.206.126.84 0.0.0.0 255.255.255.255 0
#25 192.206.126.0 0.0.0.0 255.255.255.0 0
#25 127.0.0.0 0.0.0.0 255.0.0.0 0
#25 0.0.0.0 192.206.126.82 0.0.0.0 0


#==========================================================================
26 ====COMMAND=======: # /bin/netstat -in 2>&1
#==========================================================================


#26 Kernel Interface table
#26 Iface   MTU Met    RX-OK RX-ERR RX-DRP RX-OVR    TX-OK TX-ERR TX-DRP TX-OVR
Flg
#26 eth0   1500   0   134150      0      0      0    65650      0      0      0
BRU
#26 lo     3924   0        2      0      0      0        2      0      0      0
LRU


#==========================================================================
27 ====COMMAND=======:
# for i in $(/usr/bin/lsdev | grep eth | awk '{printf "%s
# \n",$1}') ; do echo "XXXXXXXXXXXXX ifconfig for $i XXXXXXXXXXXXXXXXX";
# /sbin/ifc onfig $i; done 2>&1


#==========================================================================


#27 XXXXXXXXXXXXX ifconfig for eth0 XXXXXXXXXXXXXXXXX
#27 eth0      Link encap:Ethernet  HWaddr 00:20:78:12:70:22
#27 inet addr:192.206.126.84  Bcast:192.206.126.255  Mask:255.255.255.0
#27 UP BROADCAST RUNNING MULTICAST  MTU:1500  Metric:1
#27 RX packets:134154 errors:0 dropped:0 overruns:0 frame:0
#27 TX packets:65654 errors:0 dropped:0 overruns:0 carrier:0
#27 collisions:186 txqueuelen:100
```

```
#27 Interrupt:11 Base address:0x2c00
#27


#=========================================================================
28 ====COMMAND=======: # /bin/ls /etc/rc.d/init.d 2>&1
#=========================================================================

#28 apmd
#28 arpwatch
#28 atd
#28 crond
#28 functions
#28 gpm
#28 halt
#28 identd
#28 inet
#28 keytable
#28 killall
#28 kudzu
#28 linuxconf
#28 lpd
#28 netfs
#28 network
#28 nfslock
#28 pcmcia
#28 portmap
#28 random
#28 routed
#28 rstatd
#28 rusersd
#28 rwhod
#28 sendmail
#28 single
#28 syslog
#28 xfs
#28 ypbind


#=========================================================================
29 ====COMMAND=======: # for i in $(/bin/ls /var/spool/cron) ; do echo "XXXXXXXX
XXXXXXX cron file $i XXXXXXXXXXXXXXXXXXXXXX"; cat /var/spool/cron/$i; done 2>&1
#=========================================================================
```

```
#==========================================================================
30 ====COMMAND=======: # /sbin/chkconfig --list 2>&1
#==========================================================================


#30 keytable 0:off 1:off 2:on 3:on 4:on 5:on 6:off
#30 crond 0:off 1:off 2:on 3:on 4:on 5:on 6:off
#30 syslog 0:off 1:off 2:on 3:on 4:on 5:on 6:off
#30 netfs 0:off 1:off 2:off 3:on 4:on 5:on 6:off
#30 network 0:off 1:off 2:on 3:on 4:on 5:on 6:off
#30 random 0:off 1:on 2:on 3:on 4:on 5:on 6:off
#30 xfs 0:off 1:off 2:on 3:on 4:on 5:on 6:off
#30 apmd 0:off 1:off 2:on 3:on 4:on 5:on 6:off
#30 arpwatch 0:off 1:off 2:off 3:off 4:off 5:off 6:off
#30 atd 0:off 1:off 2:off 3:on 4:on 5:on 6:off
#30 gpm 0:off 1:off 2:on 3:on 4:on 5:on 6:off
#30 pcmcia 0:off 1:off 2:on 3:on 4:on 5:on 6:off
#30 nfslock 0:off 1:off 2:off 3:off 4:off 5:off 6:off
#30 kudzu 0:off 1:off 2:off 3:on 4:on 5:on 6:off
#30 linuxconf 0:off 1:off 2:on 3:on 4:on 5:on 6:off
#30 lpd 0:off 1:off 2:on 3:on 4:on 5:on 6:off
#30 inet 0:off 1:off 2:off 3:on 4:on 5:on 6:off
#30 identd 0:off 1:off 2:off 3:off 4:off 5:off 6:off
#30 portmap 0:off 1:off 2:off 3:on 4:on 5:on 6:off
#30 routed 0:off 1:off 2:off 3:off 4:off 5:off 6:off
#30 rstatd 0:off 1:off 2:off 3:off 4:off 5:off 6:off
#30 rusersd 0:off 1:off 2:off 3:off 4:off 5:off 6:off
#30 rwhod 0:off 1:off 2:off 3:off 4:off 5:off 6:off
#30 sendmail 0:off 1:off 2:on 3:on 4:on 5:on 6:off
#30 ypbind 0:off 1:off 2:off 3:off 4:off 5:off 6:off


#==========================================================================
31 ====COMMAND=======: # /usr/bin/lsdev 2>&1
#==========================================================================


#31 Device           DMA   IRQ  I/O Ports
#31 -----------------------------------------------
#31 cascade           4     2
#31 dma                          0080-008f
#31 dma1                         0000-001f
#31 dma2                         00c0-00df
#31 eth0                    11   c2822c00-c2822c7f
#31 fpu                     13   00f0-00ff
#31 ide0                    14   01f0-01f7 03f6-03f6 ffa0-ffa7
#31 ide1                    15   0170-0177 0376-0376 ffa8-ffaf
#31 keyboard                1    0060-006f
#31 Mouse                   12
```

```
#31  pic1                      0020-003f
#31  pic2                      00a0-00bf
#31  rtc              8        0070-007f
#31  serial                    03f8-03ff
#31  timer           0         0040-005f
#31  vga+                      03c0-03df
                                              # View session begins


#========================================================================
1 ====COMMAND=======: # /bin/date 2>&1
#========================================================================


#1 Sat Nov 25 14:27:45 EST 2000


#========================================================================
2 ====COMMAND=======: # /bin/date "+%Z" 2>&1
#========================================================================


#2 EST


#========================================================================
3 ====COMMAND=======: # /bin/hostname 2>&1
#========================================================================


#3 linden


#========================================================================
4 ====COMMAND=======: # /bin/uname -a 2>&1
#========================================================================


:q                                            # End view session
Want to re-execute any of the above commands (y/n)?n
#




# ls -l /root/checkit/checkout                # Baseline file now exists
total 32
-rw-r--r--   1 root     root      32449 Nov 25 14:27
                      sys_check.linden.Good_Output
#
```

Second sys_check Run

The following example shows the second run of the script. It checks for differences in the baseline file created by the first run (shown in the previous

code) and enables the user to view the differences between the baseline file
and the current set of output generated by a run of the script in a view
session:

EXAMPLE

```
# ./sys_check                                              # Begin second run


#========================================================================
1 ====COMMAND=======: # /bin/date 2>&1
#========================================================================


#1 Sat Nov 25 14:30:54 EST 2000


#========================================================================
2 ====COMMAND=======: # /bin/date "+%Z" 2>&1
#========================================================================


#2 EST


#========================================================================
3 ====COMMAND=======: # /bin/hostname 2>&1
#========================================================================


#3 linden


#========================================================================
4 ====COMMAND=======: # /bin/uname -a 2>&1
#========================================================================


#4 Linux linden 2.2.12-20 #1 Mon Sep 27 10:25:54 EDT 1999 i586


    (...)


#========================================================================
31 ====COMMAND=======: # /usr/bin/lsdev 2>&1
#========================================================================


#31 Device          DMA   IRQ  I/O Ports
#31 -------------------------------------------------
#31 cascade          4     2
#31 dma                         0080-008f
#31 dma1                        0000-001f
#31 dma2                        00c0-00df
#31 eth0                   11   c2822c00-c2822c7f
#31 fpu                    13   00f0-00ff
#31 ide0                   14   01f0-01f7 03f6-03f6 ffa0-ffa7
#31 ide1                   15   0170-0177 0376-0376 ffa8-ffaf
```

```
#31 keyboard               1   0060-006f
#31 Mouse                 12
#31 pic1                      0020-003f
#31 pic2                      00a0-00bf
#31 rtc                    8   0070-007f
#31 serial                    03f8-03ff
#31 timer                  0   0040-005f
#31 vga+                      03c0-03df
                                              # View session begins

                  ATTENTION!! THE FOLLOWING HAS CHANGED!!
  Original_File <<<< = /root/checkit/checkout/./sys_check.linden.Good_Output
  Current__File >>>> = /root/checkit/checkout/./sys_check.linden.Current_Output

              !!! You are using view to view this data. (:q to quit) !!!


< #1 Sat Nov 25 14:27:45 EST 2000
.


> #1 Sat Nov 25 14:30:54 EST 2000
.


< #24 /dev/hda8             1612808      46436   1484444   3% /
.


> #24 /dev/hda8             1612808      46468   1484412   3% /
.


< #26 eth0   1500   0   134150       0       0       0   65650       0    0 0 BRU
.


.


< #27 RX packets:134154 errors:0 dropped:0 overruns:0 frame:0
.


< #27 TX packets:65654 errors:0 dropped:0 overruns:0 carrier:0
.


> #27 RX packets:134411 errors:0 dropped:0 overruns:0 frame:0
.


> #27 TX packets:65798 errors:0 dropped:0 overruns:0 carrier:0
.
~
```

```
~
~
:q
Want to re-execute any of the above commands (y/n)?y  # Re-execute request
Which command number? 27
#27 XXXXXXXXXXXXX ifconfig for eth0 XXXXXXXXXXXXXXXXXX
#27 eth0       Link encap:Ethernet  HWaddr 00:20:78:12:70:22
#27 inet addr:192.206.126.84  Bcast:192.206.126.255  Mask:255.255.255.0
#27 UP BROADCAST RUNNING MULTICAST  MTU:1500  Metric:1
#27 RX packets:134452 errors:0 dropped:0 overruns:0 frame:0
#27 TX packets:65821 errors:0 dropped:0 overruns:0 carrier:0
#27 collisions:186 txqueuelen:100
#27 Interrupt:11 Base address:0x2c00
#27
#=========================================================================
Another command (y/n) ? n
#
# ls -l /root/checkit/checkout                    # Three files in directory now
total 68
-rw-r--r--   1 root root 32449 Nov 25 14:30 sys_check.linden.Current_Output
-rw-r--r--   1 root root   914 Nov 25 14:30 sys_check.linden.Diff_File.112500
-rw-r--r--   1 root root 32449 Nov 25 14:27 sys_check.linden.Good_Output
#
```

Numbered Version of `sys_check` Script

The following is the sys_check script with each line numbered. This was
created through vi by typing the :set number command in last line mode:

EXAMPLE

```
# vi sys_check

 1 #!/bin/ksh
 2 #checkout version 1.0 11/25/00
 3 #-----------------------------------------------------------------
 4 #  Define All functions below this comment
 5 #-----------------------------------------------------------------
 6
 7 # Function syntax displays correct syntax for the command line
 8 # when executing this script.
 9
10 function syntax {
11 print -u2 Usage: "${0##*/} [-n] [-h] " \
12 "\n\t -n: Print list of commands to be executed, do not execute." \
13 "\n\t -h: Print help message."
14 exit 1
15 }
16
```

```
17 # Function cleanup is used as a signal handler for CTRL+C and CTRL+\
18 # Also called at normal script termination with argument of 'Norm'
19
20 function cleanup {
21 if [[ -f ${DiffFile}.$$ ]]
22 then
23     rm ${DiffFile}.$$
24 fi
25 [[ $Noexec = 0 ]] && print -u4 "exit" # End coprocess (if it exists)
26 [[ $1 = "Norm" ]] && exit 0          # Check for normal exit
27 exit 99                              # End script with error status
28 }
29
30 # Function locate_command avoids problems with commands being in odd
31 # directories.  It finds the commands for processing.
32
33 function locate_command {
34 loc=$(find /bin /sbin /usr/bin /usr/sbin -name $1 2>/dev/null | head -1)
35 if [[ $? == 0 ]]
36 then print $loc
37 else
38         print ": ; #Can't locate $1 command. "
39 fi
40 }
41
42 # Function 'check_exist' handles cases where the script's files or
   directories
43 # don't exist.  It is not used for the system files.
44
45 function check_exist {
46         if [[ ! -f $1 ]]
47         then
48                 if [[ $2 == "D" ]] then
49                         mkdir -p $1 || { print "Can't make $1"; exit 2; }
50                         return 2
51                 else
52                         :
53                         return 1
54                 #   touch $1 || { print "Can't make $1"; exit 2; }
55                 fi
56         fi
57         return 0
58 }
59
```

```
 60 #------------------------------------------------------------
 61 #  Define All functions above this comment
 62 #------------------------------------------------------------
 63
 64 #------------------------------------------------------------
 65 #  Define All traps
 66 #------------------------------------------------------------
 67
 68 # Funtion cleanup is called when user aborts from sys_check.
 69
 70 trap 'cleanup' INT QUIT
 71
 72 #------------------------------------------------------------
 73 #  Initialize Variables
 74 #------------------------------------------------------------
 75
 76 integer x=0
 77 integer Num=0
 78 integer line_count=0
 79
 80 typeset host=$(hostname)
 81 typeset Program=$0
 82 typeset Noexec=0
 83 typeset dat=$(date +%m%d%y)
 84 typeset FunctionMarker="=FUNCTION="
 85 typeset Headcmd="====COMMAND=======: #"
 86 check_exist "/root/checkit/checkout" "D" # Check directory existence.
 87 typeset OutFile="/root/checkit/checkout/${Program}.${host}.Current_Output"
 88 typeset GoodOutFile="/root/checkit/checkout/${Program}.${host}.Good_Output"
 89 typeset DiffFile="/root/checkit/checkout/${Program}.${host}.Diff_File.${dat}"
 90 typeset CleanMsg="...${Program} ended with no changes"
 91 typeset Separator="#=============================================\
 92 =========================="
 93     # The following typeset uses a 'here document'.
 94 typeset DiffMsg=" $(cat << DATA
 95 \n\t\tATTENTION!!  THE FOLLOWING HAS CHANGED!!
 96 \n  Original_File <<<< =  ${GoodOutFile}
 97 \n  Current__File >>>> =  ${OutFile}
 98 \n\n\t\t  !!! You are using view to view this data. (:q to quit) !!!
 99 \n
100 DATA
101 )
102 "
103
```

```
104 #------------------------------------------------------------------------
105 #  Alias Definitions
106 #------------------------------------------------------------------------
107
108 alias incx="((x=x+1))"
109
110 #------------------------------------------------------------------------
111 #  Main entry point
112 #------------------------------------------------------------------------
113
114 while getopts :nh OPT
115 do
116     case $OPT in
117         n) Noexec=1 ;;
118         h) syntax ;;
119         \?) print -u2 "${0##*/}: unrecognized option \'$OPTARG\'"
120                 syntax;;
121         esac
122 done
123 shift OPTIND-1
124
125 (($# > 1)) && syntax
126
127 #------------------------------------------------------------------------
128 #  Clear output file
129 #------------------------------------------------------------------------
130 rmcmd=$(locate_command "rm")
131 $rmcmd -f ${OutFile} # -f ignores non-existent files, no errors
132
133 #------------------------------------------------------------------------
134 #  Check if the Good Output file has been created
135 #    and if not define it.
136 #------------------------------------------------------------------------
137
138 check_exist ${GoodOutFile}
139 if [[ $? = 1 ]] then
140         OutFile=${GoodOutFile}
141 fi
142
143 #------------------------------------------------------------------------
144 #  Command Array
145 #
146 #  Cmd[x] is the array element holding the command string
147 #  incx - increments the value of x the element by one
148 #
```

```
149 #  If you wish to use a function make sure you place the variable
150 #  ${FunctionMarker} in the Command Array pior to the function name.
151 #     ie  incx;Cmd[x]="${FunctionMarker} Pdisk_to_Hdisk"
152 #  Add other commands using the same format as below.
153 #------------------------------------------------------------------
154
155 #------------------------------------------------------------------
156 #  Command Array section
157 #------------------------------------------------------------------
158 cmd_loc=$(locate_command date)             # 1
159 incx;Cmd[x]="$cmd_loc 2>&1"
160 incx;Cmd[x]="$cmd_loc \"+%Z\" 2>&1"        # 2
161 cmd_loc=$(locate_command hostname)
162 incx;Cmd[x]="$cmd_loc 2>&1"                # 3
163 cmd_loc=$(locate_command uname)
164 incx;Cmd[x]="$cmd_loc -a 2>&1"             # 4
165 cmd_loc=$(locate_command echo)
166 incx;Cmd[x]="$cmd_loc \${PATH} 2>&1"       # 5
167 cmd_loc=$(locate_command cat)
168 incx;Cmd[x]="$cmd_loc /etc/hosts 2>&1"     # 6
169 incx;Cmd[x]="$cmd_loc /etc/fstab 2>&1"     # 7
170 incx;Cmd[x]="$cmd_loc /etc/passwd 2>&1"    # 8
171 incx;Cmd[x]="$cmd_loc /etc/group 2>&1"     # 9
172 incx;Cmd[x]="$cmd_loc /.rhosts 2>&1"       # 10
173 incx;Cmd[x]="$cmd_loc /etc/dhcpd.conf 2>&1"    # 11
174 incx;Cmd[x]="$cmd_loc /etc/inetd.conf 2>&1"    # 12
175 incx;Cmd[x]="$cmd_loc /etc/initlog.conf 2>&1" # 13
176 incx;Cmd[x]="$cmd_loc /etc/lilo.conf 2>&1"     # 14
177 incx;Cmd[x]="$cmd_loc /etc/named.conf 2>&1"    # 15
178 incx;Cmd[x]="$cmd_loc /etc/resolv.conf 2>&1"   # 16
179 incx;Cmd[x]="$cmd_loc /etc/smb.conf 2>&1"      # 17
180 incx;Cmd[x]="$cmd_loc /etc/yp.conf 2>&1"       # 18
181 incx;Cmd[x]="$cmd_loc /etc/ypserv.conf 2>&1"   # 19
182 incx;Cmd[x]="$cmd_loc /etc/aliases 2>&1"       # 20
183 cmd_loc=$(locate_command netstat)          # 21
184 incx;Cmd[x]="$cmd_loc -nr | grep -v \"Kernel IP routing table\" | awk '{
 printf \"%s %s %s %s %s\\\n\", \$1,\$2,\$3,\$4,\$8 }' 2>&1"
185 cmd_loc=$(locate_command cat)
186 incx;Cmd[x]="$cmd_loc /etc/inittab 2>&1"       # 22
187 cmd_loc=$(locate_command mount)            # 23
188 incx;Cmd[x]="$cmd_loc 2>&1"
189 cmd_loc=$(locate_command df)
190 incx;Cmd[x]="$cmd_loc -k 2>&1"             # 24
191 cmd_loc=$(locate_command netstat)          # 25
192 incx;Cmd[x]="$cmd_loc -rn   | awk '{printf \"%s %s %s %s\\\n\", \$1,\$2,
\$3,\$6}' 2>&1"
```

```
193 incx;Cmd[x]="$cmd_loc -in 2>&1"                    # 26
194 cmd_loc=$(locate_command lsdev)                    # 27
195 incx;Cmd[x]="for i in \$($cmd_loc | grep eth | awk '{printf \"%s\\\n\",\
$1}') ; do echo \"XXXXXXXXXXXXX ifconfig for \$i XXXXXXXXXXXXXXXXX\";
      $(locate_command ifconfig) \$i; done 2>&1"
196 cmd_loc=$(locate_command ls)                       # 28
197 incx;Cmd[x]="$cmd_loc /etc/rc.d/init.d 2>&1"
198                                                     # 29
199 incx;Cmd[x]="for i in \$($cmd_loc /var/spool/cron) ; do echo \"XXXXXXXXX
XXXXX cron file \$i XXXXXXXXXXXXXXXXXXXX\";
      cat /var/spool/cron/\$i; done 2>&1"
200 cmd_loc=$(locate_command chkconfig)
201 incx;Cmd[x]="$cmd_loc --list 2>&1"                 # 30
202 cmd_loc=$(locate_command lsdev)
203 incx;Cmd[x]="$cmd_loc 2>&1"                        # 31
204 Num=${x}
205
206
207 #-------------------------------------------------------------------
208 # Check to see if user just wants command list.
209 #-------------------------------------------------------------------
210
211 if [[ $Noexec = "1" ]]
212 then
213         print "\n\nPrinting Commands (not executing)\n\n"
214         for (( x=1 ; x<=Num ; x++ ))
215         do
216                 print "#${x} ${Cmd[${x}]}"
217         done
218         print "\n\n Exiting \n\n"
219         cleanup
220 fi
221
222 #-------------------------------------------------------------------
223 #  If the logic goes here, the user wants the whole enchilada.
224 #  Loop through the previous command array executing each string.
225 #   If the string has the variable ${FunctionMarker} in it then
226 #       run the function
227 #   else
228 #       execute the command string
229 # redirect output to screen and to a file.
230 # This sequence uses a coprocess to execute the commands
231 #       in the command array.
232 #-------------------------------------------------------------------
233
```

```
234 ksh  2>&1 |&                    # Create coprocess running ksh
235 exec 3<&p                       # Use fd 3 to read from ksh
236 exec 4>&p                       # Use fd 4 to write to ksh
237
238 x=0
239 while (( ${x} < ${Num} ))
240 do
241     incx
242     print
243     print ${Separator}          # Displays command to be executed.
244     cmd="${x} ${Headcmd} ${Cmd[${x}]}"
245     print ${cmd}
246     print ${Separator}
247     print
248     print "${Cmd[${x}]}" | grep  ${FunctionMarker} > /dev/null 2>&1
249     if [[ $? = 0 ]]             # Checks for function.
250     then
251         TmpVar=$(print ${Cmd[${x}]} | sed "s/${FunctionMarker}//g")
252         func=${TmpVar}
253         ${func} 2>&1
254     else
255         print -u4 "${Cmd[${x}]}| wc -l" # Give command to ksh coprocess
256         read -u3  line_count           # Read wc output from coprocess
257         print -u4 "${Cmd[${x}]}"       # Redo command without wc
258         for (( ; line_count > 0 ; line_count-- ))
259         do
260                 read -u3  subout        # Read a line of output
261                 print "#${x} $subout"   # Present output to stdout
262         done                            # Handles multiline output in loop
263     fi
264 done  |tee -a  ${OutFile} 2>&1          # Output of while loop piped to tee
265
266 #----------------------------------------------------------------
267 #  if we are creating the Good Output file then view it
268 #    for user validation
269 #  else
270 #    compare the current output file with the Good Output file
271 #    if the files are different
272 #      print ATTN message and VIEW the read-only diff file
273 #----------------------------------------------------------------
274
275 if [[ ${OutFile} = ${GoodOutFile} ]]
276 then
277     view ${OutFile}
278 else
279     diff  ${GoodOutFile} ${OutFile}  > ${DiffFile}.$$ # Create diff file
```

```
280     Rc=$?                                           # Store return code
281     grep -v "< ===" ${DiffFile}.$$ > ${DiffFile}.$$.$$
282     mv ${DiffFile}.$$.$$ ${DiffFile}.$$
283     if [[ ${Rc} = 1 ]]          # diff status 1 means diffs found
284     then
285         print ${DiffMsg} > ${DiffFile}   # Write ATTN message
286         grep -E "ATTENT|<|>" ${DiffFile}.$$| \
287         awk '{
288             if ( substr($0,1,10) == "> ====COMM" )
289                { Cmd_Hdr=$0 }
290             else
291               { print Cmd_Hdr
292                   print $0
293                   print "."
294               }
295           }' >> ${DiffFile}
296
297         view ${DiffFile}
298     fi
299 fi
300
301 read ans?"Want to re-execute any of the above commands (y/n)?"
302
303 while [[ $ans = "y" ]]
304 do
305         read cmdnum?"Which command number? "
306         print -u4 "${Cmd[${cmdnum}]}"  # Give command to ksh coprocess
307         while read -u3 -t1 subout       # Read output from coprocess
308         do
309              print "#${cmdnum} $subout"  # Present output to stdout
310         done                            # Handles multiline output in loop
311         print $Separator
312         read ans?"Another command (y/n) ? "
313 done
314
315 #--------------------------------------------------------------------
316 # Cleanup
317 #--------------------------------------------------------------------
318
319 cleanup "Norm"
320
321 # End of script
```

Comments on Selected sys_check Lines (10–59)

Lines 10–59 define four functions. The syntax function (lines 10–15) is used
when the script discovers some anomaly in the syntax used by the user. It

uses $0 to reference the command (./sys_check) and removes the largest matching left pattern. The result displays sys_check instead of ./sys_check. The print -u2 prints its message to stderr.

The cleanup function is used when a CTRL+C or CTRL+\ is typed to abort the script. It performs certain cleanup activities, such as deleting temporary files and killing the coprocess if necessary. Line 25 checks to see whether the Noexec variable is set to 1, and if it's not, it executes the print -u4 command following the &&. Unit 4 is an open pipeline to the coprocess. It causes the eco-process to terminate. Line 26 checks to see whether this cleanup is due to a normal termination or an abort (CTRL+C) and returns a different exit status in either case.

The locate_command function (lines 33–40) is used to find the location of UNIX commands so that, when they get executed, they provide full file specifications to the shell. This is part of the bulletproofing discussed earlier in the book. It uses the $(comm) form of command expansion to execute the find command and capture the output in a variable. Note that line 36 is not being used to print to stdout, despite what it looks like. When a function is called using the format x=$(func), any output of the function is placed in variable x. See line 167 for an example.

The check_exist function (lines 42–58) checks the existence of sys_check's directories. If the directory does not exist, it is created. Notice the -p option on the mkdir command (line 49), which creates any intermediate directories in the path to the target directory if necessary. Notice also that this function uses a more standard type of return than the locate_command function does. This function returns a number using the return statement. The locate_command function returned a string.

Comments on Selected sys_check Lines (70–102)

Two signals are trapped during the run of the script (line 70), and both signals cause the cleanup function to execute.

Three integer variables are defined on lines 76–78, while other variables are defined on lines 80–102. Lines 80, 83, and 94 use command expansion to develop a value to place in the target variable. Line 93 embeds a here document that is used to create an attention message. The document begins at <<DATA on line 94 and ends at DATA on line 100. As is true with many of the constructs shown in this example, other ways of handling this attention message are available.

Comments on Selected sys_check Lines (108–125)

An alias is created on line 108 to streamline some of the upcoming lines that repetitively increment x by 1.

The getopts while loop (lines 114–122) is used to process the command options. Only two options (-n, -h) exist, as you can see in the syntax on line 114. The selected option is placed in the variable named OPT. The loop processes the variables as they appear on the command line. The third case (line 119) handles illegal options by calling the syntax function.

The shift command on line 123 eliminates the processed portions of the command line. The test on line 125 checks whether the count of remaining items is more than 1. If so, it calls the syntax function.

Comments on Selected sys_check Lines (130–140)

Lines 130 and 131 remove a Current_Output file if it exists at this point. The script will be creating a new Current_Output file. Lines 138–140 check whether the Good_Output file exists, and if it doesn't, sets the Outfile variable to contain the name of the Good_Output file. This is the case when the script is being run for the first time or if the target directory has had all files removed.

Comments on Selected sys_check Lines (144–204)

Lines 144–204 populate an array containing the commands to be executed. You can tinker with this as you see fit. Your needs might dictate that commands different from the ones selected here execute. Use the ideas shown in the script as a template for your needs. Many calls to the locate_command function are available to try to bulletproof the commands. Most commands are terminated with the 2>&1 syntax, which sends the error messages to the same place as stdout. This enables the execution loop to work properly with the coprocess created on line 234. The wc command does not include error messages in its count of lines unless stderr is redirected as shown.

Comments on Selected sys_check Lines (207–220)

The Noexec variable is set to 1 if the -n command-line option is used. Lines 207–220 check whether the user just wants a list of commands with no execution. If so, a for loop is executed to display the commands (lines 214–217). The for loop initializes x to a 1 and checks whether x<=Num. If it does, it executes the print command and then increments x by 1 with the x++ command. When the loop is complete, the cleanup function is called to terminate the script.

Comments on Selected sys_check Lines (222–264)

Lines 222–264 form the heart of the script. They contain a loop that executes the commands stored in the command array. A coprocess is used to maximize the use of the ksh process created on line 234. The syntax to note is the |& that terminates the line. This instructs the shell to create a coprocess, which will run the ksh program. The alternative is to create a new ksh for each command executed. The two exec commands on lines 235 and 236 are used to create channels for input to and output from the coprocess—a small price to pay (in complexity) for the performance benefit gained.

The while loop on lines 239–264 works its way through the array and executes the commands. Note that the output of this loop is piped (line 264) to a tee command, which uses the -a option to provide for an append to the Outfile. Although this script uses no functions in its main loop (everything executed is a command), the syntax on lines 251–253 is prepared to check for functions and react accordingly. This enables you to alter the script such that it executes any functions you might create in the future, if you want.

The command to execute is actually presented twice to the coprocess—once to find out how many lines of output it will generate (line 255) and again to actually generate the output (line 257). The line count is obtained from the coprocess in line 256. It is then used to control the number of passes through the read loop on lines 258–262. All output of the commands is piped to the tee command (line 264) and ultimately ends up in the Current_Output file.

Comments on Selected sys_check Lines (275–281)

If the test on line 275 is true, the script reacts by executing a view command (read-only vi). This is the case when the script is being executed for the first time or after the target directory is emptied. If the test is false, the assumption that the script makes is that the user wants a report on the differences between this run and the previous run (lines 279–299).

The diff command output is placed in a temporary file with the current pid ($$) appended to the end (line 279). Line 280 stores the return code of the diff command for later analysis. The diff command returns a status of 1 if it finds differences. The grep command on line 281 eliminates some of the input file lines from the diff file (-v means invert the meaning, so lines that have < === in them are eliminated).

Comments on Selected `sys_check` Lines (285–319)

Line 285 writes an attention message to the target differences file. The `grep -E` on line 286 eliminates unnecessary `diff` output from the target file by piping its output to an awk filter, which uses the `substr awk` function (line 288) to check whether the first 10 characters match the `> ====COMM` sequence. The idea is to present command identification information as few times as possible.

Line 297 creates a view session to enable the user to get a feel for the differences between the current stats and the baseline stats. Line 301 asks whether the user wants to re-execute any of the commands. The idea is that the user might want to see more than just the lines that are different. He might prefer to see the entire command output. All commands are identified by a number, so all the user has to do is respond appropriately to the prompt (line 305) and the command is presented to the coprocess (which still exists) for processing.

The `while` loop on lines 303–313 continues until the user indicates that he does not want to see any more commands. Upon exit from the loop, the script's logic flows through line 319, where the `cleanup` function is called to terminate the script.

What's Next

Two appendices are included for your perusal. Appendix A, "Useful Commands," presents my comments on some commands that will be useful for you to keep in mind as you go forth and develop your scripts. Not that I'm trying to replace the man pages with Appendix A, but you tend to not get qualitative commentary or subjective appraisals from them. Take a look; maybe you'll find something interesting.

I also have included an appendix on vi (Appendix B, "vi Tutorial") for those who need some help over some of the hurdles vi throws into a UNIX rookie's path. Enjoy.

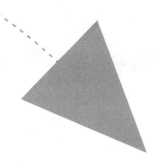

Appendix A

Useful Commands

This appendix documents many commands that you will find useful in your scripts. This is not meant to be a complete list of commands, nor do I include comments on every command option. But I think you will find that the examples are succinct and to the point, that the text is directed to the main facts, and that you will not have to wade through mountains of man pages to get what you want.

Take a look. See what you think. I have included a brief introduction to the command, a syntax summary, details on some of the command's options, a comment on some of the oddities of the command, and an example.

alias

Official Description

Defines or displays aliases.

Syntax

```
alias [-t] [alias-name[=string...]]
```

Options

-t establishes a tracked alias, providing faster alias translation. Allowed only if the trackall shell option is set (set -h or set -o trackall).

Oddities

Some implementations provide a -x option, enabling the exporting of aliases. This also enables aliases to be accessible in subshells.

Some implementations provide a -p option, which causes the word "alias" to appear before each alias name displayed.

Aliasing is performed when scripts are read, not while they are executed. Therefore, for an alias to take effect, the alias definition command must be executed before the command that references the alias is read.

Aliases can be used to redefine special built-in commands but cannot be used to redefine the following reserved words: if, for, case, then, while, esac, else, until, function, elif, do, select, fi, done, time, { }, and [[ ]].

Alias processing is performed after the reserved words listed previously are processed.

C shell alias command does not use the = in its syntax.

Example

EXAMPLE

```
$ alias                    # Red Hat Linux ksh93 alias list
2d='set -f;_2d'
autoload='typeset -fu'
command='command '
fc=hist
float='typeset -E'
functions='typeset -f'
hash='alias -t --'
history='hist -l'
integer='typeset -i'
ll='ls -la'
nameref='typeset -n'
nohup='nohup '
r='hist -s'
redirect='command exec'
```

```
stop='kill -s STOP'
suspend='kill -s STOP $$'
times='{ { time;} 2>&1;}'
type='whence -v'
$
$ alias gg=ls                  # Make an alias named gg
$ gg
!      f2            mbox       ob      oldsedtest1   scripts    sortfile
Mail   hosts         names      obr     oldsedtest2   sedtest1   sortfile2
core   locate_command newfile   obrr    oldsedtest3   sedtest2   symstats
f1     lotsofiles    newfile2   obrrr   regextest     sedtest3   temp
$
$ alias -p                     # List aliases preceded by 'alias'
alias 2d='set -f;_2d'
alias autoload='typeset -fu'
alias command='command '
alias fc=hist
alias float='typeset -E'
alias functions='typeset -f'
alias gg=ls
  (...)
$
$ alias if=ls                  # Alias won't work for shell keyword
$
$ if                           # Alias 'if' exists but won't work
>
$
$ alias gg=ls                  # Make standard alias
$
$ gg                           # Alias 'gg' works
!      f2            mbox       ob      oldsedtest1   scripts    sortfile
Mail   hosts         names      obr     oldsedtest2   sedtest1   sortfile2
core   locate_command newfile   obrr    oldsedtest3   sedtest2   symstats
f1     lotsofiles    newfile2   obrrr   regextest     sedtest3   temp
$
$ alias cat=ls                 # Make alias for 'cat'
$
$ cat                          # Alias cat works
!      f2            mbox       ob      oldsedtest1   scripts    sortfile
Mail   hosts         names      obr     oldsedtest2   sedtest1   sortfile2
core   locate_command newfile   obrr    oldsedtest3   sedtest2   symstats
f1     lotsofiles    newfile2   obrrr   regextest     sedtest3   temp
$
```

autoload

Official Description

autoload is an alias for typeset -fu.

Syntax

```
autoload function_name
```

Options

None

Oddities

autoload enables the shell to recognize a name as a function name (-f) but not bother reading the function until it is actually needed (-u leaves the function undefined). This saves shell processing time in the event that the function is never used during the script run.

Example

EXAMPLE

```
$ cat funca
function funca {
print "In funca"
}
$
$ print $FPATH

$
$ pwd
/home/obrien
$
$ FPATH=/home/obrien          # FPATH variable must include path
                              # of file containing function
$
$ autoload funca              # Make ksh aware of function funca
$
$ typeset -f                  # Not loaded yet
typeset -fu funca
mc()
{
        mkdir -p ~/.mc/tmp 2> /dev/null
        chmod 700 ~/.mc/tmp
        MC=~/.mc/tmp/mc$$-"$RANDOM"
        /usr/bin/mc -P "$@" > "$MC"
        cd "`cat $MC`"
        rm "$MC"
        unset MC;
}
$
```

```
$ funca                         # Use the funca function
In funca
$
$ typeset -f                    # Loaded now
function funca
{
print "In funca"
}
mc()
{
        mkdir -p ~/.mc/tmp 2> /dev/null
        chmod 700 ~/.mc/tmp
        MC=~/.mc/tmp/mc$$-"$RANDOM"
        /usr/bin/mc -P "$@" > "$MC"
        cd "'cat $MC'"
        rm "$MC"
        unset MC;
}
$
```

bg

Official Description

Runs jobs in the background.

Syntax

bg [*job_id...*]

Options

None

Oddities

If no *job_id* is given, the most recently suspended job is used.

Available on systems that support job control.

Used to get a stopped job to resume execution but remain in the background.

Example

EXAMPLE

```
$ cat buzz
#! /bin/ksh
integer x=17
while :
do
x=17
```

```
done
$
$ buzz
[1] + Stopped                 buzz    # Ctrl+Z
$
$ jobs
[1] + Stopped                 buzz    # Job buzz is stopped
$
$ bg %1                                # Get it going in the background
[1]      buzz&
$
$ jobs
[1] +  Running                buzz    # Job buzz is running now,
                                       # in the background
$
```

break

Official Description

Exits from the enclosing for, while, until, or select loop, if any.

Syntax

break [*n*]

Options

None

Oddities

You can supply a number (*n*) indicating how many levels of nesting to break out of.

Might not have its own man page. Look in ksh man page for information.

Example

EXAMPLE

```
$ cat buzz1
#! /bin/ksh
integer x=17
while :                    # Potentially infinite loop
do
x=x+1
if (( x>20 ))
then
        break              # Break out when x>20
fi
done
print $x
$
```

```
$ buzz1
21
$
$
$ cat buzz2
#! /bin/ksh
integer x=17
integer y=0
for (( y=0; y<5; y++ ))      # Outer loop
do
        while :             # Inner loop
        do
        x=x+1
        if (( x>20 ))
        then
                break 2     # Break out of both
        fi
        done
done
print $x
print $y
$
$ buzz2
21
0
$
```

builtin

Official Description

Displays the names of commands built into the shell itself. Allows C language function extensions to the shell.

Syntax

```
builtin [-ds] [-f file] [path/basename]
```

Options

-f *file* names a shared library file containing built-in functions.

-d deletes a built-in.

-s displays special built-ins.

Oddities

Available in ksh93 and beyond.

Example

EXAMPLE

```
$ builtin | wc -l          # Count of built-in commands
      61
$
$ builtin -s | wc -l       # Count of special built-in commands
      19
$
$ builtin | head -5        # Lists several built-ins
:
.
[
alarm
alias
$
$ builtin -s | head -5     # Lists several special built-ins
:
.
alias
break
continue
$
```

case

Official Description

Executes the list associated with the first pattern that matches the word.

Syntax

case *word* in [[(] *pattern* [| *pattern*] ...) *list* ;;] ... esac

Options

None

Oddities

The form of the patterns is the same as that used for filename generation.

Example

EXAMPLE

```
$ x=21                     # Set value of x to 21
$
$ case $x in               # Use case to check various values
> 2 )
> print 2 ;;
> 17 )
> print 17 ;;
> 21 )
> print 21 ;;
```

```
> * )
> print huh
> esac
21                               # Correctly finds the 21
$
```

cat

Official Description

Concatenates or displays files.

Syntax

```
cat [-benstvA] file... | -
```

Options

-A shows all.

-b numbers nonblank output lines.

-e shows $ at the end of lines.

-n numbers all output lines.

-s means squeeze-blank; never more than one single blank line.

-t shows tabs as ^I.

-v shows characters that typically do not print.

With no *file*, or when *file* is -, it reads standard input.

Oddities

Used to create small files (cat > xx).

Example

EXAMPLE

```
$ cat -n buzz                    # Numbers the output lines
    1  #! /bin/ksh
    2  integer x=17
    3  while :
    4  do
    5  x=17
    6  done
$
$ cat > small                    # Create small file
junk
more junk                        # Ctrl+D to end the input (at beginning of next line)
$
$ cat small
```

```
junk
more junk
$
$ cat -e small                   # Indicate line ends with $
junk$
more junk$
$
```

cd

Official Description

Changes the current working directory.

Syntax

cd [*directory*]

Options

None

Oddities

C shell cd command is slightly different.

You must have execute (search) permission in the specified directory to cd
to it.

If - is specified as the directory, the cd command changes your current
(working) directory to the directory name saved in the environment variable OLDPWD.

Example

EXAMPLE

```
$ cd /tmp
$
$ print $OLDPWD               # Previous directory is held in OLDPWD
/home/obrien
$
$ cd /etc
$
$ print $OLDPWD
/tmp
$
$ pwd
/etc
$
$ cd -                        # Uses contents of OLDPWD
/tmp
$
$ pwd
```

```
/tmp
$
$ cd                        # Uses contents of $HOME
$
$ pwd
/home/obrien
$
```

chmod

Official Description

Changes file-access permissions.

Syntax

```
chmod [option] mode file(s)
```

Options

-R causes chmod to recursively descend its directory arguments, setting the mode for each file.

-f suppresses most error messages; forces the change.

-v stands for verbose and outputs a diagnostic for every file processed.

Oddities

Has a numeric form (755) and a mnemonic form (ug+x).

Example

EXAMPLE

```
$ ls -l buzz
-rwxrwxr--   1 obrien    obrien         47 Nov 26 12:19 buzz
$
$ chmod o+x buzz           # Add execute access for others
$
$ ls -l buzz
-rwxrwxr-x   1 obrien    obrien         47 Nov 26 12:19 buzz
$
$ chmod 007 buzz           # No access for user and group,
                           # all access to others
$
$ ls -l buzz
-------rwx   1 obrien    obrien         47 Nov 26 12:19 buzz
$
$ buzz                     # Others can execute, user (owner) is denied
-ksh: buzz: cannot execute [Permission denied]
$
$ chmod u+x buzz           # Add execute access for user (owner)
$
```

```
$ ls -l buzz
---x---rwx   1 obrien   obrien          47 Nov 26 12:19 buzz
$
$ buzz                        # Owner can't read, read is necessary to execute
buzz: buzz: cannot open [Permission denied]
$
$ chmod u+r buzz              # Add read access for user (owner)
$
$ ls -l buzz
-r-x---rwx   1 obrien   obrien          47 Nov 26 12:19 buzz
$
$ buzz                        # Now the script works (Ctrl+C to end)
$
$
$ chmod g=w buzz              # Sets group to stated value (-w-)
$
$ ls -l buzz
-r-x-w-rwx   1 obrien   obrien          47 Nov 26 12:19 buzz
$
$ chmod o=rx buzz             # Sets others to stated value (r-x)
$
$ ls -l buzz
-r-x-w-r-x   1 obrien   obrien          47 Nov 26 12:19 buzz
$
```

command

Official Description

Executes command and eliminates functions from search order.

Syntax

`command [-pvV] command_to_be_executed [args_to_command...]`

Options

-p uses the PATH variable to locate command.

-vV both request that the whence command be used to locate the command to be executed.

Oddities

Available in ksh93 and beyond.

Example

EXAMPLE

```
$ function ls {          # Create function named ls (executes date command)
> date
> }
$
$ ls                     # Function ls is found before ls command
Sun Nov 26 13:55:57 EST 2000
$
$ command ls             # The command command says execute the command,
                         # not the function
!      core   locate_command  newfile2  oldsedtest1  sedtest1  sortfile2
Mail   f1     lotsofiles       ob        oldsedtest2  sedtest2  symstats
buzz   f2     mbox             obr       oldsedtest3  sedtest3  temp
buzz1  funca  names            obrr      regextest    small
buzz2  hosts  newfile          obrrr     scripts      sortfile
$
$ command -V ls          # Sees ls as a function
ls is a function
$
$ ls
Sun Nov 26 13:57:41 EST 2000
$
$ unset -f ls            # Removes ls as a function
$
$ ls                     # Back in shape now
!      core   locate_command  newfile2  oldsedtest1  sedtest1  sortfile2
Mail   f1     lotsofiles       ob        oldsedtest2  sedtest2  symstats
buzz   f2     mbox             obr       oldsedtest3  sedtest3  temp
buzz1  funca  names            obrr      regextest    small
buzz2  hosts  newfile          obrrr     scripts      sortfile
$
$ command -V ls          # May be different on your system
ls is a tracked alias for /bin/ls
$
```

continue

Official Description

Resumes the next iteration of the enclosing for, while, until, or select loop.

Syntax

continue[*n*]

Options

None

Oddities

If *n* is specified, it resumes at the nth enclosing loop.

Example

EXAMPLE

```
$ cat buzz3
#! /bin/ksh
integer x=17
while (( x<25 ))
do
x=x+1
if (( x==21 ))
then
        print "x>20"
        continue            # Prints message when x=21,
                            # then continues the loop
fi
done
print $x
$
$ buzz3
x>20
25                          # Note that x contains 25,
                            # proving that the loop finished
$
$
$ cat buzz4                 # Contains nested loops
#! /bin/ksh
integer x=17
integer y=0
for (( y=0; y<5; y++ ))
do
        while (( x<25 ))
        do
        x=x+1
        if (( x=21 ))
        then
                continue 2  # Ends this pass through inner loop,
                            # but continues outer loop
        fi
        done
done
print $x
print $y
$
```

```
$ buzz4
21
5                                  # Note that the value of y has progressed to 5.
$
```

cp

Official Description

Copies files.

Syntax

cp [-fipr] [--] *source destination*

Options (not a complete list)

-f does not prompt you when an existing file is to be overwritten (not available in all UNIX variants).

-i prompts you with the name of the file whenever the copy would cause an existing file to be overwritten.

-p preserves metadata (permissions, ownership, dates, and so on).

-r, when the source is a directory, copies the directory and the entire subtree connected at that point.

Oddities

Do not give the destination the same name as one of the source files.

If you specify a directory as the destination, the directory must already exist.

Example

EXAMPLE

```
$ ls -l buzz4
-rwxrwxr--  1 obrien   obrien          165 Nov 26 14:08 buzz4
                                              # Note date and time
$
$ cp buzz4 /tmp                               # Normal copy
$
$ ls -l /tmp/buzz4
                                              # Time has changed
-rwxrwxr--  1 obrien   obrien          165 Nov 26 14:23 /tmp/buzz4
$
$ ls -l buzz4
-rwxrwxr--  1 obrien   obrien          165 Nov 26 14:08 buzz4
                                              # Original file date
$
$ cp -p buzz4 /tmp
                                              # Use preserve option
```

```
$
$ ls -l /tmp/buzz4
                                        # Date is unchanged
-rwxrwxr--   1 obrien    obrien         165 Nov 26 14:08 /tmp/buzz4
$
```

cut

Official Description

Displays specified parts from each line of a file.

Syntax

```
cut -b list [file...]
cut -c list [file...]
cut -f list [-d delim] [-s] [file...]
```

Options

-b *list* cuts based on a list of bytes (not available on all UNIX variants).

-c *list* cuts based on a list of characters.

-d *delim* uses the specified character as the field delimiter.

-f *list* specifies a list of fields assumed to be separated in the file by a field delimiter character.

-s suppresses lines that do not contain delimiter characters.

Oddities

If you do not specify a file or you specify a hyphen (-), the cut command reads standard input.

To change the order of columns in a file, use the cut and paste commands.

On Red Hat Linux, ksh93, cut is a shell built-in version of /usr/bin/cut.

Example

EXAMPLE

```
$ cat /etc/passwd              # Standard password file
root:x:0:0:root:/root:/bin/ksh
bin:x:1:1:bin:/bin:
daemon:x:2:2:daemon:/sbin:
adm:x:3:4:adm:/var/adm:
lp:x:4:7:lp:/var/spool/lpd:
sync:x:5:0:sync:/sbin:/bin/sync
shutdown:x:6:0:shutdown:/sbin:/sbin/shutdown
halt:x:7:0:halt:/sbin:/sbin/halt
mail:x:8:12:mail:/var/spool/mail:
news:x:9:13:news:/var/spool/news:
```

```
uucp:x:10:14:uucp:/var/spool/uucp:
operator:x:11:0:operator:/root:
games:x:12:100:games:/usr/games:
gopher:x:13:30:gopher:/usr/lib/gopher-data:
ftp:x:14:50:FTP User:/home/ftp:
nobody:x:99:99:Nobody:/:
xfs:x:100:101:X Font Server:/etc/X11/fs:/bin/false
gdm:x:42:42::/home/gdm:/bin/bash
obrien:x:500:500:Dennis O'Brien:/home/obrien:/bin/ksh
$
$ cut -f 1,5 -d : /etc/passwd        # Cuts and displays fields 1 and 5,
                                     # delimited by :
root:root
bin:bin
daemon:daemon
adm:adm
lp:lp
sync:sync
shutdown:shutdown
halt:halt
mail:mail
news:news
uucp:uucp
operator:operator
games:games
gopher:gopher
ftp:FTP User
nobody:Nobody
xfs:X Font Server
gdm:
obrien:Dennis O'Brien
$
```

date

Official Description

Prints or sets the system date and time.

Syntax

```
date [-u] [+field_descriptor ...]
```

Options

-u uses a different time zone (Greenwich Mean Time).

Oddities

Can be used by the root user to set the system date and time.

Many field descriptors are available, several of which are listed here:

- %a—Locale's abbreviated weekday name (Sun–Sat)
- %A—Locale's full weekday name, variable length (Sunday–Saturday)
- %b—Locale's abbreviated month name (Jan–Dec)
- %B—Locale's full month name, variable length (January–December)
- %c—Locale's date and time format (Sat Nov 04 12:02:33 EST 1989)
- %d—Day of month (01–31)
- %j—Day of year (001–366)

Example

EXAMPLE

```
$ date
Sun Nov 26 15:38:32 EST 2000
$
$ print "$(date) is day number $(date +%j) of the year."
Sun Nov 26 15:38:48 EST 2000 is day number 331 of the year.
$
```

disown

Official Description

Prevents ksh from sending a HUP signal to existing jobs when the login process ends.

Syntax

disown [*job*...]

Options

None

Oddities

Available in ksh93 and beyond.

Performs the same function as the nohup command, but it is used after the target command has already started.

Example

EXAMPLE

```
$ buzz&
[1]     3994
$
$ jobs
[1] + Running                 buzz&
$
```

```
$ ps laxw | grep buzz
000   500  3994  3993  12   4  1812  840  -      RN  pts/0      0:13 ksh buzz
$
$ disown %1                   # The buzz job will keep running after logout.
```

echo

Official Description

Writes its arguments to standard output.

Syntax

```
echo [-n] [string...]
```

Options

-n requests that no newline is added to the output.

Oddities

Many special characters are recognized (such as \n, which means newline; \t, which means tab; and so on).

echo is not as portable as the print built-in command.

Example

EXAMPLE

```
$ type echo               # Echo is built into some implementations of ksh
echo is a shell built-in
$
$ echo -n "What now? "    # The built-in does not recognize the -n option
-n What now?
$
$ whereis echo            # The echo program is in /bin
echo: /bin/echo /usr/man/man1/echo.1
$
$ /bin/echo -n "What now? "  # It recognizes the -n option
What now? $                # Note that the prompt appears on the same line
$
```

ed

Official Description

The ed command is a line editing program.

Syntax

```
ed [-p string] [-s] [file]
```

Options

-p *string* sets the ed prompt to *string*.

-s suppresses diagnostics (which is useful for scripts).

Oddities

The default for string is null (no prompt).

Example

EXAMPLE

```
$ cat buzz
#! /bin/ksh
integer x=17
while :
do
x=17
done
$
$ ed buzz                    # Use ed to edit the buzz file
47                           # Character count is automatically displayed
2                            # Command 2 means display line 2
integer x=17
s/17/23/                     # Changes the 17 to a 23
2                            # Redisplay line 2
integer x=23
3                            # Display line 3
while :
q
?                            # Editor displays a ? when confused
q                            # Quit the editor, (w saves changes)
$
$ cat -n buzz
     1  #! /bin/ksh
     2  integer x=17
     3  while :
     4  do
     5  x=17
     6  done
$
```

eval

Official Description

The arguments are read as input to the shell, and the resulting command(s) is executed.

Syntax

```
eval [ arg ... ]
```

Options

None

Oddities

Evaluates arguments, forms a command, and executes the command.

Example

EXAMPLE

```
$ search=num
$ num=17
$ eval print /'$'$search/ | ed - buzz   # $search evals to num, $num evals to 17
integer x=17
$
$ unset num
$ eval print /'$'$search/ | ed - buzz
?
$
```

exec

Official Description

If an argument is given, the command specified by the argument is executed in place of this shell without creating a new process.

Syntax

```
exec [argument ...]
```

Options

-c clears variables before execution.

-a assigns a different name to the command being run.

Oddities

Options -a and -c are available in ksh93 and beyond.

If no arguments are given, the effect of this command is to modify file descriptors through redirection.

File descriptors > 2 opened with exec are closed when the shell exits.

Example

EXAMPLE

```
$ ksh                       # Create new ksh
$
$ print $$                  # Display pid
4088
$
$ exec csh                  # Use exec to run a different shell
%
%echo $$                    # Note pid is the same
4088
%
%ksh                        # Run a different shell without using exec
$
$ print $$                  # Note different pid
4089
$

$ exec 6<buzz               # Open acees to file named buzz using fd unit 6
$
$ read -u6 line             # Read first line into variable named line
$
$ print $line               # Display
#! /bin/ksh
$
$ read -u6 line             # Read and display more lines
$ print $line
integer x=17
$ read -u6 line
$ print $line
while :
$
$ exec 6<&-                 # Close access to buzz file
$
$ read -u6 line             # Read fails now
ksh: read: bad file unit number
$
```

exit

Official Description

Causes the shell to exit with the exit status specified by n.

Syntax

exit [*n*]

Options

None

Oddities

If *n* is omitted, the exit status is that of the last command executed.

The $? variable is changed after each command, including null commands (carriage returns).

Example

EXAMPLE

```
$ print $$                # Current pid
3972
$
$ ksh                     # Make child process
$
$ print $$                # Child pid
4128
$
$ exit 5                  # Exit from child with failing status
$ print $?
5                         # Display status
$
```

export

Official Description

Variable names are marked for automatic export to the environment of sub-sequently executed commands.

Syntax

export [*name*[=*value* ...]]

Options

-p displays variables preceded by export.

Oddities

Similar to typeset -x.

Example

EXAMPLE

```
$ myvar=den               # Create local variable
$
$ print $myvar            # Display contents
den
$
```

```
$ ksh                      # Create new shell process
$
$ print $myvar             # Variable myvar is local to parent shell

$
$ exit                     # Back to parent shell
$
$ print $myvar             # Still available
den
$
$ export myvar             # Make it an environment variable
$
$ print $myvar             # Looks the same
den
$
$ ksh                      # Create new shell
$
$ print $myvar             # Variable is available
den
$
$ exit                     # Exit from child shell
$
$ export -p                # List exported variables preceded by 'export'
export _=ksh
export HISTFILESIZE=1000
export HISTSIZE=1000
export HOME=/home/obrien
export HOSTNAME=linden
export INPUTRC=/etc/inputrc
export LANG=en_US
export LC_ALL=en_US
export LINGUAS=en_US
export LOGNAME=obrien
export MAIL=/var/spool/mail/obrien
export myvar=den
export PATH=/usr/local/bin:/bin:/usr/bin:/usr/X11R6/bin:.
export PS1='$ '
export PWD=/home/obrien
export SHELL=/bin/ksh
export TERM=vt320
export USER=obrien
$
$ export                   # Simply list the variables
_=-p
HISTFILESIZE=1000
HISTSIZE=1000
HOME=/home/obrien
HOSTNAME=linden
```

```
INPUTRC=/etc/inputrc
LANG=en_US
LC_ALL=en_US
LINGUAS=en_US
LOGNAME=obrien
MAIL=/var/spool/mail/obrien
myvar=den
PATH=/usr/local/bin:/bin:/usr/bin:/usr/X11R6/bin:.
PS1='$ '
PWD=/home/obrien
SHELL=/bin/ksh
TERM=vt320
USER=obrien
$
```

false

Official Description

The false command returns a nonzero exit value.

Syntax

false

Options

None

Oddities

Typically used to check for nonzero exit status.

Can be considered a do-nothing, unsuccessful command.

Example

EXAMPLE

```
$ until false          # Keeps looping until false returns true
                       # (never happens)
> do
> date
> done
Sun Nov 26 17:38:22 EST 2000
Sun Nov 26 17:38:22 EST 2000
    (...)
CTRL+C
```

fc

Official Description

Allows the user to fix previously executed commands through command-line editing.

Syntax

```
fc [-r] [-e editor] [first [last]]
fc -l [-nr] [first [last]]
fc -s [old=new] [command ]
```

Options

-r reverses the search order.

-e enables you to choose a different editor (the default is ed).

-l lists previous commands.

-n does not display command numbers for previous commands.

-s substitutes *new* for *old* in the command (*old* is the old string to be replaced by the *new* string).

Oddities

Typically performed using a command-line editor.

The history command is an alias for fc: history='fc -l'.

The r command (recall) is an alias for fc: r='fc -e -'.

Example

EXAMPLE

```
$ fc -l
1412    print $myvar
1413    ksh
1414    print $myvar
1415    exit
1416    print $myvar
1417    export myvar
1418    print $myvar
1419    ksh
1420    print $myvar
1421    exit
1422    export -p
1423    export
1424    man false
```

```
1425    until false
        do
        date
        done
1426    fc -l
1427    fc -l
$ fc -ln
        ksh
        print $myvar
        exit
        print $myvar
        export myvar
        print $myvar
        ksh
        print $myvar
        exit
        export -p
        export
        man false
        until false
        do
        date
        done
        fc -l
        fc -l
        fc -ln
$
```

fg

Official Description

Runs jobs in the foreground.

Syntax

fg [*job_id*...]

Options

None

Oddities

The C shell has its own version of fg.

It's useful for jobs that are in the background and need to be brought to the foreground for input processing.

EXAMPLE

Example

```
$ cd /tmp
$
$ /bin/rm -i *&              # Do a rm -I command in the background
[1]     4272
$ in/rm: remove 'buzz4'? $
[1] + Stopped (SIGTTIN)        /bin/rm -i *&
$
$ jobs                       # Command is stopped and in the background
[1] + Stopped (SIGTTIN)        /bin/rm -i *&
$
$ fg %1                      # Bring command to the foreground
/bin/rm -i *
n
/bin/rm: remove 'dentest1'? n # Respond to its needs
/bin/rm: diffs: is a directory
/bin/rm: remove write-protected file 'difftemp2'? n
/bin/rm: remove 'junk'? n
(CTRL+C)                        # Stopped the rm command with a Ctrl+C
$
```

find

Official Description

Searches for files in a directory hierarchy.

Syntax

find [*path*...] [*expression*]

Options

-atime *number* returns TRUE if the file was accessed in the past *number* of days.

-ctime *number* returns TRUE if the file inode was changed in the past *number* of days.

-exec *command*\; returns TRUE if the command runs and returns a 0 (zero) value as the exit status. The command parameter { } is replaced by the current pathname.

-follow causes symbolic links to be followed.

-fstype *type* returns TRUE if the filesystem to which the file belongs is of the type type.

-group *group* returns TRUE if the file belongs to group.

-i *number* returns TRUE if the file has the specified inode number.

`-inum` *number* returns TRUE if the file has the specified inode number.

`-ls` causes the pathname to be printed along with its associated statistics (not available on all UNIX variants).

`-mtime` *number* returns TRUE if the file was modified in the past *number* of days.

`-name` *file* returns TRUE if *file* matches the filename.

`-newer` *file* returns TRUE if the current file was modified more recently than the file indicated by *file*.

`-perm` *octal_number* returns TRUE if the file permission code of the file exactly matches `octal_number` (for example, `-perm 777`).

`-print` causes the current pathname to be displayed.

`-size` *number* returns TRUE if the file is *number* blocks long (512 bytes per block).

`-size` *number*c returns TRUE if the file is *number* bytes long.

`-size` *number*k returns TRUE if the file is *number* kilobytes long.

`-type` *type* returns TRUE if the file type is of the specified type.

`-user` *user* returns TRUE if the file belongs to *user*.

`-xdev` causes `find` not to traverse down a filesystem different from the one on which the current pathname resides. Note that System V UNIX variants may provide `-mount` instead of `-xdev`.

Oddities

`find` has its own anarchistic syntax, unlike all other commands, and follows its own set of rules.

Example

EXAMPLE

```
$ find /bin -perm -4000       # Finds files with the setuid bit set in /bin
/bin/su
/bin/mount
/bin/umount
/bin/ping
$
$ ls -l /bin/mount            # Note setuid bit (rws)
-rwsr-xr-x   1 root     root        53620 Sep 13  1999 /bin/mount
$
$ find / -perm -4000 2>/dev/null | wc -l
     42                       # There are 42 programs with the setuid bit set
$
```

float

Official Description

Declares a variable as floating-point storage (allows a decimal point).

Syntax

```
float [variable[=value]]
```

Options

None

Oddities

Not available prior to ksh93.

`float` is an alias for `typeset -E`.

Example

EXAMPLE

```
$ float                    # No floats declared yet
$
$ float hourly=4.98        # Declare hourly as a float
$
$ float                    # Displays current floats
hourly=4.98
$
$ hourly=hourly+2          # Can do float arithmetic
$
$ print $hourly            # Display result
6.98
$
```

for

Official Description

Begins a for loop.

Syntax

```
for identifier [in word...] ;do list ;done
for (( initializer; test; increment ))
```

Options

None

Oddities

The second format is not available prior to ksh93.

Example

EXAMPLE

```
$ ls b*
buzz  buzz1  buzz2  buzz3  buzz4
$
$ for x in b*              # Each loop pass is made with a new filename
                          # in variable x
> do
> print $x
> done
buzz
buzz1
buzz2
buzz3
buzz4
$
```

function

Official Description

Defines a function that is referenced by *identifier*.

Syntax

```
function identifier {list;}
identifier () {list;}
```

Options

None

Oddities

function executes more quickly than a separate script execution.

Example

EXAMPLE

```
$ function funcy {        # Create function named funcy
> print den
> }
$
$ funcy                   # Execute function
den
$
$ integer count=0
$ time while (( count<1000 ))
> do
> count=count+1
```

```
> funcy                      # Time function called 1000 times
> done > /dev/null

real    0m0.24s
user    0m0.25s
sys     0m0.00s
$
$ cat do_funcy              # Script mimicking function
#! /bin/ksh
print den
$
$ count=0
$
$ time while (( count<1000 ))
> do
> count=count+1
> . do_funcy               # Execute script 1000 times
> done > /dev/null

real    0m0.79s            # Over twice as slow
user    0m0.58s
sys     0m0.20s
$
```

getconf

Official Description

Displays system configuration variable values.

Syntax

getconf [-v *specification*] *system_var*

Options

None

Oddities

Most systems have system specific utilities to gather this information.

Example

EXAMPLE

```
$ getconf CLK_TCK          # Get specific configuration values
100
$
$ getconf CHILD_MAX
999
$
$ getconf                  # Get all configuration values
```

```
ABI_AIO_XFER_MAX=undefined
ABI_ASYNCHRONOUS_IO=undefined
ABI_ASYNC_IO=undefined
AIO_LISTIO_MAX=4294967295
_POSIX_AIO_LISTIO_MAX=2
AIO_MAX=4294967295
    (...)

$
```

getopts

Official Description

Parses command-line options (such as -x).

Syntax

getopts *optstring name* [arg...]

Options

None

Oddities

Can be flaky. I've had some incompatibilities with the Bourne shell in the past—none recently, though.

Example

Chapter 13, "Pulling It All Together," has an example of using getopts.

grep

Official Description

Searches a file for patterns.

Syntax

grep [-E | -F] [-c | -l | -q] [-bhinsvwxy]
[-p*paragraph_separator*] -e *pattern_list* [-e *pattern_list*]...
[-f *pattern_file*]... [*file*...]

Options

-E functions as an egrep command.

-F functions as an fgrep command.

-c shows a count of matching lines.

-i ignores case.

-l lists filenames.

-v inverts the meaning of the search.

Oddities

The grep command looks to stdin for the data through which to search.

Example

EXAMPLE

```
$ cat buzz
#! /bin/ksh
integer x=17
while :
do
x=17
done
$
$ cat buzz | grep 17        # Looks through piped data for 17
integer x=17
x=17
$ ls | grep buzz            # Looks through piped data for buzz
buzz
buzz1
buzz2
buzz3
buzz4
$ ls | grep 17              # Looks through piped data for 17, not there
$
$ grep 17 buzz              # Looks for 17 in the buzz file
integer x=17
x=17
$
$ grep -v 17 buzz           # Looks for lines that do not contain a 17
#! /bin/ksh
while :
do
done
$
```

hash

Official Description

Remembers or reports utility locations.

Syntax

```
hash [utility]
```

Options

-r forgets remembered locations.

Oddities

The hash command is an alias for alias -t. It sets up tracked aliases. (Not heavily used because processor speeds and caching strategies eliminate the penalty of multiple PATH lookups.)

Example

EXAMPLE

```
$ hash                      # Nothing remembered yet
$
$ hash ls                   # Remember the location of ls
$
$ hash                      # In the list now
ls=/bin/ls
$
$ hash cat                  # Location of cat will be remembered also
$
$ hash                      # Both in the hash list
cat=/bin/cat
ls=/bin/ls
$
$ hash -r                   # Refresh the list
$
$ hash                      # Names are known, locations aren't
cat
ls
$
```

hist

Official Description

Defines or displays aliases.

Syntax

hist [-E editor] [-lnr] [command range]

Options

-l lists 16 commands.

-n does not show command numbers.

-r Reverses display order.

Oddities

Command editing is typically done by emacs or vi.

Example

EXAMPLE

```
$ ls -l buzz3
-rwxrwxr--   1 obrien    obrien          116 Nov 26 14:07 buzz3
$
$ hist -s zz3=zz4              # Make a change and re-execute
ls -l buzz4
-rwxrwxr--   1 obrien    obrien          165 Nov 26 14:08 buzz4
$
$ hist -l                      # Last 16 commands
1045    ls | grep buzz
1046    ls | grep 17
1047    grep 17 buzz
1048    grep -v 17 buzz
1049    hash
1050    hash ls
1051    hash
1052    hash cat
1053    hash
1054    hash -r
1055    hash
1056    man hist
1057    ls -l buzz3
1058    ls -l buzz4
1059    ls -l buzz4
1060
```

history

Official Description

Lists the last 16 commands you executed.

Syntax

```
history
```

Options

None

Oddities

history is an alias for fc -l.

Example

EXAMPLE

```
$ history
1047    grep 17 buzz
1048    grep -v 17 buzz
1049    hash
1050    hash ls
1051    hash
1052    hash cat
1053    hash
1054    hash -r
1055    hash
1056    man hist
1057    ls -l buzz3
1058    ls -l buzz4
1059    ls -l buzz4
1060    hist -l
1061    man history
1062    history
$
```

if

Official Description

Executes the list following `if` and, if it returns a 0 (zero) exit status, executes the list following the first `then`.

Syntax

if *list* ;then *list* [elif *list* ;then *list*] ... [;else *list*] ;fi

Options

None

Oddities

At least one command must appear between the `then` and the `fi` (it can be a : if you want it to do nothing).

Place numeric tests in `(( ))`; place string tests in `[[ ]]`.

Example

EXAMPLE

```
$ x=12
$
$ if (( x == 12 ))
> then
> print "equal"
> else
> print "not equal"
```

```
> fi
equal
$
```

integer

Official Description

Declares a variable as an integer.

Syntax

```
integer [variable[=value]]
```

Options

None

Oddities

`integer` is an alias for `typeset -i`.

Makes calculations faster. Shell has to convert strings to integers before performing a calculation.

Example

EXAMPLE

```
$ a=17
$ b=22
$
$ time for (( i=0; i<1000; i++ ))
> do
> (( c = $a + $b ))         # Do calculations using strings
> done

real    0m0.26s
user    0m0.26s
sys     0m0.00s
$
$ integer d e f             # Declare variables as integers
$
$ d=17
$ e=22
$
$  time for (( i=0; i<1000; i++ ))
> do
> (( f = e + d ))           # Do calculations using integers
> done

real    0m0.16s             # Much faster
```

```
user    0m0.16s
sys     0m0.00s
$
```

jobs

Official Description

Displays the status of jobs in the current session.

Syntax

jobs [-l | -p] [-p] *job_id*...

Options

-l provides more information about each job listed.

-p displays only the process ID.

-n displays jobs that have stopped, exited, or otherwise had a change of status.

Oddities

Can optionally specify jobs with %*string*, where *string* is some characters from the beginning of the name of the command being run within the job.

Example

EXAMPLE

```
$ buzz&                    # Start two background jobs
[1]     901
$ buzz&
[2]     902
$
$ jobs                     # Display jobs
[2] +  Running                 buzz&
[1] -  Running                 buzz&
$
$ jobs -l                  # Include pids
[2] + 902      Running                 buzz&
[1] - 901      Running                 buzz&
$
$ jobs -p                  # Display pids only
902
901
```

kill

Official Description

Sends a signal to a running process.

Syntax

```
kill [-signal_name  | signal_number] process_ID...
```

Options

-l lists all signals.

-n *num* sends the specified signal number.

-s *name* sends the specified signal name.

Oddities

The kill 0 command terminates all your background processes.

Example

EXAMPLE

```
$ buzz &                    # Create three background jobs
[1]      913
$ buzz&
[2]      914
$ buzz&
[3]      915
$
$ jobs -l                   # Display the jobs
[3] + 915        Running              buzz&
[2] - 914        Running              buzz&
[1]   913        Running              buzz &
$
$ kill -n 2 914             # Send signal # 2 to pid 914
$
[2] -                       buzz&
$
$ jobs -l                   # Two jobs left
[3] + 915        Running              buzz&
[1] - 913        Running              buzz &
$
$ kill 0                    # Eliminate all background jobs
[3] + Terminated            buzz&
[1] - Terminated            buzz &
$
$ jobs -l                   # Gone
$
```

[

Official Description

Begins a comparison.

Syntax

```
[ expression ]
```

Options

-a can be used as a logical and operator in compound tests.

-o can be used as a logical or operator in compound tests.

Oddities

It has pretty much been replaced by the [[ ]] command.

It's similar to the test command.

Example

EXAMPLE

```
$ [ -x buzz ]
$ echo $?
0                            # buzz is executable
$
$ [ -x core ]
$ echo $?
1                            # core is not executable
$
```

let

Official Description

Performs arithmetic evaluations.

Syntax

```
let argument ...
```

Options

None

Oddities

((...)) is equivalent to let "...".

Example

EXAMPLE

```
$ let f=d+e
$
$ print $f
39
$
$ print $d
17
```

```
$ print $e
22
$
```

ln

Official Description

Makes a hard link or a symbolic link to a file.

Syntax

```
ln [-fs] sourcename [targetname]
```

Options

-f forces the removal of the existing target pathnames.

-s creates symbolic links. Symbolic links are sometimes referred to as *soft* links.

-n can be included to prevent the creation of the link if the target already exists.

Oddities

Hard links will not work beyond file system boundaries, nor will they work for directories.

Example

EXAMPLE

```
$ ln -s buzz ln_buzz          # Make symbolic link to buzz
$
$ ls -l ln_buzz
lrwxrwxrwx   1 obrien    obrien          4 Nov 27 08:24 ln_buzz -> buzz
$
$ ls -lL ln_buzz
-r-x-w-r-x   1 obrien    obrien         47 Nov 26 12:19 ln_buzz
$
$ cat ln_buzz                 # Use symbolic link
#! /bin/ksh
integer x=17
while :
do
x=17
done
$
```

mv

Official Description

Moves (renames) files and directories.

Syntax

```
mv [-i | -f] [--] file1 file2
```

Options

-i prompts before renaming.

-- handles filenames beginning with -.

-f forces an override of restrictions.

Oddities

It cannot mv a file to itself.

Example

EXAMPLE

```
$ mv buzz buzz9
$
$ ls -l buzz
ls: buzz: No such file or directory
$
$ ls -l buzz9
-r-x-w-r-x  1 obrien   obrien        47 Nov 26 12:19 buzz9
$
```

newgrp

Official Description

Changes the primary group identification of a shell process.

Syntax

```
newgrp [group]
```

Options

None

Oddities

The C shell has its own version of this command.

Example

EXAMPLE

```
$ grep obrien /etc/group
users:x:100:obrien
obrien:x:500:
$
$ id
uid=500(obrien) gid=500(obrien) groups=500(obrien)
$
$ newgrp users                # Change primary group
$
$ id
uid=500(obrien) gid=100(users) groups=500(obrien)
$
```

nohup

Official Description

The utility ignores hang-ups and quits. The command continues to run after logout.

Syntax

```
nohup utility [argument...]
```

Options

None

Oddities

The C shell has its own version of this command.

It does not handle pipes well.

Example

EXAMPLE

```
$ nohup ls -R / | grep bu > /tmp/bufiles  # Continues to run after exit
$ exit
```

:

Official Description

Null command.

Syntax

```
:
```

Options

None

Oddities

Formerly used to precede a comment, it was replaced by #.

The syntax after the : is expanded.

Example

EXAMPLE

```
$ x=17
$
$ if true
> then
> print $x
> else
> :                       # Null command
> fi
17
$
```

paste

Official Description

Joins corresponding lines of several files or subsequent lines in one file.

Syntax

```
paste [-d list] [-s] file...
```

Options

-d *list* establishes a delimiter list.

-s performs serial merging (one long line).

Oddities

Some implementations provide a -x option, enabling exportation.

Example

EXAMPLE

```
$ paste buzz buzz1          # Two files are in two columns
#! /bin/ksh     #! /bin/ksh
integer x=17    integer x=17
while :  while :
do      do
x=17    x=x+1
done    if (( x>20 ))
        then
                break
        fi
        done
        print $x
```

```
$
$ paste -s buzz              # Make a single line
#! /bin/ksh    integer x=17    while : do    x=17    done
$
```

print

Official Description

Shell output mechanism.

Syntax

```
print [-Rnprsu[n]] [argument ...]
```

Options

-p causes the arguments to be written to the pipe of the process spawned with |&.

-u specifies the file descriptor (unit number) to which to print.

Oddities

It's more efficient and more portable than the echo command.

Example

```
$ print $x
17
$
```

EXAMPLE

printf

Official Description

Formats and prints data.

Syntax

```
printf FORMAT [ARGUMENT]...
```

Options

None

Oddities

Available in ksh93 and beyond.

Format is similar to the C language printf function.

Example

EXAMPLE

```
$ float f=8.78
$
$ printf "Float contains %f\n" $f
Float contains 8.780000
$
$ printf "Float contains %.2f\n" $f
Float contains 8.78
$
$ printf "Float contains %10.2f\n" $f
Float contains        8.78
$
```

pwd

Official Description

Displays the pathname of the current working directory.

Syntax

pwd

Options

None

Oddities

Equivalent to print -r - $PWD.

Example

EXAMPLE

```
$ pwd
/home/obrien
$
$ print -r - $PWD
/home/obrien
$
```

r

Official Description

Re-execute a command.

Syntax

r [*command number*] | [*beginning characters of command*]

Options

None

Oddities

The r command is an alias for hist -s.

Example

EXAMPLE

```
$ history
1117    paste buzz
1118    paste buzz buzz1
1119    paste -s buzz
1120    ls -l | pg
1121    man pg
1122    pg
1123    man print
1124    print $x
1125    man printf
1126    float f=8.78
1127    printf "Float contains %f\n" $f
1128    printf "Float contains %.2f\n" $f
1129    printf "Float contains %10.2f\n" $f
1130    pwd
1131    print -r - $PWD
1132    history
$ r                              # Re-execute previous command
history
1118    paste buzz buzz1
1119    paste -s buzz
1120    ls -l | pg
1121    man pg
1122    pg
1123    man print
1124    print $x
1125    man printf
1126    float f=8.78
1127    printf "Float contains %f\n" $f
1128    printf "Float contains %.2f\n" $f
1129    printf "Float contains %10.2f\n" $f
1130    pwd
1131    print -r - $PWD
1132    history
1133    history
$
$ r 1130                         # Re-execute command number 1130
pwd
/home/obrien
$
$ r pw                           # Re-execute last command starting with pw
```

```
pwd
/home/obrien
$
```

read

Official Description

Reads a line from standard input.

Syntax

```
read [-r] var...
```

Options

-r requests that the shell not treat a backslash character in any special way.

Oddities

The -r option enables the read command to replace the line command.

Example

EXAMPLE

```
$ ls -li b*
   4054 -r-x-w-r-x   1 obrien   obrien       47 Nov 26 12:19 buzz
   4039 -rwxrwxr--   1 obrien   obrien       90 Nov 26 12:45 buzz1
   4055 -rwxrwxr--   1 obrien   obrien      152 Nov 26 12:48 buzz2
   4057 -rwxrwxr--   1 obrien   obrien      116 Nov 26 14:07 buzz3
   4058 -rwxrwxr--   1 obrien   obrien      165 Nov 26 14:08 buzz4
$
$ ls -li b* | while read -r x y      # Read first field int x,
                                     # rest of line into y
> do
> printf "%s %s\n" "$y" "$x"         # Print y, then x
> done                               # Inode number field is now the last field
-r-x-w-r-x   1 obrien   obrien       47 Nov 26 12:19 buzz 4054
-rwxrwxr--   1 obrien   obrien       90 Nov 26 12:45 buzz1 4039
-rwxrwxr--   1 obrien   obrien      152 Nov 26 12:48 buzz2 4055
-rwxrwxr--   1 obrien   obrien      116 Nov 26 14:07 buzz3 4057
-rwxrwxr--   1 obrien   obrien      165 Nov 26 14:08 buzz4 4058
$
```

readonly

Official Description

Defines or displays aliases.

Syntax

```
readonly [name[=value ...]]
```

Options

-p precedes the output with readonly.

Oddities

It's similar to typeset -r.

The -p option is available in ksh93 and beyond.

Example

EXAMPLE

```
$ readonly -p              # Displays read-only variables (none yet)
$
$ readonly x=17            # Create read-only variable
$
$ readonly -p             # Display
readonly x=17
$
$ x=24                     # Try to change read-only variable
/bin/ksh: x: is read only  # No can do
$
```

return

Official Description

Causes a shell function to return to the invoking script with the return status specified by n.

Syntax

```
return [n]
```

Options

None

Oddities

If return is invoked while not in a function or a . (dot) script, it is the same as an exit.

Example

EXAMPLE

```
$ function ob_1 {          # Create function that returns 32
> print "Can ob?"
> return 32                # Returns arbitrary number (32)
> }
$
$ ob_1                     # Execute function
```

```
Can ob?
$ print $?                      # Display return status
32
$
```

rm

Official Description

Removes (unlinks) files or directories.

Syntax

```
rm [-efirR] [--] file...
```

Options

-f forces the deletion of the file with no prompting and no error messages (good for script use).

-i prompts you before deleting each file.

-r permits the recursive removal of directories and their contents.

-- allows filenames beginning with -.

Oddities

Only when a filename is the last link to a file is the storage actually deallocated.

Example

EXAMPLE

```
$ ln buzz8 buzz9            # Create a link to buzz8's data
$
$ ln buzz8 buzz10           # Create another link to buzz8's data
$
$ ls -l buzz[891]*          # Note link count
-r-x-w-r-x  3 obrien   users        47 Nov 27 13:31 buzz10
-r-x-w-r-x  3 obrien   users        47 Nov 27 13:31 buzz8
-r-x-w-r-x  3 obrien   users        47 Nov 27 13:31 buzz9
$
$ rm buzz9                  # Prompted because file is write protected
rm: remove write-protected file 'buzz9'? y
$
$ ls -l buzz[891]*          # Link count is down to two
-r-x-w-r-x  2 obrien   users        47 Nov 27 13:31 buzz10
-r-x-w-r-x  2 obrien   users        47 Nov 27 13:31 buzz8
$
$ rm -f buzz8               # The -f option eliminates the prompt
$
```

```
$ ls -l buzz[891]*          # Link count down to one
-r-x-w-r-x  1 obrien   users         47 Nov 27 13:31 buzz10
$
```

rmdir

Official Description

Removes a directory.

Syntax

rmdir [-p] *directory*...

Options

-p removes all directories in a pathname.

Oddities

A directory must be empty before you can remove it, and you must have write permission in its parent directory.

Example

EXAMPLE

```
$ pwd
/home/obrien
$ mkdir sub1                    # Make a series of subdirectories
$ cd sub1
$ mkdir sub2
$ cd sub2
$ mkdir sub3
$ cd sub3
$ pwd
/home/obrien/sub1/sub2/sub3
$ cd
$
$ pwd
/home/obrien
$
$ rmdir -p sub1/sub2/sub3    # Remove them in one fell swoop
$
$ cd sub1                    # Gone
/bin/ksh: cd: sub1: [No such file or directory]
$
```

script

Official Description

Makes a transcript of the terminal session.

Syntax

```
script [-a] [file]
```

Options

-a appends the transcript to an existing file rather than writing it to a new file (or clobbering the existing file).

Oddities

Writes to a file named typescript by default.

If you do not specify the -a option and the file exists, it is clobbered.

Be sure to terminate your script session with an exit command. A script session left on inadvertently will eventually tie up large amounts of disk space.

Example

EXAMPLE

```
$ script                      # Start screen capture
Script started, file is typescript
$ ps
   PID TTY      S            TIME CMD
   725 console  I  +    0:00.02 /usr/sbin/getty console console vt100
   775 pts/1    S       0:00.10 -ksh (ksh)
  2729 pts/1    S  +    0:00.00 script
  2730 pts/1    S  +    0:00.00 script
  2731 pts/2    S       0:00.00 sh -is
  2732 pts/2    R  +    0:00.01 ps
$
$ date
Mon Nov 27 14:12:23 EST 2000
$
$ exit                        # End screen capture
Script done, file is typescript
$
$ cat typescript              # Displayed captured information
Script started on Mon Nov 27 14:12:14 2000
$ ps
   PID TTY      S            TIME CMD
   725 console  I  +    0:00.02 /usr/sbin/getty console console vt100
   775 pts/1    S       0:00.10 -ksh (ksh)
  2729 pts/1    S  +    0:00.00 script
  2730 pts/1    S  +    0:00.00 script
  2731 pts/2    S       0:00.00 sh -is
  2732 pts/2    R  +    0:00.01 ps
$
$ date
```

```
Mon Nov 27 14:12:23 EST 2000
$
$ exit

script done on Mon Nov 27 14:12:26 2000
$
# script -a typescript       # Append more info to existing file
Script started, file is typescript
$
$ print "############"
############
$ date
Mon Nov 27 14:13:10 EST 2000
$ exit                       # End screen capture
Script done, file is typescript
$
$ cat typescript             # Display file contents
Script started on Mon Nov 27 14:12:14 2000
$ ps
   PID TTY       S            TIME CMD
   725 console   I  +     0:00.02 /usr/sbin/getty console console vt100
   775 pts/1     S        0:00.10 -ksh (ksh)
  2729 pts/1     S  +     0:00.00 script
  2730 pts/1     S  +     0:00.00 script
  2731 pts/2     S        0:00.00 sh -is
  2732 pts/2     R  +     0:00.01 ps
$
$ date
Mon Nov 27 14:12:23 EST 2000
$
$ exit

script done on Mon Nov 27 14:12:26 2000
Script started on Mon Nov 27 14:12:54 2000
$
$ print "############"
############
$ date
Mon Nov 27 14:13:10 EST 2000
$ exit

script done on Mon Nov 27 14:13:13 2000
$
```

select

Official Description

Produces a menu of words preceded by numbers.

Syntax

select *identifier* [in *word*...] ;do *list* ;done

Options

None

Oddities

Writes the menu to stderr.

Example

EXAMPLE

```
$ select item in b*        # Set up menu containing filenames
> do
> print $item              # Print selected filenames
> done
1) buzz
2) buzz1
3) buzz10
4) buzz2
5) buzz3
6) buzz4
#? 2                       # Choose item # 2
buzz1
#? 6                       # Choose item # 6
buzz4
#? 8                       # Ignores non-existent items

#?                         # Ctrl+D exits

$ print $PS3
#?                         # Prompts with PS3 variable contents (default #?)
$
```

set

Official Description

Sets shell options.

Syntax

set [+ | -abCefhkmnopstuvx] [+ | -o *option* ...] [+ | -A *name*] [*argument* ...]

Options

-A name prepares a variable for array assignment.

-f disables filename generation.

-h causes each command to become a tracked alias when it's first encountered.

-o provides lots of options, including emacs, vi, noclobber, xtrace, verbose, ignoreeof, and so on.

-v prints shell input lines as they are read.

-x prints commands and their arguments as they are executed.

Oddities

Other arguments are positional parameters and are assigned, in order, to $1, $2, and so on.

Example

EXAMPLE

```
$ set den cheryl          # Set up positional parameters using set
$
$ print $1 $2
den cheryl
$
$ print $-                # Show currently set options (interactive,
ims                       # Jobs complete with a message, sort parameters)
$
$ set -v                  # Set another option (verbose)
$

$ print $-                # Show set options (includes v now)
print $-
imsv
$

$ set +v                  # Turn off verbose option
set +v
$
$ print $-                # Back to normal
ims
$
```

shift

Official Description

Shifts positional parameters to the left ($2 becomes $1 and so on).

Syntax

```
shift [n]
```

Options

None

Oddities

Decrements $# (parameter count) after the shift.

There is no right shift—only a left shift.

Example

EXAMPLE

```
$ set den cheryl chris scott # Set up four positional parameters
$
$ print $1                    # $1 contains den
den
$
$ shift                       # Shift to the left by 1
$
$ print $1                    # $1 now contains cheryl
cheryl
$
$ print $#                    # Parameter count is now 3
3
$
$ shift 2                     # Shift by 2
$
$ print $#                    # Count is down to one
1
$
$ print $1                    # $1 now contains scott
scott
$
```

sleep

Official Description

Suspends execution for at least the specified time.

Syntax

```
sleep seconds
```

Options

None

Oddities

Depending on system activity, the actual time of suspension might be longer.

Example

EXAMPLE

```
$ date
Mon Nov 27 14:45:37 EST 2000
$ sleep 15                   # Sleep for 15 seconds
$ print $?                   # Reports success after 15 seconds
0
$ date
Mon Nov 27 14:46:04 EST 2000
$
$ sleep 15                   # Interrupt the sleep with a Ctrl+C
$ print $?
258                          # Non-success status due to interruption
$
```

sort

Official Description

Sorts or merges files.

Syntax

```
sort [-m] [-o output_file] [-Abdfinru] [-k keydef]... [-t character]
        [-T directory] [-y] [kilobytes] [-z record_size]... file...
```

Options

-m performs a merge.

-b ignores leading spaces and tabs.

-f treats lowercase as uppercase.

-k *keydef* specifies one or more sort keys (start byte, end byte).

-n sorts any initial numeric strings.

-r reverses the order.

-u means no duplicates in output.

Oddities

No separate merge command exists.

Example

```
$ sort buzz                # Standard sort
#! /bin/ksh
do
done
integer x=17
while :
x=17
$ sort -r buzz             # Descending sort
x=17
while :
integer x=17
done
do
#! /bin/ksh
$
$ sort -k 3,1 buzz         # Use one byte found after skipping three as
                           # the sort key
#! /bin/ksh
do
done
integer x=17
while :
x=17
$
```

stop

Official Description

Stops background jobs.

Syntax

stop %*job_number or pid*

Options

None

Oddities

The stop command is an alias for kill -s STOP.

Example

```
$ buzz&                    # Create two background jobs
[1]    1181
$ buzz&
[2]    1182
$
```

```
$ jobs
[2] + Running              buzz&
[1] - Running              buzz&
$
$ stop %1                  # Stop job #1
[1] + Stopped (SIGSTOP)    buzz&
$
$ jobs -l
[1] + 1181    Stopped (SIGSTOP)        buzz&
[2] - 1182    Running                  buzz&
$
$ stop 1182                # Stop pid # 1182
[2] + Stopped (SIGSTOP)    buzz&
$
```

tail

Official Description

Displays the tail end of a file.

Syntax

`tail [-f | -r] [-c number | -n number] [file]`

Options

`-c number` requests that the output start displaying at a specified character number.

`-f` requests that the tail function does not end after it copies the last line. Can monitor file content growth.

`-n number` requestst that the output start displaying at specified line number.

`-r` reverses the display order.

Oddities

The default is to show the last 10 lines of a file.

Example

EXAMPLE

```
$ tail -n 3 buzz          # Shows last 3 lines of file
do
x=17
done
$
$ tail -c 3 buzz          # Shows last 3 chars of file
ne
$
```

tee

Official Description

Reads from standard input and writes to standard output and files.

Syntax

```
tee [-ai] file...
```

Options

-a appends output to file.

-i ignores INT signal.

Oddities

If one target file is unavailable, the output continues to the others.

Example

EXAMPLE

```
$ ls -l b*
-r-x-w-r-x    1 obrien    obrien         47 Nov 26 12:19 buzz
-rwxrwxr--    1 obrien    obrien         90 Nov 26 12:45 buzz1
-r-x-w-r-x    1 obrien    users          47 Nov 27 13:31 buzz10
-rwxrwxr--    1 obrien    obrien        152 Nov 26 12:48 buzz2
-rwxrwxr--    1 obrien    obrien        116 Nov 26 14:07 buzz3
-rwxrwxr--    1 obrien    obrien        165 Nov 26 14:08 buzz4
$
$ ls -l b* > some_file      # Can't see output when redirected
$
$ ls -l b* | tee some_file  # Pipe it to tee and it will do both
                            # (redirect and display)
-r-x-w-r-x    1 obrien    obrien         47 Nov 26 12:19 buzz
-rwxrwxr--    1 obrien    obrien         90 Nov 26 12:45 buzz1
-r-x-w-r-x    1 obrien    users          47 Nov 27 13:31 buzz10
-rwxrwxr--    1 obrien    obrien        152 Nov 26 12:48 buzz2
-rwxrwxr--    1 obrien    obrien        116 Nov 26 14:07 buzz3
-rwxrwxr--    1 obrien    obrien        165 Nov 26 14:08 buzz4
$
$ cat some_file             # Display redirected file contents
-r-x-w-r-x    1 obrien    obrien         47 Nov 26 12:19 buzz
-rwxrwxr--    1 obrien    obrien         90 Nov 26 12:45 buzz1
-r-x-w-r-x    1 obrien    users          47 Nov 27 13:31 buzz10
-rwxrwxr--    1 obrien    obrien        152 Nov 26 12:48 buzz2
-rwxrwxr--    1 obrien    obrien        116 Nov 26 14:07 buzz3
-rwxrwxr--    1 obrien    obrien        165 Nov 26 14:08 buzz4
$
```

test

Official Description

Evaluates conditional expressions.

Syntax

```
test [expression]
```

Options

None

Oddities

It's the same as [.

Example

EXAMPLE

```
$
$ test -x buzz              # Is buzz executable?
$ print $?
0                          # Yup
$
$ test -b buzz              # Is buzz a block special file?
$ print $?
1                          # Nope
$
```

time

Official Description

Times the execution of a command.

Syntax

```
time [-p] command [argument...]
```

Options

-p writes the timing output to standard error (may not be available on all UNIX variants).

Oddities

The C shell has its own version of this command.

Example

EXAMPLE

```
$ time ls b*
buzz   buzz1   buzz10   buzz2   buzz3   buzz4

real    0m0.02s             # Elapsed time
user    0m0.00s             # User mode processing time
sys     0m0.02s             # Kernel (system) mode processing time
$
```

touch

Official Description

Updates file access and modification times.

Syntax

touch [-acfm] [-r *reference_file* | -t *time*] *file*...

Options

-a changes only the access time.

-m changes only the modification time.

-r *reference_file* causes the specified file's times to be used instead of the current time.

-t *time* specifies the time to use.

Oddities

It can be used to create an empty file.

Example

EXAMPLE

```
$ ls -l d*                  # Note date
-rw-rw-r--   1 obrien   obrien      22 Nov 27 00:32 do_funcy
$
$ date                      # Current date
Mon Nov 27 15:32:30 EST 2000
$
$ touch do_funcy            # Alter date on file
$
$ ls -l d*                  # Note date change
-rw-rw-r--   1 obrien   obrien      22 Nov 27 15:32 do_funcy
$
$ touch denfile             # Create empty file
$
```

```
$ ls -l d*                    # Note size
-rw-rw-r--  1 obrien   users         0 Nov 27 15:33 denfile
-rw-rw-r--  1 obrien   obrien       22 Nov 27 15:32 do_funcy
$
```

tr

Official Description

Translates characters.

Syntax

tr [-Acs] *string1 string2*

Options

-A requests ASCII translation, with no extended character sets (might not be available on all UNIX variants).

-c requests the use of the complement of the chars in string1.

-s substitutes characters in string1 into string2.

Oddities

Specifying the -A option improves ASCII performance, but the option might not be available in all UNIX variants.

Example

EXAMPLE

```
$ cat funca               # Note the { }
function funca {
print "In funca"
}
$                         # Change to ( )
$ tr '{}' '()' <funca > funcanew
$
$ cat funcanew            # Note the ( )
function funca (
print "In funca"
)
$
```

trap

Official Description

Traps a signal to be serviced by a signal handler.

Syntax

trap [*argument*][*signal* ...] | [-p]

Options

-p prints the currently trapped signals.

Oddities

If the argument is omitted or is -, all traps associated with signals are reset to their original values.

Example

EXAMPLE

```
$ trap -p                     # No signals being trapped yet
$
$ trap 'print "Trapped"' INT QUIT # Trap INT (CTRL+C) and QUIT (CTRL+\)
$
$ trap -p                     # Print signals being trapped
trap -- 'print "Trapped"' QUIT
trap -- 'print "Trapped"' INT
$
$ Trapped                  # CTRL+C
$
$ Trapped                  # CTRL+\
$
$ trap - INT QUIT          # Back to default trapping
$
$ trap -p                  # No more special traps
$
```

true

Official Description

Returns success status.

Syntax

true

Options

None

Oddities

You can use true when you need a command but don't want it to perform any processing.

It's available as a built-in in ksh93 and beyond.

Example

EXAMPLE

```
$ true                      # Returns success status
$ print $?
0
$ false                     # Returns failure status
$ print $?
1
$
$ if true                   # Tests to see if true returns success
> then
> print "Must be true"
> else
> print "Must be false"
> fi
Must be true                # It does
$
```

tty

Official Description

Returns the pathname of the terminal device.

Syntax

tty [-s]

Options

-s suppresses reporting the pathname. (It might be useful to check for the existence of a terminal device.)

Oddities

It can be used to determine whether the standard input is a terminal.

Example

EXAMPLE

```
$ tty                       # Current terminal device
/dev/pts/0
$
$ tty -s                    # If successful, stdin is a tty
$ print $?
0
$
```

type

Official Description

Writes a description of command type.

Syntax

```
type name...
```

Options

None

Oddities

The type command must be aware of the contents of the current shell execution environment to work properly.

Example

EXAMPLE

```
$ type cat
cat is a shell builtin version of /bin/cat
$
$ type if
if is a keyword
$
$ type find
find is a tracked alias for /usr/bin/find
$
```

typeset

Official Description

Sets attributes and values for shell parameters.

Syntax

```
typeset [+ | -HLRZfilprtux[n]] [name[=value ...]]
```

Options

-f sets up a function.

-i sets up a shell variable as an integer.

-l requests that contents be stored in lowercase only.

-L requests that contents be left justified.

-p requests that all variables be printed (displayed).

-r sets a variable's characteristics to read-only.

-R requests that contents be right justified.

-u requests that contents be stored in uppercase only.

-x makes the shell variable an environment variable (marked for export).

-Z requests that contents be right justified and that any leading spaces be filled with zeroes.

Oddities

Using + (plus sign) rather than - (hyphen) causes these options to be turned off.

Example

EXAMPLE

```
$ typeset -p                    # Print typeset shell variables
typeset -i TMOUT
typeset -E f
typeset FCEDIT
typeset -x INPUTRC
typeset -i RANDOM
typeset -x _AST_FEATURES
typeset -x TERM
typeset -x HOME
typeset -x PS1
typeset HISTEDIT
typeset PS2
typeset PS3
typeset -x LC_ALL
typeset -i PPID
typeset -x USER
typeset -x HISTSIZE
typeset -x LANG
typeset -x MAIL
typeset -x LOGNAME
typeset -x LINGUAS
typeset -i OPTIND
typeset -r x
typeset -i MAILCHECK
typeset -x HOSTNAME
typeset -x HISTFILESIZE
typeset -i LINENO
typeset -x PATH
typeset -i HISTCMD
typeset -r .sh
typeset -x _
typeset -x PWD
typeset -F 3 SECONDS
typeset -x SHELL
$
$
```

```
$ typeset -RZ10 zfod          # Variable zfod is right justified,
                              # zero filled, 10 chars wide.
$
$ zfod=23                     # Initialize to 23
$
$ print $zfod                 # Note zero fill
0000000023
$
```

ulimit

Official Description

Sets or displays a resource limit.

Syntax

ulimit [-HSacdfmnstvw] [*limit*]

Options

-a lists current limits.

-c displays the maximum size of core dump files.

-d displays the maximum size of data area.

-f displays the maximum file size.

-m displays the limit on physical memory usage.

-n displays the maximum number of concurrently open files.

-s displays the maximum stack size.

-t displays the maximum CPU time in seconds.

-v displays the maximum virtual memory (kb).

-w displays the maximum swap area (kb) (not available on all UNIX variants).

Oddities

The H and S options specify whether the hard limit or the soft limit for the given resource is set.

A hard limit cannot be increased after it is set.

A soft limit can be increased up to the value of the hard limit. Warnings will be issued when exceeding the soft limit. Errors also will be issued when attempting to exceed a hard limit.

Example

EXAMPLE

```
$ ulimit -a
time(seconds)         unlimited
file(blocks)          unlimited
data(kbytes)          unlimited
stack(kbytes)         8192
memory(kbytes)        unlimited
coredump(blocks)      1000000
nofiles(descriptors)  1024
vmemory(kbytes)       unlimited
$
```

umask

Official Description

Displays or sets the file mode creation mask.

Syntax

umask [-S] [*mask*]

Options

-S produces symbolic output.

Oddities

The one's complement of the umask value is bitwise or'ed with octal 666 (for regular files) or octal 777 (for directories) to determine the permission to set on a new file or directory.

Octal? Isn't this the twenty-first century? It shows the PDP 11 origins of UNIX.

Example

EXAMPLE

```
$ umask
0002
$
$ umask -S
u=rwx,g=rwx,o=rx
$
```

unalias

Official Description

Removes alias definitions.

Syntax

```
unalias alias-name... | [-a]
```

Options

-a removes all alias definitions.

Oddities

The C shell has its own version of this command.

Example

EXAMPLE

```
$ alias cat=ls              # Make two aliases
$ alias p=ps
$
$ alias                     # Display alias list
2d='set -f;_2d'
autoload='typeset -fu'
cat=ls
command='command '
fc=hist
float='typeset -E'
functions='typeset -f'
hash='alias -t --'
history='hist -l'
integer='typeset -i'
nameref='typeset -n'
nohup='nohup '
p=ps
r='hist -s'
redirect='command exec'
stop='kill -s STOP'
suspend='kill -s STOP $$'
times='{ { time;} 2>&1;}'
type='whence -v'
$
$ unalias -a               # Blow them all away
$
$ alias                    # Gone
$
```

uniq

Official Description

Removes or lists repeated lines in a file.

Syntax

```
uniq [-cdu] [-f fields] [-s chars] [input-file [output-file]]
```

Options

-c displays the count of occurrences of the line.

-d displays repeated lines only.

-f *fields* ignores specified fields when comparing lines.

-s *chars* ignores the specified number of chars when doing comparisons.

-u displays unique lines only.

Oddities

Repeated lines must be on consecutive lines to be found.

You can arrange them with the sort command before processing.

Example

EXAMPLE

```
$ uniq utest
den
cheryl
cheryl cheryl den
mark                      # Mark shows up once
den
den cheryl
dencheryl
den cheryl
$
$ uniq -c utest
   1 den
   1 cheryl
   1 cheryl cheryl den
   3 mark                 # There were four lines of mark
   1 den
   1 den cheryl
   1 dencheryl
   1 mark
   1 den cheryl
$
$ sort utest             # Sort test file
cheryl
cheryl cheryl den
den
den
den cheryl
den cheryl
dencheryl
mark
mark
```

```
mark
mark
$
$ sort utest > utestnew      # Create sorted test file
$
$ uniq utestnew              # Eliminates duplicate lines
cheryl
cheryl cheryl den
den
den cheryl
dencheryl
mark
$
```

unset

Official Description

The variables or functions given by the list of names are unassigned.

Syntax

unset [-fv] *name* ...

Options

-f names refer to functions.

-v names refer to variables.

Oddities

Read-only variables cannot be unset.

Example

EXAMPLE

```
$ readonly                   # Display read-only variables
x=17
$
$ unset x                    # Attempt to unset a read-only variable
/bin/ksh: unset: x: is read only
$
$ y=23                       # Create a normal shell variable
$
$ print $y
23
$
$ unset y                    # Remove it with unset
$
$ print $y

$
```

until

Official Description

Executes until a condition becomes true.

Syntax

```
until list ;do list ;done
```

Options

None

Oddities

An until loop is similar to a while loop, except that the test is negated.

Example

EXAMPLE

```
$ a=0
$
$ until (( $a==5 ))          # Loop until variable a contains a 5
> do
> print $a
> (( a=a+1 ))
> done
0
1
2
3
4
$ print $a                   # Variable a contains a 5 now
5
```

wait

Official Description

Awaits process completion.

Syntax

```
wait [pid]
```

Options

None

Oddities

The C shell has its own version of this command.

Example

EXAMPLE

```
$ sleep 15&                    # Start a job in the background
[1]     1309
$ wait                         # Wait for it to complete
[1] +  Done                        sleep 15&
$
$ sleep 15&                    # Start two jobs in the background
[1]     1310
$ sleep 30&
[2]     1311
$ jobs
[2] +  Running                     sleep 30&
[1] -  Running                     sleep 15&
$
$ wait 1311                    # Wait for a particular one to complete
[1] +  Done                        sleep 15&
$
```

WC

Official Description

Counts the lines, words, characters, and bytes in a file.

Syntax

wc [-c | -m] [-lw] [*file*...]

Options

-c counts bytes.

-l counts lines.

-m counts characters.

-w counts words.

Oddities

Words are separated by whitespace.

Example

EXAMPLE

```
$ wc buzz*                          # Lines, words, chars
        6        9       47 buzz
       11       18       90 buzz1
        6        9       47 buzz10
       16       31      152 buzz2
       12       22      116 buzz3
       16       33      165 buzz4
       67      122      617 total
```

```
$
$ wc -l buzz                 # Lines only
      6 buzz
$
$ ps laxw | wc -l            # Useful in pipes
     42
$
```

whence

Official Description

Indicates how a command would be interpreted.

Syntax

whence [-pv] *name* ...

Options

-a shows all uses of name.

-f excludes functions.

-p searches the path for a name.

-v causes more verbose output.

Oddities

The -a and -f options are available in ksh93 and beyond.

Example

EXAMPLE

```
$ whence ls
/bin/ls
$
$ whence -v ls
ls is a tracked alias for /bin/ls
$
$ whence -a echo             # Displays all uses of echo
echo is a shell builtin
echo is a tracked alias for /bin/echo
$
```

while

Official Description

Executes the while list repeatedly, and if the exit status of the last command in the list is 0 (zero), it executes the do list.

Syntax

```
while list ;do list ;done
```

Options

None

Oddities

The while loop is the same as the until loop except that the test is check-ing for a true value. If it finds one, it repeats the loop. The until loop checks for a false value and repeats the loop until the test evaluates to true.

Example

EXAMPLE

```
$ a=5
$
$ while (( $a>0 ))              # Repeat the loop as long as a>0
> do
> print $a
> (( a=a-1 ))
> done
5
4
3
2
1
$
```

who

Official Description

Identifies users currently logged in.

Syntax

```
who [-a] | [-AbdhHlmMpqrstTu] [file]
```

Options

-a displays all options.

There are many other options. See the man page. Not all options in the pre-ceding list are available on all UNIX variants.

Oddities

Several commands are related to the who command that can be used to display specific information, such as the following:

who am I, which displays the name, terminal, date, and host.

whoami, which displays the login name only.

Example

EXAMPLE

```
$ who
obrien    pts/0    Nov 27 07:35
obrien    pts/1    Nov 27 07:18
obrien    pts/2    Nov 27 07:19
$
$ who am i
linden!obrien    pts/0    Nov 27 07:35
$
$ whoami
obrien
```

What's Next

I hope this appendix is of use. It should get you pointed in the right direction (at least) if you forget about some command. If you are a rookie, I'd recommend putting your feet up and flipping through this appendix a few times when you have a few minutes to yourself. Plenty of examples are included, which should stimulate your imagination and spur you on to greater script-writing heights.

The final appendix (Appendix B, "vi Tutorial") should be of use for new users of vi. Come to think of it, it will probably help shake up some of you old-timers as well. Take a look. Enjoy.

Appendix B

vi Tutorial

You wouldn't be reading this appendix if you were comfortable with the vi editor. The vi editor has many fans and many detractors. The detractors tend to be those who don't completely understand the way it works. My goal here is to explain the way vi works so you can use this editor in peace rather than in pain.

This appendix teaches you the following:

- Where vi came from
- How to start an edit session
- The modes of operation within vi
- Inserting and appending text
- Last line mode
- Exit options
- Cursor movement
- Cutting and pasting
- Searching and replacing
- How to use vi buffers
- How to change the vi environment settings

Where vi Came From

UNIX editors have gone through an evolutionary process. The first UNIX editor was the ed editor. It was strictly a line-oriented editor (as opposed to a screen-oriented editor like vi). It still exists in most UNIX variants, but it has been relegated to special-case use. As an example, if your UNIX runs in single-user mode, the editor that tends to be used by a utility with an edit subfunction, at that time, is the ed editor. Single-user mode is usually entered to accomplish some specialized system admin task. While in single-user mode, the only file system that is mounted is the root file system (unless the administrator specifically mounts other file systems).

The vi editor program has been linked against shared libraries, and the shared libraries are found in the /usr file system, which is not available in single-user mode. The bottom line is that it is difficult (but not impossible) to use vi in single-user mode. Therefore, if your responsibilities include occasionally doing some work in single-user mode, it might help to know the rudiments of ed as well as vi. I'll include a short summary at the end of this appendix.

The vi editor libraries are not found in the root file system, and therefore vi is not available in single-user mode unless the administrator mounts other file systems manually.

The ed editor is a line-mode editor. This means that the display is line oriented rather than screen oriented. (The vi editor is screen oriented.) A line-mode editor does not have many requirements that limit terminal type and characteristics. Conversely, a screen-mode editor (such as vi) requires a recognized terminal interface.

The ed editor evolved into the ex editor. Several extensions to the ed editor were added, and the resulting editor was called ex, an *ex*tension of the ed editor. It also provided a more friendly user interface, although it was still not screen oriented.

The following example shows a simple ex session that creates a file and inserts a line. Note that the insertion is terminated by a line starting with a period:

EXAMPLE

```
$ ex dentest1
"dentest1" [New File]
Entering Ex mode.  Type "visual" to go to Normal mode.
:i
hello

.
:wq
"dentest1" [New File] 2 lines, 8 characters written
```

```
$ cat dentest1
hello

$
```

To comfortably view many lines of a file while editing, the nature of the editor had to change from line oriented to screen oriented. The visual version of the ex editor is vi. This means that the engine of the vi editor is the good old ex editor. (And don't forget that ex is just an extension of ed.)

Starting an Edit Session

The vi editor is invoked by the vi command:

```
$ vi filename
```

The editor functions in one of three modes: command mode, insert mode, and last-line mode (sometimes called single-line mode, or ex mode). When the edit session starts, vi enters command mode. Several commands can change the mode to insert mode (I, i , a , A, o, O, and so on), and one command can change the mode to last-line (:).

If the file to be edited does not exist, vi reports that it is a new file and enters the command mode of operation. The following example show the startup of a vi session involving a new file:

EXAMPLE

```
$ vi junk


~

~

~

~
(...)
"junk" [New File]
```

If the file exists, vi displays a screen full of data from the file—or the whole file if it is less than a screenful. It then reports on the size of the file and enters command mode. Don't be surprised if you see a bunch of tildes (~) running down the screen. The editor uses them to indicate nonexistent lines in the screen display. A new file shows nothing but the lines containing ~s:

EXAMPLE

```
$ vi dentest1

hello

~

~
```

```
~
~
(...)
"dentest1" 2L, 8C
```

Modes of Operation

The vi editor supports three modes of operation: command mode, in which keys are interpreted as commands; insert mode, in which keys are interpreted as input to the file; and last-line mode, in which ex commands can be entered.

Command Mode

As indicated earlier, upon entering vi, the editor is in command mode. This means that you can enter any of the vi command mode commands. The typical new user complaint is that no prompt exists in command mode. In fact, this is true for two of the three vi modes. We can whine about it, or accept it and move on. Basically, the editor accepts any characters typed while in command mode as commands. The commands usually are one-letter commands. They do not echo when typed, and the editor does not prompt you for the next command. The commands also are accepted without the carriage return being entered.

The previous few characteristics are very important to understand. They are major hurdles preventing the typical user from understanding and even enjoying this editor.

The following are the most commonly used command mode commands:

- i—Switches to insert mode; inserts text before the cursor
- I—Switches to insert mode; inserts at the beginning of a line
- a—Switches to insert mode; inserts text after the cursor
- A—Switches to insert mode; inserts at the end of a line
- o—Switches to insert mode; opens the line below the current one
- O—Switches to insert mode; opens the line above the current one

Insert Mode

After the user types one of the commands listed in the previous section, the editor switches to insert mode. As the name implies, insert mode allows the insertion of characters into the file. The assumption that rookie vi users make is that after they get into the editor, they can just start typing the characters they want to place in the file. If a user did this, he would type characters until he happened to type a character that matches a command. Then, the editor would do whatever the command was supposed to do.

If a user got into vi and started to type the string Dennis, he would end up inserting an s into the file. The command mode of vi does not recognize any of the characters D, e, or n as commands. The first letter that actually is a command is the i, which means switch to insert mode. So the editor would dutifully switch to insert mode and gladly accept whatever the user typed in from that point on as characters to be placed in the file.

As I mentioned earlier, the editor does not (by default) indicate whether you are in command mode or insert mode. This can leave you very confused if you inadvertently type in something like Dennis while in command mode. By the time you look up, you see something like s is a dude onscreen. The natural question would be, "Where did the Denni disappear to?" The missing letters were all interpreted as commands (one at a time) and discarded because they did not match any of vi's commands.

ESCAPING FROM INSERT MODE

Now that you can get into insert mode (by typing i, I, a, A, o, or O), the question is, how do you get out of insert mode? You can't type in a letter because it will be interpreted as another character to be inserted into the file. You must *escape* from insert mode. If the editor is given the escape character while in insert mode, it means that the editor should switch back to command mode. Essentially, six commands cause vi to enter insert mode, and only one key sequence gets it out of insert mode (see Figure B.1). The only mode vi goes to when it exits insert mode is command mode.

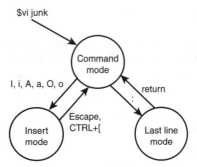

Figure B.1: *The vi editor modes and how they relate to each other.*

The Esc key on your keyboard can sometimes cause problems. It does not always appear in the same place on all keyboards, and most importantly, it does not always send the same escape sequence on all keyboards. This means that you might be in the middle of an edit session, cruising along in insert mode, decide to get back to command mode, and find that the Esc key doesn't work, or doesn't exist, or causes the character that the cursor is on to get uppercased, or some other weird action. None of the previous results are correct behavior. (There is always the possibility that it will work as advertised, I suppose.)

The incorrect behavior usually occurs because the keyboard is set up to send some bizarre escape sequence when the Esc key is pressed, rather than sending a pure escape sequence. The solution, strange as it might seem, is to NOT USE THE ESC KEY! I know that sounds radical, but it is exactly what I do. And I have successfully used vi on many terminals.

The way I get the correct escape sequence to be sent by the keyboard is to press Ctrl+[. That is, while holding down the control key (Ctrl), press the [key. Try it. You'll see that it never fails to send the correct escape sequence to the vi editor, which means it can get you out of insert mode without any side effects.

Last-Line Mode

Last-line mode is entered by typing the : command while in command mode. It is referred to as *last-line* mode because the editor actually places a small prompt (:) on the last line of the screen to indicate that it is ready for you to enter an ex command. Yes, it is expecting you to enter an ex editor command. Remember that the engine of vi is ex. Vi is a visual (screen-oriented) front end to the ex editor. Therefore, any commands you can perform in the ex editor should also work in the vi editor. But you must indicate to vi that you intend to enter an ex command, which you do by typing the : command.

Exiting from the Editor

Your first few last-line mode commands are very simple. (They can get much more complex.) You probably want to save your edits and exit from the editor. The last-line mode command sequence to do this is :wq. This is actually two last-line mode commands. It is the w, which means write the changes to the file, and the q, which means quit from the editor.

Maybe you are hung over one morning, and you start making a bunch of changes to a file, which, upon review (before exiting the editor, and as you sober up) you find to be totally incorrect. It might behoove you at that time to quit from the editor without saving your changes. This can be achieved by the last-line mode sequence of :q!. The : is issued from command mode and gets you to the : prompt, indicating that you are in last-line mode. The q means you want to exit the editor. The !, on the other hand, means you truly want to exit, and realizing that you've made changes, still want to exit and not save the changes.

If you have entered the editor to be able to read the file, and not make any changes, you can exit the editor with the :q sequence (no !), indicating that you simply want to get out. If you have indeed made changes and type the :q sequence, you are informed that you have made changes to the file and given another chance to save your work (:wq) or exit without saving (:q!).

In addition, a command to exit the editor is available directly from command mode. It is the oddly named ZZ command. It means quit the editor and save changes. I guess the person who thought that one up was a fan of Texas-based rock and roll played by guys with long beards (ZZ Top).

The following are the commands to exit the editor:

- :wq—Write changes to the file and quit the editor.
- :q—Quit the editor.
- :q!—Quit the editor and don't save changes.
- ZZ—Command mode command to write and quit.
- :w!—Write changes to the file and override permissions if necessary.

Moving the Cursor

Now that you know the basics of vi, the next step is to start honing your skills. Many of the files you edit can be large. Suppose you want to move through the file rapidly? Typically, the arrow keys on the keyboard are available to move the cursor up, down, left, and right. If you try the arrow keys and they refuse to cooperate (sometimes the keyboard mappings are not what vi expects), you should be able to use the h, k, j, and l keys to move left, down, up, and right, respectively.

Sounds like it might take many keystrokes (and much time) to move through a large file, doesn't it? Generally, if you find yourself typing repeated cursor movement keys for many seconds, you should think of another way to move around in your file. For instance, you can move forward and backward by page (rather than by line) by using several control-key sequences. For instance, you can use Ctrl+D or Ctrl+F to move down many lines at a time, and you can use Ctrl+U or Ctrl+B to move the cursor up many lines at a time.

Sometimes you might want to move immediately to the bottom of the file. The G command assumes you want the cursor at the end of the file. You can precede the G with a number to move to a specific line. I find the 1G command to be useful for moving back to the beginning of a file.

You also can move quickly within a line by using the 0 (that's a zero) command to move to the beginning of a line and using the $ command to move to the end of a line.

The following are the cursor movement commands:

- 0—Move to the beginning of the line
- $—Move to the end of the line
- h—Move to the left
- j—Move down a line
- k—Move up a line
- l—Move to the right
- Ctrl+D—Move down half a screen
- Ctrl+U—Move up half a screen
- Ctrl+F—Move down a screen
- Ctrl+B—Move back a screen
- G—Go to the end of the file
- 1G—Go to line one (beginning of file)
- 34G—Go to line 34
- w—Move forward to the next word

Deleting

Occasionally, you will reread your document an hour after creating it and decide that you need to delete a character, a word, an entire line, or an entire group of lines. The following lists the commands to handle deletions. Be aware that the dd and dw commands are two of the rare commands that actually require two keystrokes to execute.

The following are the deletion commands:

- x—Delete the character where the cursor is
- dw—Delete the word where the cursor is
- dd—Delete the line where the cursor is

Suppose you make a deletion and realize that it wasn't what you really wanted to do. The vi editor allows you to undo the last command you executed by using the u command. The u command actually takes the contents of the delete buffer (called the general purpose buffer [GPB]) and puts it back where it originated. Be aware that you can undo only the last command you performed. If you try to undo a second command, you will be undoing the undo, which puts you right back where you started!

Cutting and Pasting

One of the more common deletion-oriented edits made when working with an existing file is the cut-and-paste operation. This is useful when you have a few lines of the file that need to be moved to another area of the file. You typically cut the section to be moved, and then place it in a temporary buffer (the GPB). Next, you move the cursor to the location you want the data to be placed, and then paste it into its new home.

The sequence involves a dd command, followed by moving the cursor and entering the p command. If you want to move more than one line, you can use a line count in front of the dd command:

3dd

(move cursor)

p

The p command pastes the contents of the GPB on the line below the line on which the cursor sits. If you want to paste the data in the GPB above the current line, use the P command (capitol P).

Perhaps you want to perform a cut and paste but prefer to leave a copy of the data to be pasted at its original location. This can be accomplished by a dd command, followed immediately by a p to place a copy of the deleted data right back where it came from. It can also be accomplished by using the yy command. This command yanks a copy of the selected lines into the GPB. The difference is that it does not delete the lines:

3yy

(move cursor)

p

Using Multiple Buffers

Be aware that any use of the GPB replaces the previous contents. So if you perform a 100dd command to delete 100 lines (and place them in the GPB), and then delete another character by using the x command, the single character removed by the x command replaces the 100 lines of data in the GPB.

Your goal might have been to append some extra bytes or lines onto the current contents of the GPB. However, the result would be that you end up with the last deleted (or yanked) command in the GPB. It does not perform the append operation by default.

The vi editor provides buffers other than the GPB. Some of these other buffers have the append characteristic discussed in the previous paragraph. These buffers are referred to as *named* buffers. Their names are the letters of the alphabet (so you can have an additional 26 buffers beyond the GPB). To use them, you must precede your delete or yank command with a " (double quote) and the name of the target buffer (a letter). The following command deletes five lines and places them into a buffer named a:

`"a5dd`

You then can place the contents of the buffer named a anywhere you want by moving the cursor and typing `"`**ap**. This means get the contents of the buffer named a and insert it below where the cursor is currently. If you need to append to the current contents of the buffer named a, you can reference it with a capitol letter on the next delete or yank. The editor interprets a request such as `"A5dd` as a request to append the deleted lines to the current contents of the buffer named a. Note that the reference to the buffer named A is actually a request to *append* to the buffer named a:

`"b25dd`

(move cursor to prepare for append)

`"B5dd`

(move cursor to prepare for paste)

`"bp`

Searching and Replacing

A variation on the cut-and-paste action is the search-and-replace action. This is useful if you need to make changes to every instance of a string within a file. The first step is the search. Searching is something you will do even if you are not interested in performing a replace. The following command places the cursor on the first instance of the string Den:

`/Den/`

Notice that no : exists in front of it; it is a command-mode command. This command searches forward from the current cursor position to the end of the file. If you want to search backward, you can surround the search string with ? instead of /. If the search finds an instance of the string, and you want to search for the same string again, you can type the **n** command, which means find the next instance of the search string.

Table B.1 documents the most commonly used search commands available within the vi editor.

Table B.1: Search commands

Command	Description
/str/	Searches forward for next instance of str. (This won't work without the trailing / as well.)
n	Finds the next instance of str.
//	Finds the next instance of str.
?str?	Searches backward for str.
??	Finds the next instance (backward).

To replace a string (as it is found) with another string, you must use the substitute command. This command is a last-line mode command, so it is preceded with a colon (:). The syntax is shown here:

```
:s/original str/replacement str/
```

To cause the substitute command to operate on all lines of a file and even handle multiple occurrences of the search string found on one line, use the following syntax:

```
:1,$s/original str/replacement str/g
```

The 1,$ means start at line one and proceed until the end of the file. The g means do it globally on one line. It takes care of the situation in which the search string is found more than once on the same line and also appears on many lines within the file. As you can tell, this is a powerful construct.

The following example searches the entire file for instances of the string Digital UNIX and replaces them with the string Tru64 UNIX:

```
:1,$s/Digital UNIX/Tru64 UNIX/g
```

Table B.2 documents the most commonly used substitute commands available within the vi editor.

Table B.2: Substitute commands

Command	Description
:s/orig/new/	Replaces the first occurrence of orig with new on current line.
:s/orig/new/g	Current line; handles multiple instances of orig on same line.
:1,$s/orig/new/	All lines; first instance of orig on each line is replaced.
:1,$s/orig/new/g	All lines; all instances are replaced.

Searches can be customized by using regular expressions, such as

- ^—Search at the start of the line
- $—Search at the end of the line
- .—Match any single character
- *—Match zero or more of previous characters
- [...]—Match any character in the brackets
- [^...]—Match any character except ones in the brackets

Combining Buffers and Substitute Commands

The notion of vi buffers discussed previously can be combined with any of the ex commands to customize and streamline your session. Suppose you find yourself typing in the following command (or commands similar to this) repetitively:

```
:1,$s/orig/DEN/g
```

You can place this command in a buffer (exclude the :) and request the execution of the buffer full of commands with the :@buffer_name command. You type the command as if you are trying to insert it into your file, leave off the colon, and delete the line into one of your named buffers:

```
"add
```

This command requests a deletion of the current line and requests that the contents of the line be placed in the buffer named a. When you are ready to execute the stored command, type the following:

```
:@a
```

Changing vi Environment Settings

The vi editor has many environment settings. These can be used to customize your editing sessions to meet your particular needs and habits. One of the more popular options, especially to novice vi users, is the showmode option. When set, it displays a small message on the bottom of your screen to remind you when you are in insert mode. This eliminates a lot of the confusion and hesitation experienced by neophyte vi users.

The following example demonstrates the effect of using the showmode option within the vi editor:

```
$ vi junk

stuff
in the
```

EXAMPLE

junk file.

~

~

(...)
:set showmode

Because showmode is set, after entering insert mode, the screen looks like this:

stuff
in the
junk file.

~

~

(...)
-- INSERT --

EXAMPLE

When in doubt as to which vi mode you are in, you can always just type the escape key (or Ctrl+[). If you are in insert mode, it takes you back to command mode. If you are already in command mode, it doesn't do any harm, but it emits a small beep. Basically, after you type the escape sequence, you are guaranteed that you are back in command mode.

Here is a list of all the vi settings. This display was acquired by typing the last line-mode command :set all. Don't panic—you won't be using most of these. I just thought you should be aware of their existence:

EXAMPLE

```
:set all
--- Options ---
noautoindent         isprint=@,161-255   scrolloff=0        textwidth=0
noautowrite          joinspaces          nosecure           notildeop
  background=light   keymodel=             selectmode=        timeout
  backspace=0        keywordprg=man        shell=/bin/ksh     timeoutlen=1000
nobackup             laststatus=1          shellcmdflag=-c   nottimeout
  backupext=~        nolazyredraw          shellquote=        ttimeoutlen=-1
nobinary             lines=24              shellxquote=       ttybuiltin
  cmdheight=1        nolisp              noshiftround       nottyfast
  columns=80        nolist                shiftwidth=8       ttymouse=
nocompatible         listchars=eol:$     noshortname        ttyscroll=999
  cpoptions=aABceFs  magic               noshowfulltag      ttytype=vt320
  display=           matchtime=5         noshowmatch        undolevels=1000
noedcompatible       maxmapdepth=1000      showmode           updatecount=200
  endofline          maxmem=5120           sidescroll=0       updatetime=4000
  equalalways        maxmemtot=10240     nosmartcase          verbose=0
  equalprg=          modeline            nosmarttab         novisualbell
noerrorbells         modelines=5           softtabstop=0      warn
  esckeys            modified            nosplitbelow       noweirdinvert
noexpandtab          more                  startofline        whichwrap=b,s
```

```
noexrc                mouse=                swapfile           wildchar=<Tab>
  fileformat=unix       mousemodel=extend     swapsync=fsync     wildcharm=^@
  formatoptions=tcq     mousetime=500         switchbuf=         wildmode=full
  formatprg=          nonumber              tabstop=8          winheight=1
nogdefault            nopaste               tagbsearch         winminheight=1
  helpheight=20         pastetoggle=          taglength=0        wrap
nohidden                patchmode=            tagrelative        wrapmargin=0
nohlsearch              previewheight=12      tags=./tags,tags   wrapscan
  history=20          noreadonly            tagstack           write
noignorecase           remap                 term=vt320       nowriteany
noincsearch            report=2            noterse              writebackup
noinfercase            scroll=11            textauto            writedelay=0
noinsertmode           scrolljump=1        notextmode
  backupdir=.,~/tmp,~/
  define=^#\s*define
  directory=.,~/tmp,/var/tmp,/tmp
  fileformats=unix,dos
  helpfile=/usr/share/vim/vim54/doc/help.txt
  highlight=8:SpecialKey,@:NonText,d:Directory,e:ErrorMsg,i:IncSearch,l:Search,m
:MoreMsg,M:ModeMsg,n:LineNr,r:Question,s:StatusLine,S:StatusLineNC,t:Title,v:Vis
ual,V:VisualNOS,w:WarningMsg,W:WildMenu
  include=^#\s*include
  isfname=@,48-57,/,.,-,_,+,,,$,~
  isident=@,48-57,_,192-255
  iskeyword=@,48-57,_,192-255
  matchpairs=(:),{:},[:]
  nrformats=octal,hex
  paragraphs=IPLPPPQPP LIpplpipbp
  path=.,/usr/include,,
  sections=SHNHH HUnhsh
  selection=inclusive
  shellredir=>%s 2>&1
  shortmess=filnxtToO
  suffixes=.bak,~,.o,.h,.info,.swp,.obj
```

Besides the commonly used `:set showmode`, some others of immediate use are as follows:

- `:set number`—Displays line numbers

- `:set wrapmargin=10`—Sets margin to 10 characters

- `:set ignorecase`—Makes searches case insensitive

- `:set nowrapscan`—Searches stop at the end of the file

- `:set all`—Shows all settings

The following example shows a request to set the option for line number display within vi:

EXAMPLE

```
stuff
in the
junk file.

~
~
(...)
:set number
```

After setting the number option, the screen looks like this:

```
1 stuff
2 in the
3 junk file.
4
~
(...)
```

If you find that you are changing certain characteristics every time you enter vi, you should place your changes in the .exrc file in your home directory. (You probably will have to create this file.) This file is searched for and executed by vi each time it is invoked. Be sure that all commands placed in the .exrc file are last-line mode (ex) commands and are not preceded by the colon.

The following example shows the contents of an .exrc file, which sets the number and showmode vi options:

```
$ cat .exrc
set number
set showmode
$
```

Edit Session Recovery

If you are in the middle of an edit session when the system crashes, or some other event happens that abnormally terminates your edit session, vi provides a way to recover most of your work. When the system comes back up, you can type **vi -r** to see whether any recovery files are available. If so, type **vi -r** *filename* and save the recovered work immediately.

Miscellaneous Commands

Tables B.3–B.5 list some other commands I have found useful. Be aware that there are many outgrowths from the vi editor. Additionally, many other powerful features are not covered in this tutorial that are in the standard vi editor.

Table B.3: Other useful commands

Command	Description
xp	Transposes two characters.
.	Repeats the last activity.
J	Joins the current line with the next line.
~	Changes the case of a character.
10~	Changes the case of the next 10 characters.
>>	Moves the line about 8 characters to the left.
<<	Moves the line about 8 characters to the right.
Ctrl+G	Displays filename, line number, counts, and so on.
:r file	Reads another file into the end of the work buffer.
:0r file	Reads another file into the front of the work buffer.
:w newf	Writes the current contents to a file named newf.
:w! file	Overwrites the existing file.
:w>> file	Appends to the existing file.
:sh	Creates a shell session and exits back to vi.
!comm	Executes a shell command.
!!comm	Executes a command and output goes in the file (you might need to use :r !command in some implementations).
:2!comm	Replace line 2 with output from the command.
rc	Replaces the character under the cursor with a c.
R	Replaces characters until you escape.
mz	Marks the current position with the letter z.
'z	Returns to the position marked z.
d'z	Deletes from the current position to z.

As I promised earlier in the chapter, Table B.4 summarizes some of the commonly used ed commands.

Table B.4: Some ed commands

Command	Description
a	Enters data.
.	Must be at the beginning of a line to end insert.
w	Writes buffer out.
q	Quits the editor.
p	Shows contents of the file.
3p	Displays line 3.
2,5p	Prints a range of lines.
1,$p	Prints all lines.

Table B.5 documents some of the commonly used ex commands.

Table B.5: Some ex commands

Command	Description
i,a	Inserts data.
.	When typed at the beginning of the line, the period character ends the data insertion.
d	Deletes the current line.
.+6d	Deletes line 6 below the current line.
$-5,$p	Prints the last 5 lines of the file.
c	Replaces the existing line (might not be available in all implementations).
u	Undoes the last command.

What's Next

Because this is the last appendix, I guess the only thing left to do is to say adios and wish you the best of luck with your script writing. If you have questions or comments, please send email to Dennis.Obrien@bruden.com.

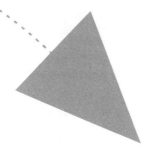

Index

C